EXMOOR

Food & Cookery

A MOORLAND HERITAGE

EXMOOR
Food & Cookery
A MOORLAND HERITAGE

BY BRIAN PEARCE

WITH HEATHER BURNETT-WELLS

EXMOOR BOOKS

In association with the
Exmoor Tourist Association

First published in 2000 by Exmoor Books

ISBN 0 86183 440 2

British Library Cataloguing-in-Publication-Data
A CIP data for this book is available from the British Library

EXMOOR BOOKS
Dulverton, Somerset

*Exmoor Books is a partnership between Exmoor Press
and Exmoor National Park Authority*

Trade sales enquires:
HALSGROVE
Halsgrove House
Lower Moor Way
Tiverton EX16 6SS
T: 01884 243242
F: 01884 243325
www.halsgrove.com

Printed and bound in Italy
by Centro Grafico Ambrosiano, Milan

❧ Contents ❧

❧ Acknowledgments ❧

This book results from the contributions of several hundred Exmoor people. Those who contributed recipes are acknowledged alongside the recipes. Some came as a result of requests through the local press and mail, some were gleaned from old books and others were given by friends and family.

Many recipes came from *The Taste of Exmoor Cookery Book*. Although every attempt was made to contact the contributors, most had moved on and we are grateful for their recipes and to the Exmoor Tourist Association for allowing us to reproduce them. Members of the Association, some of whom contributed to *The Taste of Exmoor*, made special contributions towards this book. These members included: Jackie Edwards of Westermill Farm, Exford; Tim Sandy and Daphne Criddle of Curdon Mill, Lower Vellow; Derek and Val Pritchard of Dunkery Vineyard, Wootton Courtenay; Jo Budden of Higher Hacknell Farm, Burrington; Anne Petch of Heal Farm, Kings Nympton; Richard Hunt of Periton Park Country House Hotel and Restaurant, Minehead; Jackie Payne of Huxtable Farm, East Buckland; Penny Webber of Hindon Farm, Minehead; Mark and Sarah-Jane Ravenscroft of Home Place Farm, Challacombe. Some of these members have been particularly supportive in supplying background information and photographs as well as recipes. Further information about the Exmoor Tourist Association is obtainable from: The Secretary, ETA, Mrs Kay Luckett, Periwinkle Cottage, Selworthy Green, Selworthy, Minehead.

Photographs also came from a variety of sources. Where known, sources are credited against the photographs. Steve Guscott has been extremely helpful in photographing the cooked recipes and providing background photographs. Heather Burnett-Wells was responsible for preparing much of the food for the photography. It has proved difficult to trace the owners of some of the older pictures which are out of copyright. Many came from collections and we are grateful to Michael Deering of the Exmoor Photographic Archive and Hilary Binding for archive material.

Background information was contributed by a great number of people. We are particularly grateful to Bob Deville of Heddon's Gate Hotel, Martinhoe for his recipes, information and support. Thanks also go to Michael Gee of Dartington North Devon Trust for photographs and information about local fruit and orchards and recipes arising from the Lyn and Exmoor Festival. Hugh and Sue Croft of Badgercombe, Twitchen provided settings for photographs, as did Chloe Deakin of Langleigh Farm, Cadleigh, plus recipes. Items for photography came from the Lyn and Exmoor Museum, Allerford Rural Life Museum and Dulverton Heritage Centre. Recorded interviews came from Birdie Johnson of the Exmoor Oral History Project and Michael Deering. Live interviews were made with Fred Rawle of Highley Farm, Parracombe and Pat Wright of the Moorland Larder, South Molton.

Finally, thanks go to Elaine Horton for support and assistance over several years of research and photography.

❧ Food For Thought ❧

In 1987 the English Tourist Board published *The Taste of Exmoor* cookery book. It was the result of a competition for recipes in the previous year. It attracted around a hundred entries from hoteliers, restaurateurs, schools and enthusiastic amateurs. The book soon went out of print but many people kept asking for it and we decided that there was a need for another book about Exmoor cookery.

At first it seemed easy: Heather would gather recipes and I would provide a bit of background information. However, in asking for recipes, we had to define Exmoor cookery – and that was the first problem. There are few dishes which could be said to be unique to Exmoor: perhaps the use of laver sauce for mutton, although that once became widespread; perhaps the buns which were produced for the revels at Lynton; perhaps the use of a few local ingredients such as Exmoor blue potatoes or Dunster plums. A book about such dishes would be very small. Should we count any recipes as long as they are from Exmoor people? In which case, could we include the recipes of somebody's Porlock granny for marmalade and chocolate cake or those from the Indian restaurant in Lynton? If not, should we just include local ingredients? Now that there are vineyards and ostrich farms on Exmoor, does their produce count as local?

Exmoor is an upland area and, within the limits of its climate and soils, has always produced a limited range of foodstuffs. Although these have always been supplemented by wild produce, few recipes are comprised wholly of locally produced ingredients. Also, although it has traditionally been considered an isolated area, it has never been totally removed from outside influences, especially in its coastal position. So, trying to define Exmoor cookery is a bit like trying to define the English or their language: it is a mixture of different influences, and becoming more so as its relative isolation disappears.

Exmoor food is located firmly in the West Country tradition, within which there are many localised variations. Recipes in the past were mainly for medicines rather than foodstuffs and cookery was learned by example, so that ways of cooking were passed down within families. However, this did not exclude experimentation and dishes changed with seasons and the availability of ingredients and the fortunes and outside influences on the families. Many

times I have heard people insisting that there is only one correct way to make a Cornish pasty or Devonshire junket or Somerset syllabub. The truth is that there was no standardisation and recipes varied from family to family, place to place and time to time. Those who denounce traditional English food as dull do not know of its variety and it is probably they who make it so by demanding the same food as they have always had and the same all the year round.

West Country food has developed around the few local ingredients to which the area is suited for production. It is rightly famous for its dairy produce. The relatively mild and wet climate suits the rapid growth of grass and the production of high butterfat milk from Devon or Channel Islands cattle. Cream has traditionally been used in all types of dishes, savoury and sweet, often as a substitute for butter. Exmoor, however, has never been a great dairying area. Local cattle such as the North Devon Red Ruby breed were multi purpose cattle and produced creamy milk but were usually in suckler herds for beef, not dairy production. Most farmers, however, tended to keep a house cow for their own dairy needs and from that point of view Exmoor cookery was no different from other parts of the West Country. Surprisingly, with beef cattle ever present, there are few beef dishes which can be said to be local or even regional.

Lamb and venison are the meats traditionally associated with Exmoor but, surprisingly again, they were not common food for ordinary Exmoor people until the introduction of cheap imported lamb after the Second World War and the more recent introduction of farmed venison. Until recently, although not associated with Exmoor, pork in its various forms was probably the meat most commonly eaten. Many locals, not just farmers, used to keep a pig for their own consumption, as did people in rural areas throughout the country. Exmoor has always been an area of low wages and, since the establishment of road and rail links in the late 19th century, much of its produce has been sold outside of the area where it can fetch higher prices. Only very recently has there been a revival of interest in buying local produce. Since the BSE crisis butchers have been keen to emphasise that local meat has always been produced in a largely organic fashion.

Locally caught fish, however, is still hard to find. Again, fresh fish, apart from the occasional glut of herrings, was not for ordinary people and for centuries salt fish was the norm. As with the proverbial hare, to follow recipes for many varieties of local sea fish you first have to catch your own fish. Vegetables also tend to be sent to London, from where local greengrocers have to buy other produce. Luckily a few pannier markets survive where local produce can be purchased. Many of the ingredients for Exmoor recipes, however, have to be caught or picked wild or begged from local gardeners. Whortleberries, for instance, are another mainstay of Exmoor cookery. They were once picked commercially, although not for local markets, and the only way of obtaining fresh local whortleberries now is to pick your own.

The same goes for many other local fruits such as the great number of varieties of local apples. Where now can you buy a local variety of eating apple? Luckily you can still drink local apples in the form of cider. Kingston Black is probably the best known cider apple but there are many others with fascinating names such as Foxwhelp, Cap of Liberty, Hangydown, Loyal Drain, Slack-ma-Girdle and Bloody Butcher. Near my home is an overgrown orchard of a variety named Lady Henniker. Some of the apples are normal sized green and red coloured fruit whilst others are speckled red and yellow and about three times normal size. To me they are fascinating in their variety but they are clearly not standardised enough for today's supermarkets. I am not sure whether it is the supermarkets which are responsible for such monotony or whether they are just responding to the demands of their customers. The problem is that the customers now do not demand some of these products because they do not even know they exist. Tastes have, however, broadened: look down any high street and see the variety of foreign restaurants and food outlets. There are few English ones left, let alone English regional ones.

To most people West Country cooking means pasties and cream teas. Both are relatively fast food and in that sense have kept pace with modern tastes, apart from the fashion for low fat food. Such items can now be found everywhere in the country and, indeed, throughout the world. Recently there has been the trend towards a greater variety of pasty fillings and away from standardisation, which is in the local tradition. However, the ubiquitous scones, clotted cream and strawberry jam which form the basis of a cream tea are a result of modern standardisation, not local tradition. It is what the customers expect, so that is what they are given. People do seem to be ready for a greater variety and it is a shame that it has not caught up with some so-called local food.

Another myth which seems to be perpetuated even in books on West Country cooking is that it is plain and simple. It is argued that local people only had open fires and bread ovens to cook with and limited basic ingredients so they could not make delicate or intricate dishes. The truth is that people in the past liked their food as much as we do and cooked as well as they could with what was available. One only has to look back at times of wartime rationing to see how inventive people could be. There were all kinds of ways of regulating the temperature of open fires and use was made of the dropping temperature of bread ovens to cook different items at different times. If the wood was wet for the fire, a joint would be boiled or casseroled instead of roasted, but that does not mean that it was not cooked well. For more delicate custards or creams a separate small charcoal fire would be made in a hollow in the fireplace or stillroom. Some cooks have always been old fashioned but there have also always been new inventions in cooking stoves and utensils and people who have been willing to use them.

As for basic ingredients, there has never been a time when there have not been travelling salesmen bringing exotic commodities and there have always been many pungent and powerful native herbs and spices and plants which were put to uses we have now forgotten. Local produce was once much more varied than now. Food was much more seasonal and the seasons produced a variety which was relished and celebrated. We have come to expect the same things year round, which means we can no longer expect most of our food to be produced locally. We also expect it to be at least partly prepared for us so we no longer even recognise what we are eating. Then there are all the regulations which make it difficult to produce certain foods on a small scale, and with small scale goes variety.

So, after all this rambling, did we ever get to define Exmoor cookery? Well, cookery is part of culture. Some have defined culture as the interaction of people with their environment and others as the total collective experience of a community. If you follow the first definition, you follow the theory that Exmoor cookery must contain locally produced ingredients. If you follow the second, you must allow for the many outside influences on the area in that Exmoor people have always travelled and brought back ideas from elsewhere, that many people have come to live on Exmoor from elsewhere and that produce from outside the area has always been available locally. If we followed that theory we would end up with an extremely cosmopolitan cookery book with little regional identity. So, we have gone for the first definition, with some compromise in that we have concentrated on locally produced or gathered main ingredients whilst allowing for the import of secondary ingredients. By locally produced we mean a greater Exmoor area stretching roughly from Taunton in the east to Bideford in the west and Tiverton in the south, for people on the moor itself have always relied heavily on surrounding areas for foodstuffs.

It has been difficult to find modern recipes which satisfy our criteria. As a result, the trend of my research has been towards the history of Exmoor cooking, although this had not been intentional. The main intention was to relate the ingredients and methods of cookery to the place and explain what is special about Exmoor cookery. Research has taken several years and many pleas for contributions. It could have continued for ever without publication had it not been for the financial assistance and incentive of the Exmoor Tourist Association. The Association is naturally keen to make Exmoor cooking more widely known and to improve the experience of visitors to Exmoor by making it more locally distinctive. Their financial contribution was to keep the price of this publication down, thereby making it more widely available.

I must confess that I tried many, but not all of the recipes in the book. Some are tried and tested family recipes which have been sent in and others have been cooked by Heather for our regular articles in *Exmoor – The Country Magazine*. Some are recipes which were contained in *The Taste of Exmoor* cookery book. The Exmoor Tourist Association has the copyright to this

book and recipes have been reproduced with their consent. Where we have been able to track down the contributors for their permission to reprint their recipes we have done so but many have moved on and our apologies to those we have been unable to locate. Some have been sent in by members of the Exmoor Tourist Association and Exmoor Producers Association. Some information has been obtained by interviewing local people and much has come from book research.

It is difficult to know who, if anyone, has copyright on recipes. Very old recipes I have reproduced as I have found them in old books. More recent recipes, those less than fifty years old, I have adapted to my own methods where the author has proved impossible to trace. I have acknowledged the person who has passed the recipe on, even though it may have been an old recipe for which the original source is unknown. The address given for the person, however, is often out of date and, with the old recipes, the person may be long deceased. Usually there are so many variations on any recipe that it is impossible to track down the original inventor. I have tried to divide them into three

Picnic in the woods near Luccombe, 1941   Exmoor Photographic Archive.

categories: traditional methods where I have perhaps found ingredients and cooking methods but no precise details of quantities or oven temperatures; old recipes, which have more detail but for which the origins are obscure; and modern recipes, which may have old roots but which have been handed on by people who have tried and tested them and used them with modern methods.

I have kept measurements and quantities for most recipes as they appeared where I found them, although I have given alternative temperature scales where possible. So, traditional methods and old recipes are invariably in imperial measures and often in quantities unsuited to modern small families. The modern recipes will generally be given in both metric and imperial measures. The idea is that most cooks adapted recipes to suit available ingredients and their own cooking methods and tastes: so, with the older recipes at least, we expect you to experiment with them rather than follow them slavishly.

Some of the old recipes are difficult to reproduce nowadays: getting the smoky flavour of a peat fire into the clotted cream; the various concoctions for curing a whole pig, using salt from the Bay of Biscay and essence of smoke; getting the cormorants for the cormorant pie or the five hundred squabs for the banquet at Dunster Castle, not to mention the medieval taste for dolphin or puffin! Thus, it is not the intention that you should reproduce all of the recipes. Some are there to explain the history of Exmoor cooking and to show that variety is the spice of life and, whilst we are pursuing that variety through our global culture, we are actually losing much of it through ignoring what is on our doorstep.

From Mammoths ⚜ to McDonalds

EARLY DAYS

All that we can say about prehistoric times is that we do not know what people ate on Exmoor. We can only speculate from evidence of other areas what might have been the case. Until we have scientific evidence from Exmoor, perhaps it is best not to even guess but there is a little circumstantial evidence. The first traces of human presence on Exmoor are flint implements found in gravels dating back to the last cold phase of the Ice Age. At that time Britain was still joined to the continent and it is thought that hunting people followed migrating herds of animals over to Exmoor in the brief summers. Bones of mammoths dating from similar times to the earliest human relics have been found close to Exmoor and these could have been hunted, along with elk, reindeer and even Exmoor ponies, although there is no hard evidence of this.

The first actual settlers may have come in the Mesolithic Period. Their settlements were probably in low-lying coastal areas now flooded by rising sea levels. A site at Westward Ho! which has been dated to about 4600BC suggests from the remains of their rubbish heap, known as a kitchen midden, that they ate shellfish. We can only guess that they were fishermen also, but no fish bones have been found in their refuse. The area had become well forested with the warming of the climate since the Ice Age and red and roe deer, wild pig and wild dog now inhabited Exmoor. In other areas these animals were hunted at that time and there is evidence from near Dartmoor that wild oxen were also hunted.

During the last period of the Stone Age, the Neolithic, the first farmers arrived on Exmoor. Evidence from other areas suggests that such peoples cleared woodland to plant corn. Pollen evidence from Exmoor suggests woodland clearing at that time but we do not know why. We know that such peoples planted barley and ground it between two stones. The top stone would eventually wear a trough in the lower stone, to form what is known as a saddle quern. No such stones have been found on Exmoor, where the earliest grinding stones date from about 300BC. By then, flour was made with a more sophisticated rotary quern. This device had a lower, plate-shaped stone and an upper, bee hive-shaped stone which could be rotated backwards and forwards on the lower stone. Grain was dropped between the stones through a hole in the upper stone. Remains of small cakes from Glastonbury show that in late prehistoric times people there made a kind of unleavened bread from wheat and barley mixed, probably unintentionally, with the seeds of weeds such as wild oats. The bread was made up as a stiff porridge, rolled into balls, flattened and baked. It is even suggested that the Bronze Age people made beer from the grain and drank it communally from the beakers found in their burial mounds but, again, there is no hard evidence of this.

The Romans had a staple diet of porridge and bread and the remains of several so-called bread ovens have been found at the fortlets at Martinhoe and Old Burrow. Like more recent ovens of the same name, they were almost certainly used to cook much more than just bread. They were circular or oval hollows in the ground lined with clay, then sandstone slabs. Over this were domed ash or hazel stakes, nailed together and plastered with clay. As well as firing the ovens and baking in the residual heat of the stone, they were found to have been used for roasting with beach pebbles and warming food and drink on earthenware plates and in jugs.

Exmoor was never well suited for the growing of corn but the most suitable sites were on the gentler slopes above valley sides and the 'balls' of hillsides. The valley sides themselves were too steep for ploughing, the valley floors too wet and hilltops too exposed. It may not be coincidence that some of the earliest settlement sites on Exmoor, from the indigenous peoples just before and during the Roman occupation, are in such locations. Many such sites also show evidence of enclosures for animals. By the Bronze Age we can guess that Exmoor farmers had domestic cattle, horses, pigs, sheep and goats. All may have been eaten and the sheep and goats used for milk. Residues of fats from earthenware pots found elsewhere suggest that stews with a meat base were continually simmering and added to on Bronze Age hearths. We look forward to the results of continuing research on this. Small pots were often heated by dropping into their contents pot boilers: pebbles heated in the fire. Evidence so far suggests that such pots were used for storing foods from milk to jellied pigs' trotters. We know that prehistoric people in the region also hunted deer and wildfowl and fished and collected shellfish. Almost certainly they collected birds' eggs and honey and ate large quantities of hazel nuts and berries. They probably feasted on a wide range of other wild food but this is speculation, not least for Exmoor, where there has been little scientific excavation.

The peoples of early medieval times were certainly good herbalists, as we know from Saxon documents, and made use of many wild plants which we would not consider eating now. However, they relied heavily on corn to last them through the winter. They ground the grain in small hand querns but also developed larger mills. Bread was baked in earth ovens like those of the Romans or under an iron kettle on the hearth. They produced barley, oats and wheat and the grist or crushed grains made porridge, often made as a pudding by boiling it with milk and sweetening with honey. The grain was also used to make oatcake and beer. They were good dairy farmers and produced cheese, cream and butter. They also had orchards and, like us, would have had apple sauce with their pork. They introduced many seasonal feasts and were certainly involved in the tradition of wassailing which continues on Exmoor today. However, as with prehistoric times, we do not know what happened locally on Exmoor.

In these times cattle were for dairying and pulling carts and ploughs rather than eating. Veal was not normally eaten and we know that, in more recent times at least, it was considered an extravagant waste on Exmoor. Neither was lamb normally: sheep were for wool and meat but they tended to eat mutton from old sheep whose breeding days were over. The main meat which was eaten was pork, a tradition which continued on Exmoor until very recently. Of course, farmed pork could be supplemented with wild boar. Hunting was just for the pot rather than sport. Big changes, however, came with the Normans, linked with the feudal system and the demands of their wealthier landowners for hunting over farmed land and for the better meat, from animals which were normally preserved for breeding.

Like their early medieval predecessors, people after the Norman invasion had one good cooked meal a day which was eaten communally. Living rooms were multi-purpose cooking, eating and sleeping areas and tables were trestles which could be easily moved and adapted to other purposes, such as beds. The wealthy started to use tablecloths and everyone would have their own set of cutlery: spoons, knife, spike and cup. Much would have been familiar to us in the big houses: there would have been salt cellars on the table and napkins were set in shapes like today. A waiter would hold flat bread cakes in a napkin wrapped over his shoulder and under his arm and serve two to each guest, one on each side of the platter. There were dishes of water and towels for wiping fingers and sauces were served on saucers made for dipping meat into.

The Normans introduced new spices and wines but for most Exmoor people subsistence farming continued. From the thirteenth century, when the church grew powerful and owned much land and there were many connections between abbeys throughout England and with France, trade routes grew. It became possible for Exmoor to concentrate on producing what it was most suited for: wool. Although most foodstuffs continued to be locally produced it became easier to trade for produce from other areas.

THIRTEENTH TO SIXTEENTH CENTURIES

So far, all has been speculation about what might have happened on Exmoor. From the thirteenth century onwards we have documents which help us to know more for sure. Much of what we know about late medieval Exmoor comes from accounts of the de Mohuns and Luttrells, the lords of Dunster. Dunster was a thriving market town and borough and its wide main street accommodated a Friday market and row of shambles or lock-up shops. The market area was marked with a stone cross at each end. One became known as the Butter Cross, as that was where dairy produce was sold. Court proceedings show that market days were rough and lively affairs. Short measures from the traders were common and the Keepers of the Shambles and the Bailiff kept order whilst bread weighers tested the weight of loaves and ale tasters checked the quality of every barrel before it was tapped for sale. Best ale was 1½d per gallon and the not so good sold at 1d. Drunken brawls were commonplace. According to the season, samples of corn, capons and fish were proffered and tested. Salt and spices, butter and cheese, loaves and sweetmeats were all touted by traders.

Fresh fish were a much more common part of the medieval diet than they are now. Hake was common and large shoals of pilchard, sprats and mackerel frequented the Exmoor coast. 'Mullewelles' and 'lyngys' were a common part of the catch at Dunster Haven. In the early fifteenth century Hugh Luttrell had this milwell and lyng, along with salmon, conger, scalpin, and hake salted and barrelled and sent out to his men who were fighting in France. When they returned they brought back French wines. Led by the local monasteries, Exmoor people were encouraged to abstain from eating meat on Fridays and Wednesdays, at Lent and other religious festivals. This had the practical purpose of conserving meagre meat supplies and supplementing meat with fish. Large fish traps were built all along the Exmoor coast. These consisted of low V-shaped walls of beach boulders topped with wattle fences. At the apex of the V, nearest the sea, would be a net spanning a gap in the walls. The trap would be completely submerged at high tide but as the tide receded the water would be funnelled out through the gap and any fish trapped in the net. Where the traps were at river mouths, salmon were caught in this way, and possibly also sturgeon.

Tastes were more exotic than at present. On the coast it was common to eat porpoise, dolphin and seal. Such meat did not keep well, even when salted, and was mostly eaten fresh. Seabirds and their eggs were a large part of the diet of people who lived near the breeding colonies. Young gulls, kittiwakes and cormorants were eaten. Some were taken and fattened for a while on liver or corn to remove their fishy flavour. The eating of small birds, particularly blackbirds and larks, was a common practice up until the twentieth century. The practice of bird batting probably did not change in all that time. Roosting birds were caught at night in a fine net. The net would be held on poles on one side of the hedge the birds were roosting in, with a lantern behind it. People would then beat the other side of the hedge with sticks or clap boards. The birds would fly towards the light and be trapped.

Few animals could be kept over winter and meat was frequently salted. As well as fish, Hugh Luttrell had mutton and beef sent out to his troops in France in great pipes, plus beer and live oxen. Spices were valued for disguising rancid meat. In the fourteenth century Joan de Mohun was forced by the king to hand back a shipload of raisins, prunes, cinnamon, pepper, white sugar and ginger (green and cured with lemon juice) she had seized when the ship sought refuge at Dunster during a storm. Domesticated pigeons, or culvers, were a constant source of fresh meat, but only for the wealthy. The birds were allowed to strip the crops of the peasants but there were severe penalties against them protecting their crops by taking the birds. Game was valued for the same reason. In addition to pheasant, grouse, woodcock, partridge, plover, snipe and quail, other birds such as swan, curlew, heron, crane and larks were also considered game. The de Mohun family had rabbit warrens around their property at Dunster, their own deer park and fish pond stocked with carp – another winter treat. The red deer were strictly royal property but landowners introduced fallow or park deer to their own deer parks for sport and meat. In 1355 Sir John de Mohun lodged a complaint against nine Exmoor inhabitants, including the parson of Selworthy, for taking away deer and young sparrowhawks from his parks at Dunster and Minehead, and hares, rabbits, pheasants, and partridges from his warrens in Carhampton parish.

The climate in medieval times varied as it does now but for much of the period it was generally milder than it has been in recent centuries. Vineyards existed long before varieties of grape were developed to cope with the British climate. Dunster Castle had its own vineyard on the slopes of the Tor and the south facing slopes of Grabbist Hill, now wooded, were later terraced for vines. The vineyards seem to have been introduced by the Normans. The work was labour intensive: Dunster Castle records of 1266 refer to 34 villeins each digging half a perch of ground in the vineyard. In addition to their rents, the burgesses of Dunster together paid the Lord annually a tun (252 gallons) of wine, worth forty shillings. Wine was even exported to France but labour costs or possibly the changing climate saw the end to the industry and by the mid fifteenth century French wine, mainly from Gascony, was being sold in Dunster at 6d per gallon.

Dunster was a borough, which meant that lining the village street were burgages rented from the Lord of the Manor by traders, who were free men. Each burgage included a long, thin plot behind the house. This valued piece of land helped the traders grow food for their own subsistence when times were hard. The plots were walled or fenced against theft or straying animals. Commonly they would have grown fruits ranging from apples, pears and cherries to mulberries, medlars and quinces. The Lord himself had much larger gardens and would have had orchards for these fruits, plus carefully planned groves of walnuts and chestnuts. Some of the first orchards were planted by monks and those at Cleeve Abbey may well have continued on the same site for 800 years. Cider orchards were known as pomararia and records show that the church owned such orchards and was receiving tithes from cider makers from the early thirteenth century or before.

Bread was still the staff of life. Corn was grown on the Lord's fields and some of his tenants cultivated this in lieu of rent. A document of around 1300 sets out the duties of Roger Tracey of Minehead, a tenant of William de Mohun. Roger had to spend three hours a day for two days a week weeding William's corn. Each year Roger had to plough an acre of the Lord's land for wheat with his own oxen, assuming he had some. He then had to buy seed and sow and harrow the acre, work worth three farthings. Later in the year he had to plough another half acre of the Lord's land for oats and spend another day winter ploughing, for which he was paid a penny. He also spent another full day harrowing the spring corn and several days reaping and carting away the corn. Seed was not necessarily saved from the previous year's crop and one day a year he had to travel to Taunton, Bridgwater or Watchet to buy fresh seed. Roger had other duties unrelated to the growing of corn, such as the gathering of brushwood faggots in winter and travelling once a year to Lyme Regis for sea salt. He was given a dinner on return in lieu of payment for this duty.

SIXTEENTH AND SEVENTEENTH CENTURIES

Although this was a time of great discoveries, the diet of common people became rather more monotonous. Vegetables and fruit were around but mostly unusual, expensive and highly seasonal. Potatoes did not become greatly used until the eighteenth century and in those days bacon and bread formed the staple diet. Pigs are easily fed on scraps and almost every family in town or country had one or two. Bacon, salted and sometimes smoked, kept well and smallholders frequently had no other livestock. Most farmers fed their labourers on fat bacon. Along with wine, salt was one of the main imports at Minehead harbour in the sixteenth century.

A trundle salter was mentioned in the inventory of the goods of Richard Hill, tenant of Simonsbath Farm, taken after his death in 1694. Other items on the inventory included two brewing vats and six flagons, an old cheese press and four cheese vats, along with various metal pots, pans, dishes and fire irons. Napkins and table cloths suggested that he was a gentleman farmer. The other items suggest that he supplemented his income by selling cheese. The beer was probably used for payment of workers rounding up and castrating ponies on the Forest. The farm became licensed as an inn a hundred years later but it was probable that Hill's beer was also sold to passing workmen and traders. Later, his wife passed on some of the goods to their daughters in her own will. Daughter Joan received her 'largest and least Copper Boilers my round Mahogany Table Board my large Oaken Table Board my largest Salter except one… my largest Trendle three of my largest Pewter Dishes… two Half Hogsheads two new Quarter Barrels silver Tea Tongs Silver Salt and salt Spoon.' A grand-daughter received 'half a Dozen Clome Saucers' which would have been sauce boats.

Most common people ate from wooden treen trenchers. During the wealthier times of the sixteenth century pewter plates were introduced and trenchers became used more by the poor or servants, although by the seventeenth century even they usually had a few items of pewter. Earthenware 'cloam' crockery became more common at the same time but china was not commonly used until the nineteenth century. Cooking pots were usually of brass or bell metal, an alloy of tin and copper.

Vegetables and grain later became more important. Pulses were a large part of the diet in those days. Peas were grown widely and in large quantities. They were largely hastings or runcivall peas, similar to today's marrowfats, but garden peas were also grown. They were used in stews and pease pottage. Field peas or 'hogs peas' were also grown to fatten pigs. Beans were less common but were also grown to provide winter feed for animals, including horses. Most familiar vegetables, including cabbage, spinach, carrots, parsnips, onions, leeks and radishes were commonly grown. Varieties of huge cabbages, often fed to cattle, were poor man's food. Leeks became more common over the next two centuries and were widely used in many Exmoor recipes. Fruit, including raspberries,

strawberries and gooseberries, were also grown but were generally kept in small quantities as there was no means of preserving them. Like many of these vegetables, they were garden rather than farm produce. Farmers had little time for gardening unless they had plenty of servants to help.

EIGHTEENTH CENTURY

Marshall described the diet of the West Country farm labourer as 'barley bread, skimmed milk cheese and potatoes.' Meat was now a treat for the poor, although it had previously been relatively cheap, especially when animals were slaughtered and salted in the autumn. Most local markets such as at Porlock and Dunster had their rows of butcher's stalls, known as shambles. Records from the fifteenth and sixteenth centuries show that there were literally dozens of stalls at Dunster but by the early nineteenth century there were only three or four. In 1758 Charles Wesley spent a night with a family in North Molton whilst preaching there. The honoured guest was treated with meat but he found that 'The bacon and hen were such as my teeth could not penetrate.'

Salt fish became a common part of the diet as the rich fisheries off Newfoundland became exploited. Most West Country fishing ports sent boats to the Newfoundland Banks in the spring, to return in the autumn. Although nutritious, the salt fish, mainly cod, smelt foul and did not look much like fish. Locals called it 'toe rag' – a common derisory term used today in many parts of the country. As it was highly portable, it was used much by men working long periods away from home, such as sailors and shepherds at summer pastures. By the end of that century salt fish and potatoes became a frequent dish on farmers' tables.

Sweetmeats also became more popular as the price of sugar fell. It had been available since medieval times but only to the wealthy and the usual form of sweetening was honey. Bee boles are common around the fringes of Exmoor but the hives were generally only brought up onto the higher ground for late summer. Metheglin and mead were common drinks. Sweet pies and tarts, particularly of apple and mincemeat, started to become popular, although usually reserved for entertaining. Spices, oranges, lemons, raisins and currants could all be bought at local markets. Jams were practically unknown until this time.

The diet of wealthier farmers was much more varied and changed with the seasons. Menus were often determined by religious festivals, which also marked the turning of the seasons. During Lent the wealthier families would eat salt fish, mainly herring. After Easter would come bacon and at Martinmas salt beef. In summer would come fresh beef and mackerel and by

Michaelmas fresh herrings, goose and mutton. By All Saints Day there was fresh pork and sprats and then came winter and Christmas with salt meat, poultry, game and dried fruit. Christmas was a time when wealthier farmers were expected to entertain and provide better quality food for the labourers. It was also a slack time on the farm with little to do except feed stock and there was time to shoot game.

Joan Hayes, housekeeper at Nettlecombe Court around 1755, kept careful accounts. Whatever was in season was brought to the kitchen door: lobsters, crabs, prawns, oysters, whortleberries, damsons and mulberries. She bought chickens and eggs from local farmers and yeast from the local pub. The will of Thomas Estcott of Sandhill, in Withycombe parish, who died in 1765, gives, through an inventory, an insight into the workings of the household of a wealthy Exmoor farmer. The rooms are listed with their contents. The kitchen was furnished with a long table, a settle by the fire, forms and one chair for the head of

cages and on two huge dressers, which also held sieves and other equipment. Food was mostly stored in food safes in the buttery, although four hams were hanging in the cool of the dairy and upstairs there was a cheese chamber holding 24 raw milk cheeses and 108 scalded milk cheeses. The room also held equipment for cheese making and a glass cucumber frame stored for the winter. The more valuable cooking items were kept in a lockable cupboard in the parlour. These consisted of spices and a pestle and mortar to grind them, silver cruets for salt, pepper and mustard, two coffee pots and a tea chest. The tea chest was a small wooden box divided into compartments for the extremely valuable tea. The hall was furnished with several table boards – rather like trestle tables – 12 chairs and 10 joint stools. There were six more table boards in the parlour, and more chairs, and there was a total of 39 chairs upstairs. All these dishes and tables and chairs suggest that the farmer would be used to feeding a hundred people or more on occasions such as harvest time, when most of the village would turn out to help.

Interior of a cottage at Oare, by W.W. Wheatley

the table. Cooking was done over an open fire or in a bread oven at the back of the fireplace. All the fireplace furniture is listed: a jack, five spits for roasting joints, billows, tongs, iron dogs and dripping pan together with bell metal pots and kettles. Some 102 pewter dishes and plates were stored in dish and trencher

Vancouver, writing in 1808, deplored the harvest festivities for being drunken and disorderly. Every able bodied person in a village would join in at harvest time and their pay would be as much food and drink as they could consume at the time and an invitation to a Christmas binge. According to the Rev. W.H. Thornton in his nineteenth century account in *Reminiscences of an old West Country Clergyman*, most village men and women, including the blacksmith, carpenter and postman, would join in. A harvest day would begin with a large breakfast at the farm and work would not commence until about 9am. Anyone could join the work before midday, by which time many were already merry from the ale and cider available in the fields. Dinner, as the midday meal was called, consisted of the best meat and vegetables. It was served in the fields between 12 and 1 o'clock, along with more ale and cider. Work commenced again at 2pm and at 5pm drinkings were brought into the fields in panniers. These were cakes and buns and all such articles as the confectionery skill of the farmer's wife could produce, plus yet more drinks. From about 6pm they continued work and at sunset one would bind one last sheaf and set it up. Retiring to some distance, everyone still standing would throw their sickles at it to try to knock it over. When this was achieved, there would be cries of 'we ha in' and revelry for about half an hour before all retired to the farmhouse for supper, where the drink continued to flow until the small hours of the morning.

The next morning all would commence again at breakfast and the procedure would continue until the harvest was in. When the last sheaf was cut, a necklace-shaped corn dolly was made from it and a ceremony called 'crying the neck' would commence. This varied from parish to parish but usually a young man was chosen to try to run back to the farm or church with the 'neck' without getting caught or doused with water by the rest of the harvesters. After all this, the company would start doing the rounds of the other farms in the parish.

The amount of ale and cider contained in Thomas Escott's house suggested large numbers of labourers to pay and entertain. There were one hogshead and 3 barrels full of ale and cider in the buttery; 2 barrels of beer and 1 of ale in the milkhouse; 6 hogsheads of cider and 3 half hogsheads of beer in the ciderhouse and 2 hogsheads of cider in the hogshead chamber. A hogshead usually contained 50\60 gallons and a barrel about 35 gallons. Thus there were well over 735 gallons of cider, beer and ale in the house at the time, not to mention several empty hogsheads and barrels and 60 empty casks, making a capacity of over 1000 gallons. All seems to have been home made, which was usual for that part of Exmoor. The ciderhouse contained an apple mill and cider press, empty butts, chairs and tableboard. The brewhouse contained a furnace, 5 vats, 6 tubs, a brass pan and a malt mill.

This compared starkly with the lot of the poorer end of the spectrum. There were great demands on the poor relief provided by each parish. The elderly, widows, orphaned children and those who, through incapacity, were unable to work were often forced into the parish workhouse, with its cramped, prison-like existence. At Minehead there had been a workhouse near the church since at least 1734. Many Exmoor parishes had church houses which seemed to act as a combination of village hall and pub, where ales were served to help church funds. By the eighteenth century some of these funds at least seemed to be going to the poor and church houses were being converted to poor houses to accommodate the poor whilst pubs were growing up elsewhere in the parishes. An inventory of 1772 lists the 'principle goods' in the Minehead workhouse. In the parlour was a 'brake board for kneadynge dough'; in the store was a salter; in the cellar were two barrels and two fats; in the kitchen were 'two boylors fixed in ye wall', two fats, three tubs, two lade pails, two buckets, one wooden horse, two stools, a coal box and sufficient earthenware bowls for the use of the occupants. There was no specific mention of cutlery or other utensils. Presumably most things – soups, stews and porridge – were cooked in the fats or vats. The barrels could have contained beer, but most provisions came in barrels. Other workhouse accounts show that beer and cider were there to pay contractors for work rather than supply the inmates with drink.

At the Ilfracombe workhouse, provisions included milk, potatoes, wheat, cabbage, cheese, groats, beer, occasionally beef or mutton, and herrings. The cook there was a man, presumably an inmate. The suppliers of food each had to sign a contract guaranteeing a regular supply of whatever they offered. Prices remained constant throughout the middle of the century until the great changes caused by wars with France. The meat was often only given to the sick, as were other treats such as wine, cider, milk, raisins and sugar. The sugar and drinks such as beer were administered to help the foul tasting medicine go down. Brimstone and treacle seemed to be the panacea for most sicknesses. The inmates were mostly too old or sick to work but beer was sometimes given as a reward for work, as it was to contractors. The incentive given for most women to work was tobacco.

NINETEENTH CENTURY

The end of the eighteenth century saw the beginning of the Agricultural Revolution which affected even far flung Exmoor. A combination of wars in Europe and a growing urban population forced up food prices and more and more land was taken into cultivation. Britain was now importing rather than exporting wheat and French ships blockaded food supplies. In 1800 a labourer's average wage was 1s 2d per day whilst the cost of a loaf of bread was 1s 1d. Exmoor people were dying of starvation. Some tried to take the law into their own hands to force down the price of bread and there were demonstrations. Two men from Withycombe were hanged for stealing bread from the bakery at Old Cleeve. They had taken the bread, paying 10d per loaf for it, which they thought was a fair price. A similar thing happened at South Molton in 1801, when people rose in a mob and made farmers sell their produce for much lower prices and making them sell only in their own parishes. For a while nothing went through South Molton market but within weeks wheat was being taken in from other parishes and sold at a guinea a bushel, far beyond the means of most cottagers. The vestry bought ship corn from Barnstaple, wheat and barley from Exeter, adding to it rice, potatoes, herrings and butter to be sold to the neediest at cheap rates.

In 1821 overcrowding at the Minehead workhouse forced it to take over the house next door. Such problems were echoed throughout the country, forcing a Government enquiry which resulted in the Poor Law Amendment Act of 1834. This attempted to tackle the problem through trying to reduce the number of claims on poor relief by stigmatising poverty and through economy of scale, combining parishes into Unions and building large centralised workhouses. Most Exmoor parishes fell within the three Unions of Williton, Dulverton and South Molton. The Dulverton Union tried to continue to give poor relief to people in their own homes, arguing that it was cheaper than accommodating them in a workhouse. They were given money according to the amount of their incapacity to work (up to a maximum of two shillings per week for totally bed-ridden people) and each had a voucher for a loaf of bread per week. Against the familiar counter argument that they were just encouraging idle scroungers, the Poor Law guardians were eventually forced to build a workhouse in 1851, later than most other Unions.

The slang for workhouse was 'grubber'. However bad they were, they had to be better than life in the outside world for the paupers to go there and the prospect of three meals a day was the main incentive for them. The food was regulated by approved dietary tables and those for Dulverton and Williton can be found in the Somerset Record Office. Portions were strictly regulated according to the class of inmate: man, woman or child; old, young, healthy or infirm. The nineteenth century diet for an adult male at Williton was as follows:

Monday: *Breakfast,* 6 ozs bread, 1½ pints broth. *Dinner,* no meat, 1 lb. potatoes, 1½ pints soup. *Supper,* 6 ozs bread, 2 ozs cheese.

Tuesday: *Breakfast,* same. *Dinner,* 5 ozs meat, 1 lb. potatoes. *Supper,* bread same, 1½ pints broth.

Wednesday: *Breakfast,* same. *Dinner,* as Monday. *Supper,* as Monday.

Thursday: *Breakfast,* same. *Dinner,* as Tuesday. *Supper,* as Tuesday.

Friday: *Breakfast,* same. *Dinner,* 14 ozs suet or rice pudding. *Supper,* as Monday.

Saturday: *Breakfast,* same. *Dinner,* as Monday. *Supper,* as Monday.

Sunday: *Breakfast,* same. *Dinner,* as Monday. *Supper,* as Monday.

All solid food was served on wooden platters. Only a portion of the daily bread ration was offered to inmates who, unlike Oliver Twist, could ask for more – up to their full allowance. Any unserved bread was returned to store to be duly accounted for. Water was served only at dinner and salt with all meals but pepper, vinegar and mustard were given only to certain classes of inmates, as approved by the guardians. There was no equality of sexes and women received less than the men. Women over 60 were allowed 1 oz tea, 5 ozs butter and 7 ozs sugar weekly in lieu of broth for breakfast if deemed expedient to make the change. At Dulverton the breakfast broth was replaced by 1½ pints of oatmeal gruel and women automatically were given tea and butter in lieu of this every other day. They were also given cocoa at supper in lieu of the broth which men were given. Men only had tea and cocoa on Sundays. Surprisingly, contrary to religious custom, they all had meat on Fridays and the suet pudding came on a Tuesday. Dulverton seemed to be more generous than most workhouses and some classes of inmates even had a lunch break for bread and cheese.

On Exmoor the inclosure movement came later than in most parts of the country but was combined with the most up to date methods of farming. Knowledge of new methods of cultivation, new crops, root growing, sheep feeding and crop rotation spread quickly to the area. A sort of crop rotation was already practised on Exmoor to the extent that grassland was often ploughed when it became too weedy and planted with oats to clear the ground. Crops of wheat and turnips were now also taken before a return to grass. The main changes were effected by the use of machinery for deep ploughing and draining; fertilising with lime, bone meal and superphosphate (made by dissolving bones in acid); and the selective breeding of crops and stock.

The greater production through these new methods kept prices and wages down. The Exmoor agricultural labourer earned only about two thirds of the wages of labourers on more productive land. On Exmoor this meant about 6s per week. A head man could earn £10 per annum with board and lodging. The labourers were hired annually at Christmas for starting the following Lady Day. They were slightly protected from dropping wages by some of the perks of the job. Men were usually given three or four pints of cider per day and allowed to buy wheat at 6s per bushel and barley at 3s, whatever the going rate outside. They also usually had a cottage at low rent or rent free accommodation and 'potato ground' at a yearly rent of

£8 per acre which the farmer would manure free. This would generally allow the labourer to keep a pig for annual consumption. The quality of the perks was, however, very variable. Drink was always a perk but those without other perks were generally paid more, about 1s 4d per day, in compensation.

Wages were usually linked to a loose piecework system where a certain amount of work was expected in a day and no more, so there was no incentive to work harder. Thus the spare time in the summer evenings was supposed to be used for cultivating one's own garden, if it was not spent drinking. Poorer people would have allotments or field gardens donated by charity or rented cheaply, but these were often inconveniently far from their homes. Such allotments now form the Woodcock Gardens nature reserve near Wootton Courtenay. Great time and effort must have been expended by villagers walking with lime and manure to and from these gardens on the edge of Dunkery. They were last used in the 1920s, a period of recession in agriculture and high unemployment. William Sturge, writing in 1851, advocated that every cottage should have at least 20 perches of garden adjoining as: 'This would tend to give the labourer an interest in his home, and keep him from the public house – would afford him the means of teaching his children industrious habits, and to make the most of labour at times when otherwise unemployed, and provide him with a wholesome supply of vegetables.'

Betsy Bushen of Minehead was interviewed in 1901, when she was 92 and she recalled some of her memories of the early nineteenth century. She remembered that house rents and the potato ground were relatively cheap. Food, however, was not. Wages were around 6s a week and, in comparison, a loaf cost 1s. Wheat was a guinea a bushel; potatoes 20s a bag; tea 10s-12s a pound; loaf sugar 1s to 1s 2d a pound; moist sugar 8d to 9d a pound. It is easy to see how people would starve if they could not grow food for themselves. They ate cheaper barley bread rather than wheaten bread. Tea was out of the question for poor people, who used to burn a crust of bread and put it in a tea pot. They would often use infusions of herbs such as herb organ (sweet marjoram) and peppermint. Salt was a necessity and Betsy remembered going to a Captain Perkins of Porlock Weir with 11s to buy a quarter hundredweight (28 lbs) bag of salt. In order to salt a pig, Betsy's mother had to sell a quarter of it to pay for the salt.

For most labourers, breakfast and lunch would usually be bread and skimmed milk cheese, eaten in the fields. The evening meal was usually the only cooked meal of the day. It was still the job of the wealthier farmers to provide food for special occasions, such as shearing and harvest times, when there would be large suppers at the end of the work. A good, if sentimental,

Betsy Bushen of Minehead

description of shearing, locally known as sharing, festivities at Brendon was given by Chanter in 1887:

As soon as the weather is warm enough the sheep are washed and shorn, and great is the bleating of lambs and sheep, and the barking of dogs. Great also are the preparations on the part of the farmer's wives; the larders requiring much additional replenishment to feed the hungry shearers. First comes the breakfast, for many of the guests have been riding since daybreak, and were shearing late the day before, therefore require a meal before they begin their work. Each man has a roll of white linen overclothes strapped to his back, these when donned, protect their holiday suits from the grease of the sheep. They all collect in a large barn, which most of the farms possess amongst their out-buildings, and the work begins. It is a very pretty sight, with the picturesque surroundings of a Devon farmyard; the jokes of the men, the many different notes of the bleating sheep, the incessant clipping of the shears, forming a truly rustic accompaniment.

Then comes the mid-day dinner; and all the shearers wash their hands in a great bowl of herbs which the women have prepared beforehand, slip off their outer garments, and sit down for a hearty meal. The women do not eat this meal with the men, but busy themselves with the waiting. After dinner there is more work; then tea, and again more work. After that there is supper, and the fun of the day. Songs from both sexes, many of them are remarkable as to tune and words. The Punch Bowl is a great favourite, having a fine tune and quaint words, the first verse commencing Come all ye brave heroes, give ear to my song, and immediately calls for attention; to hear this trolled forth by a fine bass voice in unadulterated Devon, is to hear it to advantage. If a fiddler be present he is seated on a table, and endless polkas and country dances are indulged in; while the elder ones of the party sit still and smoke their pipes, and talk about the comparative price of wool and crops. Then steeds are saddled and mounted, and the shearers depart on their homeward road.

During harvest, farmers' wives and their maids would bring teas to the workers in the fields. These were the original cream teas, with jugs of tea, cutrounds, cream, jam and fruit cake all brought out to the fields in large wicker maunds or hampers. Tea only just became affordable for the poor at the end of the eighteenth century and was still considered a luxury. Towards the end of the nineteenth century it was about 2s 6d per pound, compared with the average wage of about 6s per week, so it was affordable in small quantities but beer was more popular.

Women and children would also generally eat a cold lunch. Children were expected to earn some of their keep and there was much absenteeism from school at times such as 'wort' and apple picking. They were then frequently absent through illness from eating too many unripe apples. Children would take a packed lunch to school but school meals were introduced towards the end of the century. Dunster school records for the 1880s show how the Luttrell family provided a room so that the children could be served hot lunches in the winter. For a penny they could have bread and soup or suet pudding. Smaller children could have half portions for a halfpenny. A few wealthy benefactors bought lunch tickets for children in large poor families. At Carhampton School, like many others, there were frequent absences through illness and the headteacher provided all the pupils with oranges for Christmas at his own expense. The Government provided an extra grant for schools where children passed a simple cookery examination and the same room was used to provide cookery classes for girls only.

Many wealthy landowners like the Luttrells were idealists and there was a general belief that ill fed labourers did not work well. Meat was supposed to be necessary for those involved in heavy work such as ploughing. Sir Thomas Acland took a particular interest in the welfare of farmers and labourers on his Holnicote Estate. The Rev. William Thornton spoke of him:

Sir Thomas was, in comparative terms, a good employer; others were not. I have known seven shillings a week given, with cider and a cottage and a garden, but with no extra privileges, except extra food in harvest time. He had a keen interest in diet, visiting cooking schools in London and supervising the cooking of friends and neighbours. He sent a cooking teacher around to the villages on his estate and often gave away cookery books, particularly a little book by Miss Guthrie Wright. He would experiment with diets on his own staff but would always try these for himself. At one time he just drank a thin oatmeal gruel for days to prove that it was healthy and good for adults who could not get milk. His efforts were not always appreciated. One day he carried a dish of rice and cheese, on which he laid great store, to a family in a Selworthy cottage. Next Sunday on his way to church he met one of the lads who had eaten it. When asked how he had liked it, the lad replied: Gave us heartburn dreadful, Sir Thomas.

Fish and potatoes were still the mainstay of the diet along the Exmoor coast. Much of the food of common people was still heavily salted – bacon, fish, cheese, butter – and labourers drank prodigious quantities of ale and cider, a gallon or more per day. This was partly provided by their employers and considered by labourers as an essential condition of their work. Farmers thought it kept the labourers happy and kept their mind off the fact that they were paid amongst the lowest wages in the country. William Hannam, who farmed at Cornham in the 1850s, wrote in his diary: 'I had no difficulty to gett my Hay made or Grass cutt and gave all Parteys sattisfaction In the first two or 3 years gott my Grass cutt at 1s per Acre and gave them sometimes a Bottle of Sidur and I could gett aney Quantitey of Meen to help about the Hay by giving them a little Bread and Cheese and sidur.'

Sir John Acland, writing about 1850, suggested that farmers deducted about a sixth of the wages of labourers for the amount of cider drunk. Generally the cider available for farm workers in the West Country was unlimited but on Exmoor, where beer was more available, it often had to be purchased. Sometimes cider was used like a carrot on a stick, as a bribe for each amount of work accomplished, often leaving a flagon at the end of a field to be ploughed or tilled. Shepherds carried their cider with them in a small barrel or firkin tied to their belts. Elsewhere known as a costrel, it held about four pints, the daily ration. Each labourer would traditionally have a small horn cup. In some areas the tradition was to share the same cup, which was passed around the firkin in a clockwise direction. The average labourer was given two hogsheads (120 gallons) of cider per year, in lieu of

Gardeners for the Luttrell family at Dunster Castle, 1890s

about 15% of his wages. The more enterprising employers, aware of the debilitating effects of cider, began to pay extra wages in lieu of cider. This meant that some saved and worked better for their employers and those that did not had to buy their cider from their employer, who then made a profit anyway.

Cider drinking tended to be deplored by the clergy and gentry. It often led to drunkenness, illness and alcoholism, frequently resulting in cider being stolen. The Dunster Church of England Temperance Society suggested that expenditure on drink increased greatly during the century. By the 1880s expenditure on drink was averaging 2¼ d per day, or, leaving out children, 4½ d; whereas 2 d per day was spent on bread, 1 d on butter or cheese, less than 1 d on milk, less than ½ d on sugar and less than ¼ d on tea, coffee and cocoa. The Knight family, who had acquired the former Royal Forest around Simonsbath, were not supporters of local tradition and they limited the hotel at Simonsbath to the sale of wine, which did not suit the tastes or pockets of the thirsty miners and shepherds on their estate. In small parishes a few influential persons could dictate whether or not inns were to be licensed and in this case Frederic Knight owned the whole parish. However, this generally just transferred the problem to surrounding parishes or encouraged home brewing.

The beer they drank at inns was not as strong as today's and was usually made on the premises. It was not until the end of the century that communications allowed the delivery of beer from large breweries.

Throughout this time the farmhouse kitchens had changed little. An auction of household goods at Challacombe Mill in 1852 read like inventories of two

Old kitchen implements at Huxtable Farm, West Buckland

Steve Guscott

centuries earlier. Offered for sale were: Iron Pot and Boilers; 2 Brass kettles; Milk Scalder, a Copper Tea Kettle; Salters and Trundles; 2 Cheese Presses. The wealthier farmers and landowners ate well and consumed large quantities of meat. William Hannam, who farmed at Cornham was financially and mentally broken by his lease on the Knight estate. When he went to Lynmouth to talk to Charles Knight about his difficulties in paying his rent, he was given a treat of a meal: 'I had not been long sat doing to a part of a Cold Leg of Mutton and a Jug of Strong Beer when I had a piece of warm Road Beef and part of a Decanter of wine sent out.' When the poor man was finally forced to sell up he felt obliged to produce a similar meal to attract the right sort of bidders to the auction.

Working hard and long hours in the open air gave men prodigious appetites as well as thirsts. A typical story is of a Brendon Hills farmer who went to Taunton with his solicitor on legal business. The two stopped for lunch at a well known restaurant and the farmer quickly disposed of his meal, remarking: 'They don't zim to gi' anybody overmuch to eat yer' and called to the waitress: 'Hey miss, vetch me another 'elping will ee?' Consuming that as quickly as the first he turned to his solicitor, who was toying with his meal, and said: 'You don't zim to be gettin' along very well wi' your dinner.' When the solicitor replied that he was not very hungry the farmer consumed his meal with equal gusto.

TWENTIETH CENTURY

The end of the nineteenth century saw the beginning of a long depression in local farming. From the 1880s there was a series of bad harvests. Because of the advent of cheap imported grain from North America the price of local grain did not rise and the bottom fell out of the market. This had a knock on effect on cattle feed and cattle production was further affected by the advent of refrigeration and cheap imported meat from Australasia and the Americas. Farmers were paid very little for beef or mutton and little changed until subsidies came in the 1930s. A 50% liming subsidy, introduced in 1937, revitalised the industry. Exmoor farmers survived by turning more to dairying, reducing labour and becoming almost self sufficient. Family owned farms survived better as few could

afford rents. Remoter farms could not sell their milk except locally. When a firm from the Torridge valley started collecting milk from Challacombe in the 1930s, nearly every farmer in the parish jumped at the chance to sell, even though only 5d or 6d per gallon was offered in the summer. The Milk Marketing Board collected by lorry from everywhere after 1945.

Workhouses were still going strongly until the 1930s and were not totally replaced until the National Assistance Act of 1948, which was part of a series of legislation following in the wake of the Beveridge Report. Obviously, workhouse diets were a little better but still very rigid and the accent still very much on the midday meal:

Breakfast:
Every day: 8 ozs bread, 1½ ozs margarine, one pint tea.

Dinner:
Monday: 3½ ozs boiled beef, 6 ozs bread, two vegetables and 6 ozs fresh or dried fruit pudding.
Tuesday: 4½ ozs roast mutton, 4 ozs bread and two veg.
Wednesday: 3½ ozs roast or boiled pork, 4 ozs bread, two veg. and 8 ozs rice or sago pudding.
Thursday: 4½ ozs roast beef, bread and two veg.
Friday: 4½ ozs cold meat, bread and veg.
Saturday: Cottage pie, two veg. and bread pudding.
Sunday: 16 ozs meat pie.

Supper:
Every day: 8 ozs bread and ½ oz margarine with the addition of 1½ ozs jam and 2 ozs cheese one weekday and 3 ozs cake on Sunday.

This contrasted with the menus of the wealthier families in the area. Many details survive from the records of the Fortescues at Castle Hill and the Chichesters at Arlington Court. A typical menu of the latter is as follows:

le 10 juin 1910

Consommé

Sole au gratin

Timbales de Volaille

Filet de boeuf

Meringues

Pailles de fromage

French cuisine had obviously become fashionable with the wealthy. Interestingly, however, the recipes for

Ilfracombe butcher c1925

each course show that, apart from the Timballes de Volaille (chicken creams), the food was still cooked in an English, if not local manner. The consommé was made with beef stock and roasted marrow and chicken bones. The sole was cooked in a traditional local manner: skinned but left on the bone, with the top fillet just lightly parted from the bone. It was served with a sharp sauce made from shallots, herbs, vinegar and Worcester sauce. The beef was a whole fillet wrapped in larding bacon and roasted. Pailles de Fromage were simply cheese straws, although Parmesan cheese was mixed with Cheddar.

For farmers life remained much as it had been until the First World War, which was a great turning point in most peoples lives. Hazel Eardley-Wilmot in her *Yesterday's Exmoor* tries to conjure up the atmosphere of the farm kitchen before the changes:

> The old-fashioned farm kitchen was at the heart of the house, unchanged for centuries (because money was not readily spent on any indoor comfort). It was the living-room, and friends and neighbours would troop into it after helping with shearing or haymaking, corn-harvest or threshing, and crowd the benches at the refectory table which stretched along one wall. The shearing-party was the best, when the wool-harvest was safely home; the men who had been working hard all day were feasted, and the fun went on, with drink and song and dancing far into the night. As in Shakespeares day, success depended upon the warmth of the welcome, and on the generous preparations made. The table would be spread with good farm produce – home-cured ham, home-brewed cider, home-baked bread, butter and clotted cream fresh from the dairy, blackberry jam or whortleberry tart, cake and buns made with new-laid eggs.

Old-fashioned farm kitchen at Sparhangar

In the early part of the century it was usual for a farmer not to handle cash but to deal largely in cheques paid at

certain times of the year. Often it was up to the farmer's wife to supply not only her own keep but also the wages the farm labourers and food for them and the family. She would also have to provide large suppers for extra helpers at shearing or harvest time and crockery and kitchen utensils from her own cash. Until about the 1930s she usually had at least one maid to help her and she would supervise her own family business. It was usual for her to earn money by selling bacon, poultry, eggs, butter, cheese and cream at the local pannier markets, such as at Barnstaple and South Molton. This often coincided with the cattle market, so the wife could

Barnstaple pannier market

travel in with her husband but many women had long hard journeys by foot. Produce was sold early in the day, so she was often back by lunchtime having walked twenty miles or more. They would often bring their produce in large wicker hampers known as maund baskets. Some baskets, unique to the area, had oval bases but rectangular openings and lids. They would have their own family stalls and make market day a social occasion. Customers had to take their own containers for cream or whatever produce they expected to buy. Bert Verney in his *Reflections* remembers going to Barnstaple market in the 1920s:

> On market days the horse and trap were used to take my parents to Barnstaple. My mother used to have a stall (as most farmers wives did) in the Pannier Market. The stalls would consist of a large hamper, made of wicker, interwoven, some three feet deep, four feet wide and five feet long, with handles for carrying at each end. There were always men waiting to help carry, when you arrived at the market, and others who took charge of the horse and trap, stabling the horse and housing the trap at one of the many inns in the town.
>
> To display one's goods, the hamper was opened on a hinged top. The far end of the top had two holes, through which two stays were placed. These took the weight of the lid on their cross-pieces. The lid then became a table, for displaying ones goods, i.e. the butter, cream, often a boiling hen, rabbit, sprouts, peas, beans,

apples and at pig killing time hog's pudding and pork sausages.

The main business of the market was done by one o'clock, when one would throw a rug over the stall and do ones own shopping in the town. Nothing was ever stolen from the stalls, although left unattended for long periods. At the far end of the Pannier Market was the Corn Exchange, where farmers and merchants carried out their business,

Outside the market was Butchers Row, with some thirty butchers shops displaying huge carcasses of beef, lamb and pigs. These too were a magnificent sight, with their displays of meat. At Christmas poultry, holly and mistletoe were displayed.

On the Somerset side of the moor pannier markets were not the norm. Farmers wives and daughters would walk to nearby towns to sell their wares from door to door. They would have regular customers they supplied and when in town would undertake shopping for neighbours.

Maud Harding of Winsford remembers helping her mother do the cooking at Torr Farm between the wars. There were fewer servants after the First World War and the two of them did all the cooking and housework, even when they brought in hired help for farm work:

It was haymaking or shearing. When we had in extra help we always provided the food for them. I remember I got a bent knife taking the food up in baskets for harvesting – the harvest fields up on top. Take it up hot – peas, vegetables and meat – a proper meal, on a plate with a knife and fork and something to drink – tea or coffee then. Well they carried cider – take that with them. We always had to buy our cider, either Fanny would be making hers before they had soft drinks. Cider and beer were our main drinks. Because years ago they brewed their own beer in Winsford. All the farms did. That was before my day actually, because of the excise licence. The brewhouse stood on your own farm. Each farm, not since I've been grown up and married. But farmer Milton at Edbrooks making his own beer. They do it in the big furnace – like some clothes used to get boiled in – a copper. They were built in, weren't they? Every farm had them built in like the oven. We had a bake oven. We never used it, not here – but out at Stoke Pero it was used up till I went up for bread making. We used to make the bread in the range. Run on coal and logs mainly.

Bert Verney remembers his mother's home help in the 1920s:

She always lit the hearth fire and fried the breakfast for eight people: fat bacon from our

Haymaking picnic for the Bawden family at Cloggs Farm, Hawkridge

own pigs, eggs and potatoes left over from the day before, and often batter pancakes. If anyone wanted toast, it had to be toasted on long-handled forks over the open fire. The taste was superb, and when covered with home-made butter, jam or marmalade, was really a meal on its own. She cooked or fried the breakfast in a huge frying pan, holding ten eggs at a time, balanced on a brandis over an open fire.

He also remembers taking food out to contractors working in the fields at harvesting and other occasions:

At ten o'clock, a break of some twenty minutes was taken. A tin kettle full of tea (about two gallons), mugs and cups of all shapes and sizes. A huge market basket full of cooked or baked food. Yeast cake (well buttered), bread and cheese were always there, sometimes home-made sausage rolls. The men never washed but ate the food, dust muck and all with great zest. At one o'clock they came into the house to a baked meal. Beef, potatoes, sprouts, swede, turnip or cabbage, whatever was in season. Followed by apple pie and cream and tea.

Even up to the 1950s most Exmoor food and drink was locally produced. Most locals had gardens and produced their own vegetables. In the lower lying areas many had fruit trees – apples, pears, plums and even figs. What could not be produced at home could often be purchased from a neighbour or nearby farm. In the *Exmoor Review* of 1995 Stella Carroll recalls her wartime days at Withypool as an evacuee:

Withypool at that time was almost self sufficient, with everyone growing vegetables and salad stuff. Bread, butter and milk were all home produced, fruit too; even the lambs tails were cooked.

Gardening was commonly taught at school. In *Within Living Memory* by Margaret Bate a farmer known as Herbert recalls his schooldays at North Molton:

All the bigger boys, twenty or thirty, each had a small plot of land which belonged to the school, down where Jubilee Gardens is now. We used to

Gardening party at Dunster School, 1930s

grow rows of potatoes, cabbage, peas, beans and carrots. Then the biggest boys would take large baskets and sell them round the village. Perhaps a cabbage for a ha'penny.

Walter Isaac in *The Way 'Twas* remembers Chittlehampton School in the 1920s:

> The school garden played an important part in preparing us for the future. This was of particular interest to me and in fact I won a gardening prize. Allocated two to a plot, we would plan, plant and harvest crops, meticulously recording every detail, such as dates, varieties and yields.

Farm workers wages in the 1920s and '30s were 28-30 shillings per week. However, they often had a cottage and garden rent free and food was fairly cheap: beer was about 2d per pint, eggs 6d to a shilling per dozen, a large joint of meat about 2s 6d and herrings in season 6d per dozen. Most farm workers worked a nine hour day five days a week, a half day on Saturday and a few hours on Sunday checking and feeding stock. The only holidays were Christmas, Boxing Day and Good Friday. The latter, along with evenings, was spent in the garden. Bert Verney remembers:

> They kept a few hens in a house and pen in the corner of the garden. The house usually was

made of flattened, empty tar barrels or old and galvanised rusty sheets. Many also kept a pig, as most farm cottages had a sty where one could be kept. They were allowed to plant one cwt bag of seed potatoes in the farmers field: usually allowed one pint of milk daily, given apples at picking time and allowed to catch a rabbit when they needed one, and allowed swede or turnips from the field.

Rabbit shoot, Porte Farm, Kentisbury c1930

Exmoor Photographic Archive

There would often be traders selling more exotic produce such as oranges and bananas at cattle markets. Fairs were the usual places to buy earthenware crockery and, in more recent times, china. Much food was delivered. It was not until the 1920s that bus services came to the area and few locals travelled far. From the mid eighteenth century many Exmoor villages had been linked with nearby villages by carriers cart services. In the mid nineteenth century the development of better roads following the setting up of turnpike trusts meant that such services were extended to larger towns. For instance, in the 1840s there were two weekly services from Dunster to Taunton. The carrier took shopping commissions, leaving orders at several shops which would then deliver to a central collecting point before his home journey. This was to some extent replaced by the bus services in the twentieth century, but carriers continued trading in the area until the 1940s. One such person was Tom Sparks of Porlock Weir, who carried between there and Minehead. He would take a penny commission for shopping, which compared well with the 1 shilling bus fare for housewives to shop for themselves. Some provisions were brought from Bristol to Minehead by boat and then by smaller boat to Porlock Weir, from where the carrier would deliver them to outlying farms at a rate of 4 pence per hundredweight. Common deliveries were cases of sugar, corn, oranges, bananas, cheese, flour and bacon.

Few people had cars and not all had horses, so it was usual for traders to come to them. Frank Summers, who was born at Oldways End in 1911, recalls various traders calling in the 1920s. He remembers the butcher from Dulverton delivering weekly by cart. A grocer from Dulverton came by bicycle on a Tuesday to take orders and delivered them on the following Friday. Bread was delivered by bakers from Bishops Nympton, Oakford and Rackenford. One called Fridays and Wednesdays, one Tuesdays and Saturdays and the other called Thursdays. Sometimes fish was delivered, but not often as it did not pay. Sometimes a man would call with a basket of oranges, which he sold at 1d each. Walter Isaac recalls the same period at Cobbaton:

> Traders provided a service in rural areas which is unrivalled today. Will Ashton from Barnstaple was one such who called regularly for grocery orders which he would deliver later. While writing down each item he made himself quite at home at our table in his usual place. Stoeman the grocer at Landkey usually called late on Thursday evening with his large van laden with almost everything. Alf Cole from Townsend Bakery of Chittlehampton was another regular caller with his horse drawn bread cart. There was also Lewis's Bakery in East Street (South Molton).

An account of life in an Exmoor village (Luccombe) in the 1940s is given in W.J. Turner's *Exmoor Village*. Here

John Legg of Winsford delivering bread to Exford c1920

Exmoor Photographic Archive

are some extracts from the daily routine of Mr Tame, a farmworker:

> He and his wife get up at 6am each morning. Mrs Tame heats water and cooks breakfast with the aid of a primus and a methylated spirit stove. Mr Tame goes to work on his bicycle, getting there at 7am. After feeding and mucking out the horses he sits down to eat his own breakfast, which he carries with him in the form of sandwiches and a quart-sized bottle of tea. The tea will still be hot for the breakfast drink, but by midday it will be cold. However, Mr Tame does not mind and prefers to drink his tea cold than to have it in a thermos. But Mrs Tame makes use of a thermos. Last thing at night there is always plenty of water boiling on the hob, so she fills up her two large thermos flasks, and in the morning the water only takes a minute to boil up again for the first pot of tea. At about 12.30am Mr Tame knocks off for about an hour and has his lunch. Mrs Tame has no real meal until her husband returns between 6 and 6.30pm. He arrives back at Porch Cottage to find Mrs Tame putting the finishing touches to a two-course evening meal – stewed steak and onions, potatoes, cauliflower, and rhubarb tart on a typical evening. Water is drunk with the meal, and later on, about 9.30pm, they both have a cup of Bovril before going to bed. After supper Mr Tame goes straight out into his garden, for there is always plenty to do there. For Mrs Tame after the meal comes the washing up and the cutting of sandwiches for Mr Tame to take to work the following day. He likes cheese, supplemented by one or two of his wifes jam tarts or cakes. By the time she has cleared away it is getting on well into the evening and she goes out to watch her husband gardening.

Gardens proved very important through the two World Wars, when they were intensively cultivated. Farmland too came into more intense cultivation and heathland was ploughed for corn. In the Second World War there was a threefold increase in the amount of arable land, which became half the total. On the moors, however, despite heavy liming, fertility declined rapidly after the first two crops. For centuries locals had made assarts, cultivating a bit of heathland and letting it revert after two years. Now the attempt to grow corn on Exmoor was largely abandoned after the bad weather and harvest of 1943. Efforts were concentrated on getting more grass and food for livestock and root crops such as potatoes and sugar beet. The new moorland assarts were turned over to grass and subsidies for hill stock encouraged farmers to lime high ground. By the end of the war the nation was producing 80% of its food needs instead of 20% at the beginning. With the lack of male labour the Womens Land Army helped out and the 'War Ag'. completely took over some farms. Their inspectors may

A cottage vegetable garden at Twitchen

Brian Pearce

have known little about Exmoor farming but had power to dispossess farmers who refused to co-operate with their plans.

Bert Verney remembers the war years near Landkey:

> Whereas we used to grow 20 to 25 acres of corn we now grew 80 to 100 acres. Where we grew no potatoes we now grew 5 acres. This meant a reduction in the numbers of sheep and cattle kept on the farm. We had double summer time at that time and were often working in the harvest field until 11.30 pm or midnight. At the end of 1940, the girls of the Land Army became available to help the farmers. They were, on the whole, hard-working and happy and a great help at busy times, such as harvest, threshing, apple picking and the potato harvest.
>
> In the winter we had a little more time to spare, with less livestock to look after. Now my brother was away, I had to have someone to help me keep the rabbits under control. An ex-farmer helped me with ferreting, fitting nets in holes on his side of the hedge and catching any rabbits trying to escape that way. I had nets and guns on my side and between us we managed to keep the rabbits under control.

Late in the second war a week's ration for one person amounted to 1 egg, 2 pints of milk, ½ lb meat, 4 ozs bacon, 2 ozs tea, 4 ozs sugar, 4 ozs sausages, 2 ozs butter, 2 ozs lard, 4 ozs margarine, 3 ozs cheese and a small amount of offal. At the end of the war the lard ration went down to 1 oz. The meat often included whale and horse meat. Many ponies were rustled for their meat and the Exmoor ponies nearly disappeared from the moors in the first war. Before the second war sheep, pigs and poultry had declined because they were fed on imported food. Now locals kept hens and rabbits in their gardens and many an old pigsty was revived. Children would collect acorns, house and garden refuse for pig feed and bracken for bedding. Some villagers who could not have a pig of their own got together to form pig clubs. They bought shares in pigs which were sold for profit. Even the pig manure was sold for gardens. Local councils subsidised the making of meat pies, which were baked in local bakehouses and delivered by volunteers. A profit of ½d per pie was made, which went to charity. The schemes continued throughout the period of rationing.

After rationing there was much less emphasis on local produce and more and more food became imported. There was also a move away from working on the land and greater urbanisation. Austerity also meant that not only were there fewer people in the countryside but there were fewer housewives, as many women started going out to work. In turn this meant less time spent on cooking and Exmoor cooking, like most British cooking

went into the doldrums. The balanced meals, the importance of which was emphasised in the war continued, with meat and two veg. being the standard main course. Much of this changed in the 1960s with the fashion for skinny models and slimming. At first it was the starchy foods which were targeted and people ate less bread and fewer potatoes.

Bob Deville remembers his parents guest house in the early 1950s:

> My mother did the cooking and my father the washing up. They charged four guineas per person per week half board. The food was very basic by todays standards, but most things were still on ration – guests gave up their ration tokens for the time they spent with us. The gong was sounded at 6pm sharp and dinner started with a bowl of the ubiquitous Maggi soup, put on the table whether or not anyone was seated. It was followed by dishes such as shepherds pie and peas, bought puff pastry mince pies and cream and a minuscule cup of Camp coffee. Friday's dinner was the highlight of the week: tomato soup, tinned salmon salad, and trifle topped with tinned peaches.

By the late 1960s he was running his own hotel, the Heddons Gate at Martinhoe, currently renowned for its quality local food:

Dallyn family at tea, Killington Farm, Martinhoe, 1954

Our weekly tariff was 11 to 12 guineas per person for half board. A lunch of lamb chop and chips followed by ice cream could be had for three shillings and sixpence and morning tea cost one shilling per person. Dinner, not the refined affair it is today, was served in a most spartan dining room with brick wallpaper, bentwood chairs and chipboard tables covered with a cheap tablecloth; not much of the crockery and cutlery matched. Tables were advertised as separate but were about an inch apart. Guests dined on soup, a roast with one vegetable, generally peas, cabbage, carrots or runner beans (courgettes were unknown) and about a pound of potatoes each, followed by fruit pie with custard, and, because it was Devon, clotted cream. The floor was covered by thick rubber treated with Linopaint. If you lingered over your cheese you might find your chair firmly stuck to it. The room was heated by a small fan heater which I turned towards whomever complained most vociferously about the cold.

None of us had much knowledge about wine. Our list had about a dozen wines, stored in an unused fireplace; the most popular were Sauternes, Mateus Rose and Liebfraumilch. After dinner, guests crowded into the bar; there was a great consumption of spirits, accompanied by a hubbub of conversation and laughter. In these sophisticated days far fewer spirits are taken after dinner, and though things are still pleasant, the absolute conviviality has gone.

In the countryside old traditions died harder, although there seemed to be a great decline in home baking. Typical was farmer Dick French, of Brendon Barton, who died in 1997. His wife, Lorna, cooked a full roast dinner most days for Dick and anyone else who was around the farm, summoning them with a hand bell. Dinner meant between 1pm and 2pm and anyone not arriving at that time missed out completely. Breakfast was also a full cooked breakfast but a more flexible feast. Dick would often come home late from the pub in the evening, help himself to the remains of the mid-day joint, sleep until mid morning, have his cooked breakfast and then come back soon for his roast dinner. Tea was often a cream tea, although with bread instead of scones and large quantities of bread were consumed at in-between times. The evening session at the local or daytime at the cattle market could also involve the consumption of large quantities of brown ale, with no obviously adverse effect.

Part of the revival of interest in local food came with the Exmoor Tourism Development Action Programme, out of which sprang *The Taste of Exmoor Cookery Book* in 1987. The book was followed up with a campaign known as 'The Whortleberry Trail' which helped to

market businesses serving food with locally produced ingredients. About the same time was running 'A Taste of Somerset', an annual exhibition of local produce. This eventually became incorporated into the much larger 'Taste of the West' exhibition, which started as the 'Festival of West Country Food and Drink' at Exeter in 1993.

In 1996 the West Country Tourist Board, the NFU, Food from Britain and Taste of the West joined forces to launch 'West Country Cooking', which aims to help growers, producers and chefs to work closer together. They want hotels, restaurants, cafes, pubs and tearooms across the West Country to use more local food in their cooking. To help them they have been researching and compiling local recipes to remind people of the West Country's culinary heritage. Leading in this were the owner of Taunton's Castle Hotel, Kit Chapman and his chef Phil Vickery. The hotel has the reputation of being one of the top places to eat in the West Country. Kit says: 'The way forward is to create regionalism in food. The saddest thing is that if you ask twenty people to name a traditional West Country dish, the best most of them can do is to suggest a Cornish pasty. Yet ones they eat are likely to be produced under a flag of convenience somewhere else in Britain and bear no relation to a real pasty.' Phil has been adapting old recipes for the restaurant and Great Western Trains Co., which also set up in 1996, is using West Country produce and recipes on its menus. The aim is to produce a form of accreditation for food outlets which support the aims of 'West Country Cooking' and meet exacting standards. Such outlets are listed in an annual guide. 'West Country Cooking' has also sponsored a series of recipe books by food writer Michael Raffael.

When giving a talk about the qualities of Devon cattle in 1995, Albert Beer, Secretary of the Devon Cattle Breeders Society, arranged with the chef to provide the following menu, all of local produce and showing what can be done:

Dunkery nettle soup

———

Juniper and rabbit terrine
with apple and blackberry chutney

———

Smoked trout muffin
with watercress and fennel salad

———

Cider and apricot water ice

———

Fillet of Devon beef
with julienne of vegetables
with English mustard and pear sauce

———

Whortleberry tart
with clover and honey ice cream

and Devonshire clotted cream

———

Selection of Devonshire cheeses

Local wines were served with the dinner.

A typical local business trying to provide customers with a taste of Exmoor is Huxtable Farm at West Buckland, run by Anthony and Jackie Payne. Anthony's mother, Barbara, was the overall winner of 'The Taste of Exmoor' recipe competition with her Whortleberry Cream dessert. Jackie says:

> I love to use the wild produce found in the hedges and fields of Huxtable and on Exmoor, with the knowledge that these products would rarely be sampled by our visitors and to share with them our wonderful source of natural food, e.g. in Autumn the sloes, whortleberries, elderberries, crab apples, hazelnuts, wild mushrooms, partridge, pheasant, rabbit and venison; in Spring the elderflowers, nettles and wild strawberries; in Summer the rose and herb petals together with the vast variety of fruit, herbs and vegetables grown on the farm.
>
> Three years ago we put half of our 80 acres into woodland to encourage the return of wildlife to the farm. We keep about 60 sheep, lambing in Spring and occasionally obtain our own lamb for consumption. Other livestock includes four goats and a few chickens. We have a large fruit garden from which we make delicious puddings, jams, jellies and wines. Fruits include rhubarb, gooseberries, raspberries, loganberries, redcurrants and blackcurrants. The orchard produces apples, plums and crab apples. The herb garden produces sorrel, lovage, lemon balm, mint, rosemary, bay, coriander, fennel and thyme; the greenhouse sweet basil, parsley and cherry tomatoes. A few years ago we kept three Jersey house cows and pigs. We made clotted cream, yoghurt and cottage cheese from the cows milk and fed the pigs on the skimmed milk. The new legislation has prevented us from continuing with these methods, a sad loss to us and to our visitors.
>
> Our four course dinners are always served with a complimentary glass of home-made wine, home-made bread rolls, fresh farm and local produce, Devon clotted cream, a selection of Devon cheeses and home-made fudge with the coffee.

Jackie suggests a typical menu for her farmhouse dinners, the recipes for which are contained in this book:

Cream of wild mushroom soup with
herb croutons

———

Venison casserole in cider and cream
with parsley dumplings and sloe jelly

———

Elderflower, gooseberry and hazelnut tart
served with clotted cream

———

Whortleberry and elderberry cream fudge

Jackie says she is always looking for local recipes to try for her guests and would like more to go with the few she has found. Tourism is now the main industry on Exmoor and it would be a shame if providers for tourists cannot provide 'A Taste of Exmoor' for their guests through lack of ideas, which is one reason why this book is much larger than its predecessor. Also, the landscape of Exmoor that tourists come to see has been created by generations of farmers. The traditional methods they have used to maintain the landscape are geared to the production of food. If people do not support local produce they may be contributing towards the changing of the distinctive landscape they come to see. That is not to say that the landscape should not change as it has always done or that food should not change with the times. The complete Exmoor cookery book will, hopefully, never be written, as Exmoor cookery will continue to evolve. The essence is that variety is the spice of life and that going on holiday is about going somewhere that is refreshingly different. Supporting distinctively local food helps to support the whole culture of an area and to provide re-creation in the true sense of the word for the visitors to that area.

Not only does it enhance the special nature of Exmoor for visitors to eat local food but they often wish to take some home with them as a souvenir. Few visitors actually want souvenirs made in other areas: they often have no choice. To help to highlight local products, for residents and visitors alike, the Exmoor Producers Association was set up in 1995 with funding from the European Regional Development Fund, Rural Development Commission and Exmoor National Park Authority. In helping to increase the market for local produce, it keeps local people in employment in the area, thereby helping to sustain the Exmoor way of life. The Association includes a wide range of craft industries as well as food manufacturers. Members' products include flour, bread, sweets, preserves, honey, cakes, biscuits, cheeses, fish, poultry, beef, lamb, pork, tea and spring water. In 1997 the Association undertook a survey of local food outlets to see if there was potential to improve sales of local products. Nearly two thirds of the respondents replied that they were already committed to selling local produce or would prefer to. Of the products which were already being sold, drinks, both alcoholic and non-alcoholic, were most popular, but the greatest growth potential seemed to be for organic meat and vegetables. Besides the growing interest in organic food, one of the reasons

Locally reared meats from Heal Farm, Kings Nympton

for this is that businesses still tend to buy such products from local shops whereas most other items are purchased from large supermarkets and wholesalers. This has resulted in the Association launching into wholesaling of local food products.

Despite the growing interest in local produce and healthy food, there is still the problem of cost and competitiveness for small scale producers. There is no simple answer to this: small is in most cases bound to mean more expensive. The producers can only do so much: it is up to the customer to decide how important food is to them and their health. It is also up to them to understand a little more about where food cames from and how it is produced. I am sure that Exmoor food would be much more popular if people knew what they are eating. I have already spoken of definitions of culture. The dictionary definitions all refer to development, training and state of knowledge. In essence, if Exmoor culture is to survive it depends upon education, education and education. The essence of culture, however, is that the knowledge and experience lives within the people and not in books. I can only hope that this book is a first stage and not an end in itself.

Hindon Farm, Minehead, a modern organic meats, local produce and accomodation enterprise   Penny Webber

Exmoor Houses and their Kitchens

BUILDING MATERIALS

Exmoor houses were usually made of materials dug on site. As the local materials tended to be poor, houses were often sited near the supplies of better materials. Most local subsoils, however, make reasonable cob. Much of Exmoor is covered with 'head', a mixture of stone and clay produced by frost weathering and soil creep during the Ice Age. Such material can become very hard and is the foundation and building material for many Exmoor cottages. Where built of stone, most older houses have a mortar made of cob or a mixture of lime and cob. Cut stone (ashlar) was not usually of local material and expensively imported to the area. Timber for roofs and spars for thatching mostly came from the cutting of hedgerow trees.

FARMHOUSES

The basic plan of the traditional Exmoor farmhouse derives from the ancient 'cross passage' plan. This consists of a simple single storey rectangular building with a passage running straight from front to back. The passageway connected a front and rear door, usually leading to a yard, and internally there were doors from the passageway to rooms on either side.

Longhouse-style farmhouse at Higher Mannacott, Martinhoe

In its simplest form there were only two rooms, making what is known as a 'longhouse'. One room was for the family and one for their animals and the front door was shared by both. This must have been very mucky and later shippons had their own outside doors. The building was built down the slope of the land with the lower end for the animals, making it easier for 'mucking out' along a central channel with an opening in the end wall. However, such houses were more common on Dartmoor and only two or three such houses survive on Exmoor, although traces can be found in abandoned sites, such as the so called 'Doone houses' in Hoccombe Combe. The term seems to be commonly applied to almost any old farmhouse and most current 'longhouses', with two, three or more rooms in a row, never housed cattle and are not strictly longhouses. Farmhouses with three rooms in a row were for centuries the most common design on Exmoor and either side of the Bristol Channel. Cattle were normally housed in separate buildings, although never far from the house. Cattle were extremely valuable in centuries past and needed to be well housed and looked after. Not every farmer could afford an ox for ploughing and plough teams were often shared commodities. Milking cows also needed to be kept close for convenience.

Until late medieval times no Exmoor cottages had fireplaces or chimneys, which did not become common until the sixteenth and seventeenth centuries. Many are known as 'hearth houses' as in the hall or living room there was a central hearth for a wood or peat fire. This was generally set in an earthen floor. The smoke escaped either through a simple hole in the roof or worked its way out through the thatch. The rafters became blackened with the soot, as in the 'black houses' of Scotland and Ireland, and such evidence is often sought in determining the age development of a house. Such houses would have been very dark and smoky and mainly just used as places to sleep in. Great care was taken to keep firewood dry, so that it was less smoky. Even the grandest houses generally did not have wall fireplaces with chimneys until the fifteenth century, although they were not a new invention. They may, however, have had a louvered canopy over the roof opening, sometimes with hinged louvres like Venetian blinds which could be adjusted according to the wind.

Central hearths survived locally well into the seventeenth century. In some cases where large fires were required for cooking, the oven or kitchen building was situated outside the house to reduce the risk of sparks setting the thatch alight. This was probably the origin of the communal bakehouses found in some Exmoor villages until the twentieth century. Most ovens were placed outside the main house until the hearths were moved against the walls. Anciently, ovens were simply holes in the ground where fires were made and the food put in with the embers and covered over. They gradually became more sophisticated, being lined with stone or clay and later being constructed of similar materials above ground.

Generally, central hearths suited houses with high roofs to give space for the smoke to escape. They were occasionally placed against a wall using a stone fireback or in stone houses, but the building of fireplaces and chimneys against the wall generally went hand in hand with enlarging the accommodation into the roof space by creating a first floor which rendered a central hearth impractical. Such improvements were often funded by profits from the wool trade in the sixteenth and seventeenth centuries. The industry was past its height locally but wool prices were rising whilst wages remained static and it was a time of increasing wealth for yeoman farmers. The size of local timber was a limiting factor in house size and there was a great demand for English oak at the time, as opposed to smaller types of trees. Cruck framed houses, supported by tall, one piece, curved timbers from ground to ridge, are almost absent on Exmoor. It was much more common to build walls of cob or stone and set smaller, jointed cruck timbers on top of these for the roof space.

In the seventeenth century hearths were taxed and only the wealthier families had more than one. Records of taxes at the time at Combe Martin show most houses having only one hearth, but those of wealthier families having four or five and the Lord of the Manor having eight. Those with only one hearth had the fireplace positioned as centrally as possible for maximum effect. This was sometimes to the rear of the building, but usually to the front with the chimney projecting from the facade as a status symbol. It was usually from the living room, just on the upslope side of the doorway. The chimneys appear tall as they are freestanding from the eaves, but are generally no taller than chimneys which project through the roof ridge. They need to reach above ridge height to prevent downdraughts caused by the wind turbulence created by the roof, also to carry sparks away from the thatch, which was prone to catching fire.

Many cottages were still of the cross passage design, but this died out in the eighteenth century. Usually the living room was split into two to create a bedroom or parlour, often with its own fireplace and chimney on the end wall. Where the house was built along a slope, the 'lower room' as it was called, was often a store room or work room. This was usual on Exmoor but many houses were built along the slope according to the dictates of drainage or aspect. Fashion and greater wealth meant that many newer houses were built across the slope with the living rooms facing south. A dairy was often then built along the darker, cooler rear of the house. In *Within Living Memory* by Margaret

A cottage chimney at Selworthy

Bate an old lady describes her farmhouse at North Molton:

> This is one of eleven Devon long houses in this parish which were built facing south. All the windows are on the south side except two at the back, one for the dairy and the other for a store room where the wool used to be kept at one end and the other end used as a granary. Sometimes bullocks that were being fattened were kept there. The floor and shelves of the dairy are of blue stone which keeps it cool. Our well is under what is now our kitchen and we have a pump. It was my grandmother who had alterations made on the ground floor, which used to be the kitchen and one large room with a central fireplace and the stairway. She wanted more privacy as family and domestic help all had to go through the large room to get upstairs. So a passageway was made at the back and two good rooms in the front each with its own fireplace.

In the nineteenth century and before most farmhouses were home to labourers and servants as well as the farmer and his family. Most farmhands lived on the farm until they were married and poor wages often delayed marriages. A dozen occupants to a farmhouse was average and all ate the same food. It was common for three or four to occupy the same bedroom and those working with animals would often sleep in a loft above a shippen or stable. Mechanisation and the largely Victorian concept of privacy put an end to this. From the late eighteenth century farmers and labourers gradually became more separated and small old farmhouses lining village streets became labourers' cottages. Often a farmhouse would be partitioned into several cottages, each requiring its own fireplace and chimney. These frequently became slums for the poor whilst remaining farms grew fewer and larger. Today it is common for a farm to be worked by one man and his son or a labourer housed in the nearest council or housing association houses. Often the old farmhouse has been sold to wealthy incomers and the barns converted for stables. The farmer more often lives in a modern bungalow with large modern barns at a little distance from the house.

Farmhouses were usually enlarged by adding rooms on the ends, hence the so-called 'longhouses'. From the eighteenth century it was quite common to create a 'double pile' house by adding another block with its own roof to the rear of the original building. The old Hunter's Inn was extended in this manner. The larger farmhouses often grew to contain several specialist rooms. There was the dairy, cheese room or 'wring house', still room, smoking chamber, buttery for the butts or barrels, apple cellar and malt chamber. The Agricultural Revolution, however, brought new, planned farmhouses. Like the Knight farms in the former Royal Forest, they often had a 'villa' style farmhouse with a central doorway and symetrically arranged windows on two floors. This would have a slated kitchen and dairy and farm buildings would be arranged behind around a quadrangle.

The book *Exmoor Village* by W. J. Turner shows the plan of a typical Luccombe cottage in the 1940s. It clearly shows the original cross passage plan, with one side of the passage removed to enlarge the living room, which is also the kitchen. The animal room has become the parlour and the roof has been raised to add a first floor with bedrooms and landing, with staircase coming up from the parlour. A brick extension has been added to the rear for scullery, kitchen and wash house, with a separate chimney for the copper boiler. Such boilers were mainly used for washing clothes, but also for cooking where large quantities of water were required, such as in preparing pigs for salting, boiling potatoes for pig food, boiling large puddings or boiling mash for brewing. The copper was usually heated from underneath with faggots of furze, which made a quick, hot fire. Often these were called 'black sticks' because the spines had been burnt off to make cutting easier. The toilet was an earth closet in the garden. Water came from a rain butt by the back door. Many houses had water piped from springs, but it was usual for the house only to have one cold tap, in the scullery.

KITCHENS

The old hall of medieval houses or main room of cross passage houses remained the kitchen as it was the room with the large fireplace. From the late eighteenth to late twentieth century most houses were built with several fireplaces. However, it was usual only to keep one fire going – the one for cooking. This was usually in the living room but where there was a separate kitchen, this tended to be used as the living room because of the constant heat. The fire in the parlour or sitting room was usually only lit on Sundays or other special occasions and fires in bedrooms usually only when there was illness.

Kitchen fireplaces were often so large that they incorporated stone seats – inglenooks – or space for wooden stools. Most heat went straight up the chimney and away from the fire. Kitchen seats were often high-backed settles which provided some protection from

Settle at Allerford Rural Life Museum

draughts, especially as occasionally a door had to be left ajar to help the fire draw. Some had storage space under the seats and a few had cupboard backs where sides of bacon could be hung, although it was more usual to hang salt or smoked meat from ceiling hooks. Such meat, usually cured beef, mutton or ham, was commonly called 'roofmeat'. Sometimes there was a 'kitchen chamber' – a small room above the kitchen used for storing cheeses, grain, flour or wool and often used by the maid for sleeping. There was often a bench built under a window. This was uncomfortable, as one had to sit upright against the wall, but was mostly used to sit at table at mealtimes. It was usual to sit on benches at the large kitchen table. The table was often laid on trestles so that it could be taken down and stored against a wall.

In hearth houses floors were often of bare clay. Later, most Exmoor kitchen floors were laid with cobbles or local slate slabs. The latter were easy to clean and acquired a natural polish with wear. They were often sanded. The sand 'filed the dirt out' as it was trodden in and when it had been swept away the floor appeared scrubbed. Often the housewife would take a piece of white hearthstone and make a pattern of squiggles, circles and squares around the edge of the newly swept floor. This was said to give good luck and keep the witches away. The practice is recorded up until the Second World War. During the eighteenth and nineteenth centuries lime ash floors became common in larger houses near the coast or elsewhere where there were lime kilns. Lime was mixed with ash to form a sort of concrete. Some say it was wetted with blood or cider to harden it, but this is difficult to substantiate. When hardened, the floor would take a polish with a wet mop, but tended to be dusty. In some households they were sealed with egg white, which also gave a good polish. Such floors often underlie modern tiled floors. Carpets were rare until recent times and rushes and herbs were commonly strewn on kitchen floors.

Cottage dining room, Badgercombe, Twitchen

Steve Guscott

WOOD FIRES

Exmoor has not been well wooded since prehistoric times, although it is relatively well wooded compared with England as a whole. The woods largely survive on the steeper cliffs and valley sides not suited to cultivation or improvement for pasture. They are generally dominated by sessile oak, which has been selected through centuries of coppicing. The wood was largely used for charcoal production and the bark for tanning. The timber was small and rarely straight, so was not much used for construction, for which hedgerow trees were better suited. Hedgerows were also the main source of firewood for cooking, although short rotation coppice and the trimmings from other coppicing were also used.

Wood fires were often kept alight continuously and a large branch would burn slowly. It would be set alight at one end and gradually pushed forwards into the fireplace as it burned through. This suited cooking, as logs laid horizontally burn with less flame than when they are set upright. Smaller logs were also common and were

cheaply purchased as off-cuts from sawmills. Faggots and smaller branches were used for the more intense heat required for most cookery. The wood was usually supported on fire 'dogs', which prevented burning logs from rolling out and gave a draught under the fire.

In his book *The Way 'Twas*, Walter Isaac recalls his childhood at the Elizabethan South Cobbaton Farm, to the south of Exmoor:

> There was a pump house, lead pump, stone trough and boiler with room for wood faggots, a large kitchen with an open fireplace and earthen oven. I can recall my mother using this oven by first heating with faggot wood before putting in the bread. Eventually a large Bodley was fitted with oven and water fountain with brass tap. The ceiling bore evidence of numerous repairs, and the centuries of use of faggot wood left its mark in the form of a thick layer of nut brown or dark tan stain.

The draw of smoky fires was not eased by the large size of the fireplace. The fireplace needed a large hood to catch the wood smoke. It also needed to accommodate the bread oven and the large branches used for the fire. There was a long iron bar across the length of the fireplace inside the hood from which the crooks and other utensils could be hung. Often meat was hung from this for smoking. The smoking required oak chips on the fire and adjustment of the draw of the chimney by a small door to the outside, which could be opened to let smoke out or closed to let it hang around whatever was being smoked.

On Exmoor fireplaces were usually supported by a huge clavel beams of oak. These had to be large enough to support much of the chimney and the oak usually became extremely hard with age and drying. Above the clavel was the 'clavey tack', or mantlepiece. It often had a cloth pelmet draped underneath and supported boxes of tinder, salt, tea and tobacco and anything which needed to be kept dry. Sometimes these were kept in a cupboard built into the thickness of the wall near the fireplace.

Behind the clavel in the lower part of the chimney was an iron bar or bars across the length of the fireplace from which the crooks could be hung. On these cauldrons, griddles and kettles could be suspended and their height above the fire adjusted using a ratchet on the crook so that the speed of cooking could be adjusted. The kettle often had a pivot and long handle by which it could be tipped to pour without taking it off the crook. Sometimes there would be `crane irons', which were pivoting brackets which enabled utensils to be swung away from the fire. Iron cauldrons could be used to cook complete meals. Each part of the meal could be cooked in earthenware jars standing on a wooden board in the cauldron or wrapped in cloth and suspended in the boiling water by cords. The relatively clean water could then be used for the washing up.

In front of the fire would be a roasting spit with a drip tray under for basting. At its simplest it would have been painstakingly turned by hand – a job usually given to a child. The child, usually a boy, would sit behind a screen to keep himself away from the heat. Later spits were of clockwork with weighted or spring driven mechanisms. There were devices for hanging meat over the fire for barbecuing but generally they were placed in front of the fire to avoid the meat being smoked or drying out or burning. They always had a drip tray underneath and the 'dripping' from the meat was used for frying. Spits had spiked contraptions to hold the meat or holes for tying it on. In medieval times the spit was often used to skewer fruits along with the meat like kebabs. Sometimes the whole would be basted in batter as it cooked, to develop a pastry crust. The meat would then be carved straight from the spit, which was taken to the table.

Around the fireplace would be arrayed a variety of cooking utensils. A skillet was a large, three legged saucepan which could be stood over the fire. Smaller saucepans were usually placed on a trivet or tripod over the fire. Where this had a triangular surface for resting the pan it was called a brandis. Three cornered fields were often given this name, which may also be the origin of Brandish Street, where three roads bound the settlement. Frying pans were also placed on the trivet. Crocks were often not clay dishes but expensive pans of brass or bell metal. A griddle was a flat iron plate suspended from a crook. A gridiron was also suspended from a crook. It was a grill with large bars shaped like gutters which enabled the meat juices to be run off. Kettles could be as described above or cauldrons used for baking. Baking kettles would be upturned on an iron plate on the fireplace and surrounded by burning peat, 'vags' or wood embers. In the nineteenth century 'bakers' or 'hearth ovens' were introduced. These were cast iron ovens, about 18 inches high, which stood on the hearth with the fire on top of them. They were a cheap alternative to ranges. The ovens had two compartments – one above the other. The bottom compartment contained an ash pan. This was filled with hot embers from the fire so that the baking compartment was heated from below and above. Fred Rawle of Parracombe remembers one first being used by his family and described it as a 'wonderful new invention' as it made baking food easier and until then baking was only for the bakehouse or one day a week.

BREAD OVENS

Generally on Exmoor these were used as part of large open fireplaces and their backs project through the outside wall as rounded bulges from the base of the chimney, sometimes with their own slated roofs. Often they remained in use when ranges were built into the fireplaces and occasionally they were built separately in a back kitchen or bakehouse. Sometimes they were lined with stone, but these were generally replaced by a single beehive-shaped piece of earthenware. They were then known as a 'cloam' oven from the local term for clay. 'Barnstaple ovens' were one piece cloam ovens, made from Barum pottery. There are stories of them being packed in straw and sent by boat or pack horse all over the region. Dating from the seventeenth century onwards, they originally they had clay doors, but these were easily cracked or broken and new ones seldom fitted well, so most were replaced by a cast iron 'oven stopper' – an iron door with two handles which was lifted into position. Most which survive today have had a modern iron doorway with hinged door inserted. Brick linings were introduced in the eighteenth and nineteenth centuries and commonly survive today.

The oven worked on the storage heater principle, with the brick or clay retaining heat from a wood fire. When expertly heated, the oven would retain enough heat for eight hours cooking and up to two days of drying. Enough baking for a week or fortnight was generally saved for each session and it was normal to have a weekly 'bake day'. The food was introduced to and removed from the hot oven on a wooden 'peel', which looked like a long-handled paddle. The food was all prepared together, ready for the cooking session. As the oven gradually dropped in temperature, the heat which things required usually determined the order of cooking. Often starting with pastries, pies, bread and cakes, the lowering oven heat was utilised at each stage, continuing with cooking meat, stewing and bottling, then drying herbs and grain and finally drying brushwood for the next firing. The method was well suited to the baking of cakes, which require a dropping temperature. If there was not a large amount of food to be cooked, it was all put in together, with that which required the longest cooking time at the back and the shortest cooking time at the front. Meat, such as a rabbit pie, would take about three hours to cook. Buns and pastries would take about half an hour and were placed near the front. Bread took anything from one to three hours. It required a high temperature and, if several batches were to be cooked, the oven would have to be refired between each batch. This usually only happened with a commercial bakery.

Bert Verney in his *Reflections* remembers his mother's kitchen the 1920s and '30s, when bread ovens were on their way out:

> It had the great plus of gravity-fed cold water and when the range was lit in the morning room (or best kitchen) as it was most days, it gave an ample supply of hot water. It was called the

'best kitchen' because Mother used to do all the cooking on or in the stove during the week, except on Sundays, when the cloam oven was used.

On Saturday breakfast was cooked as usual over an open fire in the hearth. The cloam oven, at the end of the hearth, was kindled with small faggots until the walls were white with heat. When this was achieved, the ash was removed using an iron scraper, letting the ash fall on the hearth beside and below. It was later carried away to a bin outside, and stored to provide potash for the flower and vegetable garden. Into the oven Mother put a huge dish with a large joint of meat, twenty or so potatoes with three or four chopped onions. A little later, pies of whatever fruits were in season, or large apple dumplings coated in pastry. If you have never tasted a meal cooked in one of these ovens, you have missed a good deal! The taste, compared to modern ovens, was of a different class.

While this was cooking, large pans of home-made bread and yeast cake were kneaded and left in front of the hearth to rise. When the dinner was taken out, the cakes and bread were put in. So, Saturdays were baking days in the farm kitchens.

Brushwood Fires

There has been an abundance of branches from the maintenance of hedges, particularly since the fashion for beech hedgebanks during nineteenth century moorland reclamation and enclosure. Faggots of small branches were often used for cooking. They burn quickly and produce much heat and can be stood upright for even more intense burning. An ashen faggot is traditionally burned on Christmas Eve for luck and health in the year to come and is linked with the custom of wassailing. The sticks were usually bound with withies. The binds were pulled tight around the sticks and tied in a sort of knot by twisting them together, doubling them back and poking the ends into the sticks. In the ashen faggot ceremony each bind is toasted as it burns through, so as many binds as possible were put on that particular faggot. The faggots were usually stored outside in a 'hoodrick' (woodrick), looking like a corn rick but underneath a waterproof cover. Larger poles were stored upright in pyramids which would dry out. Faggots were a very commercial commodity and farmers would sell any surplus, which would be delivered to local homes.

Faggots were used for the heating of bread ovens. They were usually lit with burning branches from the main fire. Gorse, known locally as furze ('vuz'), was usually used as it burns quickly and produces a great heat.

Stouter branches and occasionally logs, usually of ash, were added after the furze had burned down as it took an hour or two to warm the oven sufficiently. The hot ashes were spread all over the floor of the oven, as it was important to heat it evenly. When the oven was heated enough it appeared white. If it was not white, another faggot had to be burned. Then the ashes were raked out quickly into a tray and returned to the main fire. A way of testing if the oven was at the correct temperature was to strike the bottom of the oven with a stick from a faggot. If it gave out sparks, the oven was hot enough.

Some ovens had a slot in front of the door so that the ash could be shovelled out from a hole below without producing too much dust. A long mop, known as a 'mawkin', was then dipped in hot water and used to mop the remaining dust from the oven whilst introducing some steam. The door was then immediately closed to even out the heat again. After a short while the food was introduced and the door kept closed until the first dish was ready to be removed. The door was closed quickly after opening to retain the heat. An ill-fitting door would sometimes be sealed with dough from the bread mix. Most ovens had a shelf in front of the door. This was so the door could be 'sealed with ashes'. Hot ashes from the main fire would be piled against the door to cut down escaping heat.

Hot ashes from the main fire were often taken elsewhere in the house for small jobs such as heating a bedroom or a bed warming pan, or cooking something slowly such as scrambling an egg, warming wine or invalids' food. Sometimes the embers were placed in special utensils or simply on flat stones, but most Exmoor houses had 'creamers': hollowed out stones built into walls. These could be near fireplaces but were often elsewhere in the living room or in another room entirely and were used for a variety of slow cooking, including making clotted cream. They were often used in conjunction with 'crock' pans which would be warmed in the main fire first, so the smaller fires would simply help to retain the heat.

Peat Fires

The centre of Exmoor has been virtually treeless throughout historic times and peat was once an important source of fuel for persons living in that area. It is found in valley bogs throughout the area, but has generally been cut from the blanket bog of the Chains, Exe Plain, Great Ashcombe, Warren Allotment and Brendon Common. On the Royal Forest it was cut by right of the Free Suitors, who were like commoners. Between the late seventeenth and early nineteenth centuries the rights were sold annually to the highest bidders and substantial quantities of peat were removed.

Peat digging on Brendon Common c1950   Exmoor Photographic Archive

Later in the nineteenth century the Knights, then owners of the former Royal Forest, brought sheep and shepherds from the north of England and from Scotland to the area. The shepherds would have been well used to cutting peat for a multitude of uses: bedding for animals, smoking of fish and hams, dyeing wool and staining skins. The ash was used as fertiliser for root crops, often in combination with its use as the 'earth' in earth closets. Large quantities of shallow peat were pared from the surface of the ground, burned and the ash returned to the soil after ploughing as part of moorland reclamation. Fred Rawle of Parracombe remembers cutting turf on Homer (Challacombe) Common. It was shallow 'turf' cut with a special spade which was pushed along with the legs, using irons to protect the legs from chafing. The spade had various attachments to cut different shapes of turf and turn them. Fred says that it was easier to work in twos with one digging and one turning the turf. He used the peat to stand sheep on for shearing, to help keep the wool clean. It was later burnt and the ashes used for planting turnips. A man was expected to cut about a thousand turves per day but this was often doubled when on piece work. The nineteenth century record went to Tom Elworthy, who cut 7000 in two days at Kittuck, walking the five miles over bog from Duredon and back each day.

It has been a privilege of tenants of the Knight and, latterly, Fortescue estates to take peat for fuel and it is still cut on Lanacombe. On Brendon Common peat cutting has been continued for centuries as part of commoners legal right of turbary, a right which must be registered and which few retain. The peat is cut with a traditional spade into thin square slabs. Spine turf, where the deposits are shallow, is cut on a slant. Pit turf, where the peat beds are deeper, is cut straight down. The darker, more dense turfs from deeper in the cutting were cut more brick shaped. It was harder to harvest as the sodden turves easily broke up into lumps. These lumps, known locally as 'biddocks' were bagged separately and prized for their strong heat. The cut sods were left on the common through the summer to dry before being collected, traditionally on wooden sleds or by packhorse. It was stored under cover and the sods finally dried around the fireplace and broken into smaller pieces as required.

Turf burns slowly, gives a gentle heat and produces much ash and smoke. Such fires were generally kept burning continuously. Phosphorous matches are a comparatively recent invention and it was not easy to kindle a peat fire with a tinderbox. Bellows, or sometimes a more sophisticated rotary fan were necessary to start the fire and generate enough heat for cooking and it was usual to keep peat fires alight continuously throughout the year. The lighter peat from near the surface was kept separate as it burns quicker and produces more heat for cooking. The peat was generally used for baking on a flat stone hearth. Although occasionally used for bread ovens it gave out too little heat to cook most food in this way. The hearth was warmed with the fire and a space swept clear for the bread or dish. This was then covered with an earthenware 'pot oven' or 'iron kettle' and the fire built up over the pot. The hearth often had a sloping stone fireback or reredos built on a frame against the chimney wall. The space behind the fireback was often used as a smuggler's hiding place, accessible through loose stones in the fireback or wall.

The peat was said to suit Bodley ranges. Farmer Dick French continued to cut peat and use it at home until he died in 1997. At that time he was using it in his Rayburn. The comparatively gentle heat of the peat, however, meant that it could not be adapted to all types of cooking, and many Exmoor recipes evolved to suit such conditions. Peat was ideally suited to the production of clotted cream, to which it imparted a smoky flavour which became much sought after. It was also ideal for smoking fish and meat in the chimney above.

COAL FIRES

Exmoor is not a coal producing area and coal fires for cooking or heating are a recent introduction here. Coal certainly would not have suited the open fireplaces but coal fired cookers were introduced in the nineteenth century. Coal does not burn like wood and has to be raised so that the ashes can be raked out from under the fire. It cannot be used for heating bread ovens, so Exmoor people often tried to keep their bread ovens and open fireplaces and have the coal fire in another room. As a result, kitchens developed separate from living rooms. The old cauldrons and pots were unsuited to the raised coal fires and it became common to incorporate a boiler with the fire. Where the cookers were placed in the old fireplaces it became impossible to use the bread oven and ovens became incorporated into the fires as well to form a complete kitchen 'range' of cooking fire, boiler and oven. Early coal fires required a variety of contraptions for roasting and hanging spits were developed for the more upright fires. Screens of polished tin were placed behind the spits to reflect heat. Meat cooks surprisingly well in this way, with little shrinkage and the fat is well preserved. The dripping, collected in a basin below, does not boil and remains clear, making it suitable for pastry making and a variety of other uses.

The coal could be supplemented with wood, but Exmoor people became reliant on deliveries of Welsh coal from the coastal harbours. Often isolated country properties could not have coal delivered and purchase of a range depended on access to a suitable cart to pick up coal from the nearest depot. The Rev. Walter Halliday of Glenthorne had his own boatload of coal delivered from South Wales and distributed it to his tenants, for whom he installed ranges. The tenants were not convinced of the benefits of the ranges and tried to keep their open fireplaces as well. One insisted that the range be placed against an unused back door and just knocked a hole through the door for a flue.

The ranges developed over the years but few are still in use. The usual Exmoor type was known as a Bodley,

Hanging spit at Allerford Rural Life Museum

Brian Pearce

after the Exeter firm of Bodley's which made them. They usually had integral water boilers on the opposite side of the fire from the oven, although capacity was limited to a couple of gallons and larger quantities were usually heated in the 'copper' boiler in the scullery. The range was regularly polished with 'black lead', usually weekly, and the flue needed regular sweeping because of the soot. However, there was not the thick tar produced by wood smoke and the flue could be narrower and more efficient, without the tendency for the smoke to cool before it reached the outside and descend the chimney.

The coal range had the advantage that, for a comparatively small fire, it could bake, boil, fry and roast. Its efficiency varied considerably with the draught up the flue. Much depended upon the design of the chimney and many Exmoor cottages can be seen with brick additions to stone chimney stacks to improve the draw of the fire when ranges were introduced. As bricks had to be carried some distance, they did not become common Exmoor building materials until the spread of railways in the late nineteenth century. The heat could be directed to the oven or boiler by means of dampers, but much of the control of the oven temperature was related to the stoking of the fire. The more coal in the fire box and in contact with the oven, generally the hotter the oven, but oven temperature had to be maintained by regular

Kitchen at Driver Farm 1929

Alfred Vowles Collection

Granny Baker's kitchen at the Dulverton Heritage Centre

Brian Pearce

applications of coal. As the fire was generally to one side of the oven, temperature in the oven was uneven, necessitating turning of the food during cooking.

Many estates had ranges specially made for their tenants. The Fortescue Estate made their own. The following account of Luccombe comes from W. J. Turner's book *Exmoor Village*, published in 1947:

> The cottages in Luccombe are fitted with coal-ranges by the Holnicote estate; and no open fireplaces are in use for cooking; the ranges are supplemented by paraffin and methylated-spirit stoves. The lack of gas is not felt seriously by housewives who have never used it, and though Calor gas in cylinders has long been available in country districts, so far as could be ascertained, the nearest Calor stove is at Horner. Mrs Prestcott, who does all her cooking and heats her water on the range, says she would like to have Calor gas now; before the war she used to use three to four hundredweights of coal a week, but now she is only able to get one, and finds some difficulty in making do.

OIL FIRES

Paraffin burners and ovens were commonly used in Exmoor kitchens between roughly the 1920s and 1950s. They were particularly marketed at country dwellers. They could be smelly and slow, but improved as the fuel became more refined. Ranges were produced with up to four burners, oven and automatic oil feed. The oven was usually placed over one or two of the burners and could be removed for full use of the hotplate. Being lightly constructed, the ovens usually heated up quickly and lost heat quickly. The temperature dropped suddenly when the door was opened, which was a problem for some baking. They did not have grills, but grilling or toasting was not a common method of cooking on Exmoor.

TODAY'S KITCHENS

Ranges were not as sociable as open fireplaces and eventually came to be fitted in kitchens rather than living rooms. Insulated coal cookers like today's Rayburns and Agas came to Exmoor about the 1930s and became popular from the 1950s. They burned coal or coke much more efficiently and cleanly and reduced heat loss from the oven. The oven temperature was much more constant and controllable.

Mains gas has only reached the fringes of Exmoor and the Aga or Rayburn is still the norm in an Exmoor farmhouse kitchen, supplemented perhaps by a hob burning bottled gas and a microwave cooker. The ovens are greatly valued by the owners – and their pets – for their constant source of warmth and use for drying wet clothes. Many have now been adapted for oil burning and central heating. They are unbeatable for many forms of baking and slow cooking and can be considered an essential part of today's Exmoor cookery. The constant warmth means that the kitchen tends to be the most used room in the house and is multi-functional. Although television, like elsewhere, has pervaded mealtimes, the kitchen remains the social hub of the house where family and guests meet and as such is important for the continuance of an Exmoor culture.

❧ Fish ❧

Freshwater Fish

SALMON

These can be found on the main Exmoor rivers but are not particularly common and, as everywhere else, are becoming less and less common as the ocean currents which bring them to Exmoor are changing. Claude Wade talks of them lying as thick as herrings in pools on the East Lyn in the nineteenth century. Even then, however, there were complaints of them disappearing, largely through poaching. Where the river ran narrow it was easy to snare the fish with a cord attached to a stick with a slip knot. The process was known as jerking as it required such a movement to pull the snare tight. Snatching was where a line with a weighted hook or triangle of hooks was thrown over the fish and pulled to hook the fish on the body. Lynmouth people were accused of taking so many in this way that they were killing the goose that lays the golden egg in reducing fish stocks so that the visitors who paid for the fishing and for the fish were turning away. Eventually the riparian owners got together to enforce strict rules. However, poaching still goes on and often in a big way by gangs from outside the area using nets and fish stocks are still diminishing.

Salmon run when the rivers are in spate in late summer and autumn, but can run as early as July on the East Lyn, where they are mostly found on the lower reaches. They are still caught in the fish weir at the mouth of the

Salmon weir at Lynmouth

Brian Pearce

Lyn. The rights to this currently belong to the owner of the Bath Hotel, which is the only place where you are likely to find Exmoor salmon on the menu. Catching Lyn salmon further up river is tricky as fly fishing only is permitted and the overhanging branches restrict casting. They vary in size up to a maximum of about 20 lbs, although they are generally small and not particularly good eating. Fish of up to 40 lbs were recorded in the nineteenth century.

The most common way of cooking a salmon locally is to put it in a large pan or fish kettle with cold water and perhaps a little oil or butter. The water is then brought to the boil, left simmering for five minutes and the salmon is left in the water to get cold.

RICH SALMON SOUP

Steve Guscott

Recipe from Bob Deville of Martinhoe. Bob says: 'This recipe was born out of Exmoor desperation! Hotel keeping in a remote area always requires very careful planning and when things go wrong one cannot look to nearby shops for a solution, but only to ones wits. On this particular day we had made a fish terrine. When I came to slice it up at 5pm the whole thing fell apart and was useless. All that I could find in the fridge was some cooked salmon and the remains of a homemade tomato soup. Onions are a very good base for a soup and we had a sack of those. The solution to the problem had to be quick and fish-based. Using a food processor I combined the three ingredients we had and heated the resulting liquor up. We got lots of compliments that night and requests for the recipe! I had no idea of the quantities and it took many months of experimentation to get the same result, but here it is':

To serve four persons:
4 ozs raw fresh salmon (leftover lightly
cooked will do)
4 ozs roughly chopped onions
4 ozs tomato juice
Pinch cayenne pepper
Salt to taste

Process all ingredients in a liquidiser or food processor until very smooth. At this point you can refrigerate for later in the day. Place in a saucepan and heat gently until hot but not boiling (it will become gritty if you do). Just before serving you can add 4 ozs double cream – entirely optional but lovely. Serve in cups or small bowls with an accompaniment of crusty bread. A sprinkle of chives on the soup would be good. You can substitute the salmon with pink trout.

EXMOOR SALMON AND SMOKED TROUT PATÉ

Recipe from Daphne Criddle of Lower Vellow:

For 6 persons:
4 ozs\100 gms salmon
4 ozs\100 gms smoked trout
½ pt\300 mls fish stock
1 oz\25 gms butter
1 oz\25 gms plain flour
1 egg, separated
½ oz\12 gms gelatine
¼ pt\150 mls cream
2 hard boiled eggs

Flake the fish. Make a roux with the butter and flour and add the stock. Dissolve the gelatine in 3 tablespoons of water. Whisk the cream and beat the egg white. Chop one hard boiled egg very finely. Add the fish to the sauce and dissolved gelatine, drop by drop. Fold in the cream, egg white and beaten yolk. Pour into a greased mould and allow to set. Decorate with cucumber, salmon trimmings, chopped egg white and sieved yolk and serve with homemade brown bread.

CURDON FISH PIE

Recipe from Daphne Criddle of Lower Vellow:

Ingredients for 6 persons:
8 ozs\225 gms Exe salmon
4 ozs\100 gms shelled prawns
1 egg
¼ pt\150 mls cream
2 ozs\50 gms butter
12 ozs\350 gms puff pastry
6 ozs\175 gms chopped mushrooms
Chopped parsley

For the sauce:
1 oz \25 gms butter
1 oz\25 gms plain flour
½ pt\300 mls cream
2 egg yolks
2 shallots
Dijon mustard, lemon juice,
parsley, tarragon, chervil

Line a pie dish with 8 ozs of the pastry and bake blind for 10 minutes. Flake the salmon and place in the bottom with the prawns and mushrooms. Whip the egg with the cream and pour in. Season, sprinkle with chopped parsley. Roll out the remaining pastry for lid, seal down well and brush with egg glaze. Bake for 30 minutes at 400°F\200°C\Gas Mark 6, then cover top with cooking foil and bake for a further 20 minutes.

For the sauce, gently fry the chopped shallots in the butter, add herbs and mix in flour to absorb fat. Cook for a minute, add a teaspoon of mustard and cream, heating the mixture to boiling point. Beat the egg yolks with a tablespoon of cream and add to the sauce before serving with the pie.

LYN SALMON HOTELIÈRE

Recipe from Kevin Charlton of Lynmouth:

Ingredients for 2 persons:
1X8 ozs\225 gms salmon steak
2 ozs\50 gms butter
1 oz \25 gms prawns
½ oz\15 gms flaked almonds
2 inches\6 cms piece of cucumber
1 lemon
Seasoned flour, salt and butter

Melt half the butter in a shallow frying pan, coat the salmon steak in flour and cook slowly until both sides are a light, golden brown. Slice the cucumber and cut into thin strips. Remove the salmon, take out the backbone, drain off the butter and return to the heat. Add the remainder of the butter and replace the salmon. Add the cucumber, prawns and almonds, the juice of half the lemon and a little light seasoning and cook for about a minute. Serve, garnished with the remaining lemon thinly sliced.

SALMON PEAL

These are elsewhere known as grilse and are young salmon which run up Exmoor rivers from the sea. The time of the run varies as, although they usually run in summer, they like to have plenty of water in the river. They run earlier on the Lyn as they are close to the sea. They can actually only reach about a mile upstream here – to Peal Pool, where their run is blocked by a waterfall. It is possible to catch them with a maggot, minnow or even a woodlouse, but fly fishing only is allowed. A common fly to use is the Infallible. They are considered better fishing and eating than the larger salmon, especially when fresh run from the sea. They vary in size from about ½ lb to 3 lbs.

SEA TROUT OR PEAL

These run up the East Lyn in July and August, usually at night and do not require a fresh spate of water like the salmon or salmon peal. A fish of two and a half pounds would be considered a fair size today, but four pounders were common in the last century. Wade, writing in 1903, stated:

'One of the prettiest fish I ever saw was a thick sea trout, silvery bright, covered with spots and weighing two and a half pounds. This fish was caught by a school fellow of mine, in the deep hole just above the

Brian Pearce

bridge at the junction of the East and West Lyn. He was fishing standing in the road from the bridge itself, and I well remember it because it was in 1867, and I think the first year of salmon licences. He had not taken out a licence, and we were terribly afraid of the Coastguard, but luckily that gentleman did not turn up, though we had to fetch a ladder from a neighbouring yard, put it down into the pool and climb down it from the bridge with a landing net before we secured our fish.'

He later recalls how he saw four or five peal in the same pool on a Sunday, when fishing was not permitted. In order to outwit the local fishermen, he went out at midnight to catch them and caught all within an hour with worm bait. Each weighed about a pound.

BAKED SEA TROUT

Old recipe:

1 sea trout
6 ozs breadcrumbs
Milk
Anchovy essence
6 ozs shelled prawns
4 ozs butter
2 eggs
2 tablespoons chopped spring onions
¼ pt white wine

Gut and clean the fish. Make a stuffing by mixing the breadcrumbs, anchovy essence, eggs, prawns, spring onions and 2 ozs of the butter with a little milk. Stuff the fish with the mixture. Place in a buttered ovenproof dish. Pour the wine over the fish and dot with any remaining butter. Cover with a lid and bake at 325°F\170°C\ Gas Mark 3 for about an hour. Strain and reduce the cooking juices to use as a sauce for the fish.

TROUT

Exmoor trout are the native brown trout. They are usually small – little more than six inches long – but good sport for the angler and much better tasting than the farmed fish. Anything larger than this is a rarity but cannibal trout can reach up to four pounds on Exmoor. Fishermen are keen to get rid of them as they can rapidly depopulate an area of other fish. Farmed trout on Exmoor are generally the North American rainbow variety, although some are crossbred for even larger size. There are several fish farms in the area now. The largest, the Exe Valley Fisheries at Exebridge, was started by an enterprising farmer who dug out some ponds in his fields in 1885, making it one of the oldest trout farms in Britain. The business prospered under T. F. Tracey, a skilled trout breeder who took over in 1900. Trout are hatched and grown and sent to stock lakes all over Britain.

Visitors can catch fish from three lakes or purchase fresh and smoked fish and paté from the farm shop. The fishing season runs through the summer but the

Blakewell Trout Fisheries at Muddiford

Brian Pearce

spring months, when the fish are rising to take flies, offer the best fishing. Only fly fishing is permissible. Flies commonly used are known as the Killer, Infallible, Silverhorn, California and Blue Upright. As the fish are small but good sport, light but strong tackle is usually used and the flies are small.

There are many accounts of fishermen taking prodigious quantities of these small trout in the nineteenth century. Almost all ended up in a frying pan and some would even take a pan and stove out fishing with them. The Rev. Robert Gould of Ilfracombe is supposed to have caught so many trout on Badgworthy Water one day that a horse and cart were needed to carry them away. A vicar of Stoke Pero was reputed to have caught 370 in one day in the same area. Parson Froude caught 315 and Nicholas Snow, who owned the fishing rights, could only manage a maximum of 215. Today it would be difficult to catch more than 100. The Rev. William Thornton spoke of his fishing in 1848:

I always had a liking for small and crabbed waters, for no one fished them; in them the good fish live, and are unsophisticated withal. I liked to visit the very topmost waters, fish with a short line, fine gut, and a single fly, often a red one with a white tip to the body. I would throw myself down quite flat, and wriggle up to the brookside like a snake, throwing my fly into the small pits and narrow stickles most successfully.

In those days I generally carried a basket which held fourteen pounds weight of trout, and, after learning to fish, I did not consider that I had done well if I did not succeed in filling it. No one in these latter days, on those same upper waters, could do as much. But, dearly, also, did I love the woody, tangled brook which runs down from Holnicote, through Bossington, to the sea, near Hurlstone Point.

Sometimes with a worm, sometimes with a bluebottle, sometimes with infinite pains with artificial flies, I would fish that tiny brook, and its trout, if not numerous, were large and fat.

There were many complaints from such fishermen towards the end of the nineteenth century that, as the tourist trade was growing, hotels, particularly in Lynton and Lynmouth, were employing professional anglers to supply their kitchens with local trout and rivers were being systematically stripped. Whatever the case, such large catches have never been seen since.

SMOKED TROUT ROULADE

Smoked trout are expensive but smoking kits are easy to obtain from tackle dealers and you can smoke your own trout.

Recipe from Helena Strong of North Molton:

Ingredients for 6 persons:
2 ozs\20 gms plain flour
4 large eggs, separated
2 tablespoons water
4 ozs\125 gms Cheddar cheese, grated
4 tablespoons Parmesan cheese, grated
Salt and pepper

For the filling:
1 oz\25 gms butter
1 oz\25 gms plain flour
⅓ pint\200 mls milk
8 ozs\250 gms smoked trout fillets, cooked, skinned and flaked
1 hard-boiled egg, chopped
1 tablespoon chopped parsley

To garnish:
Herb sprigs

Sift the flour into a bowl and beat in the egg yolks and water until smooth. Stir in the Cheddar cheese, half the Parmesan cheese and salt and pepper to taste. Whisk the

egg whites until stiff and carefully fold into the mixture. Spread evenly into a lined and greased 12X18in (30X20cm) Swiss roll tin and bake in a preheated moderately hot oven at 400°F\200°C\ Gas Mark 6 for 12-15 minutes until well risen and golden brown. Meanwhile, melt the butter in a pan, add the flour and cook for 1 minute, stirring. Gradually stir in the milk and cook, stirring for 1 minute. Season with salt and pepper to taste. Fold in the trout, chopped egg and parsley. Sprinkle the remaining Parmesan cheese over a large piece of greaseproof paper. Turn the roulade onto this, removing the lining paper. Spread the filling over the surface and carefully roll up like a Swiss roll. Serve immediately, while still hot, garnished with herbs.

TROUT AND MUSHROOM BAKE

Recipe from Dorothy Ball of Wootton Courtenay: Dorothy says: This dish is especially tasty when made from freshly caught trout, field mushrooms and herbs from ones own garden.

Ingredients for 4 persons:
1½ – 2 lb trout
½ lb mushrooms
½ pt white sauce (½ pt milk, 1 oz flour, 1 oz butter, salt, pepper)
4 ozs fresh white breadcrumbs, herbs and chopped onion
½ oz butter
Bay leaves, herbs (e.g. mixed parsley and sage)

Place trout in a baking tin on two layers of foil with bay leaves and herbs. Seal parcel well and bake for 15-20 mins. Make white sauce and add finely chopped mushrooms (or you can add mushrooms to half or full fat crème fraîche and simmer). Sauté finely chopped onions in butter. Add breadcrumbs and herbs. When cool enough, remove skin and bones from the trout. Place the fish in a buttered ovenproof dish, cover with the mushroom sauce or crème fraîche and sprinkle the breadcrumb mix over the top. Return to oven for five minutes.

POTTED ROADWATER TROUT

Recipe from Tim Sandy of Williton:

130 gms trout fillet diced in 1 cm squares
60 gms butter
15 gms chopped shallots
2 gms whole mace
1 red chilli, finely chopped
2 gms chopped fresh dill
20 mls white wine
Juice of 1 lime
15 gms grain mustard
30 gms mayonnaise
Dash of Worcestershire sauce

Gently sweat the shallots in the butter, adding the mace and chilli. Mix together the white wine, lime juice and Worcestershire sauce. Quickly toss the trout into the frying pan and turn with a wooden spatula: cook rare. Take off the heat and mix with all remaining ingredients, being careful not to break up the trout pieces. Fill up ramekins with the mixture and leave to set, covering with melted butter when cold. Serve with hot toast or pickled cucumber.

NOMBLED MUFFIN

Recipe from Paul Lilly of Great Torrington:

To serve 6 persons:
2 lbs\1 kg trout or salmon
8 ozs\225 gms breadcrumbs
¼ pt\150 mls milk
5 ozs\125 gms grated cheese (Cheddar
or Curworthy)
6 muffins
1 dessertspoonful vinegar
2 pints\1 litre court bouillon
Ground cloves, ginger, salt and pepper

Poach the fish in enough court bouillon to cover. Skin and flake it, placing skin and bones back into the liquid with cloves, ginger and milk, and bring to the boil. Mix the fish with the breadcrumbs (white or half white\ half wholemeal) add enough strained court bouillon to bring to the consistency of thick scrambled egg. Add vinegar, salt and pepper to taste. Toast the split muffins. Spread the tops with the mixture, cover with grated cheese and brown under the grill.

TROUT AND PARSLEY PASTIES

Recipe from Adrian White of East Buckland:

Ingredients for 4 persons:
2 trout
½ lemon
A little butter

For the sauce:
1 oz\25 gms butter
1 oz\25 gms flour
½ pt\300 mls milk
1 tablespoon lemon juice
Bay leaves, parsley, seasoning

For the pastry:
1 lb\450 gms Dunster wholemeal flour
½ lb\225 gms lard
1 egg
A little water

Clean the trout, stuff with small lumps of butter and slices of lemon, wrap in greased foil and cook for 20 minutes in a moderate oven. While it cools, heat the milk with two bay leaves, make a roux with the flour and butter, then add the milk to make a smooth sauce, finally adding chopped parsley and lemon juice. Skin the trout, flake the flesh and add to the sauce. Make up the pastry and roll into four 6 inch rounds. Place a little of the mixture in the centre of each, fold over and seal, glaze with beaten egg and cook in a moderate oven for 45 minutes or until golden brown.

EXMOOR TROUT IN CREAM
AND CHIVE SAUCE

Recipe from Julia Brown of Winsford:

Ingredients for 6 persons:
6 fresh trout (approx. 6 ozs\150 gms each)
3 ozs\75 gms butter
½ pt\300 mls double cream
3 large tablespoons finely chopped fresh chives
1 lemon
Seasoned flour, black pepper

Steve Guscott

Gut and clean the trout, roll in seasoned flour and arrange in buttered, ovenproof dish. Place the remainder of the butter, cut into small pieces, over the trout and bake in a moderate oven for 15-20 minutes, basting with melted butter from time to time. Heat the cream in a small saucepan, season with a little salt and freshly ground black pepper and stir in the chives. Lay the fish on a serving plate, spoon the sauce over and decorate with lemon slices.

EELS

These are not caught on Exmoor rivers nowadays, but small quantities still run up from the sea as elvers. The Parret is better known for its eel fishing and elvers are matured in tanks at Hinkley Point.

The Rev. William Thornton wrote of his days fishing in the 1840s:

When it rained hard and thunder was to be heard, several of us would make a clot with worms and worsted, and go down at night with a bag and lantern to catch eels. From some cause or other the clear streams in the north of Devon are much more tenanted by eels than are the rivers in the south; and great was the scrambling of pupil and farm boys at midnight, and in streaming rain, the eels would disengage themselves from the worsted, and glide about in the long grass of the meadow, endeavouring to escape and get back to their homes. At other times I would go down to the ditches at Porlock marsh to catch eels with an eel spear, ever so many at a time.

When curate at Lynton in 1855, he lived at Lynmouth and wrote:

> I witnessed a strange sight in the month of May. The water was quite black with little eels coming up from the sea to the river. I ran down to the scullery steps and ladled them out in my fishing basket by the hundred, and Mrs Bevan my landlady, converted them with the aid of a little batter, into an imitation of whitebait, and very excellent eating they were.

FRIED ELVERS

On the Somerset Levels they make elver cakes. The elvers are exposed in the rhynes when they are drained to cut the willows. The cakes are made in the same way as the following recipe, with a little chopped onion and herbs added, but the whole is turned into a dish, pressed down and left to cool. The mass of elvers becomes almost textureless and can be cut into slices like a cake.

Traditional method:

Wash and dry the elvers. Fry some streaky bacon in a pan with some lard. Remove the bacon when crisp and add the elvers to the pan. Season and add beaten eggs. Cook for a few minutes until the elvers have become opaque and the eggs set. Serve with the bacon and sprinkle with vinegar.

EEL STEW

Old recipe:

1½ lbs skinned eel cut into 2 inch pieces
2 small onions
3 ozs butter
14 fl ozs dry white wine
1 carrot
½ teaspoon ground mace
Seasoning
Bouquet garni
1 egg yolk
¼ pt double cream

Garnish: button mushrooms, button onions, croutons

Slice the onions thinly and fry half of them in 2 ozs of the butter until soft but not brown. Add the eel pieces and cook gently, turning until light brown all over. Add the wine and simmer. Slice the carrot and add to the pan with the remaining onion, mace, herbs and seasoning. Cover and simmer for half an hour. Meanwhile, trim mushrooms, skin button onions and fry in remaining butter. Remove eels, arrange on a serving dish and keep warm. Beat egg yolk and cream together with a little of the fish liquid and blend with the sauce in the pan, stirring until it thickens. Pour the sauce over the eels and garnish with the mushrooms, onions and croutons.

SEA FISH

Sea fishing was a major industry on the Exmoor coast from Norman times until the end of the nineteenth century, although it had been in decline for most of that century. Even before the First World War there were complaints of pollution and large fleets of foreign vessels making fishing uneconomic for locals.

A fisherman with his own boat or foreshore fishing rights was the equivalent of the yeoman farmer and saw himself as a cut above an agricultural labourer. This created social divisions and it was unusual for fishing families to marry outside their own kind. Towns like Minehead, Porlock, Lynton, Combe Martin and Ilfracombe had quite distinct agricultural and fishing settlements. Even dialect could be different and an Ilfracombe fisherman could more easily understand his Porlock Weir counterpart than a farmer from his own area. Banking and credit facilities were widely provided for masters and owners in regular ports of call and it was common to marry into fishing families in those ports, as the Irish, Welsh and Cornish surnames in Exmoor coastal villages testify.

Commercial fishing from the shore was as common on Exmoor as boat fishing, especially as small harbours limited the size of vessels and fleets and the large tidal range limited the times of sailing from the harbours. All along the coast was developed an extensive network of weirs and pools. The largest of these, important from early medieval times, gave its name to Porlock Weir. A harbour and dock was built there in the fifteenth century. A fish weir lay across a pebbly shore and was made of two long banks of stones in which were held stakes woven together with wattle along the top of the stones like a hedgebank. The two banks came together in a V shape pointing in the direction of the falling tide. There was a small gap in the apex across which was strung a net. Fish would enter the pool made by the weir at high tide and be trapped in the net as the tide receded. There were often two parallel rows of weirs on

Steve Guscott

Seafish counter at Ocean Catch, Minehead

the shore, one for neap and one for spring tides. Natural ridges, streams, pools and gullies were also adapted for these purposes and draped with nets. They had names such as Owl Pool, Crab Pool, Big Weir, Old Man's Weir, Brazier's Gulley, Iron Gun and Martin's Weir. These have all disappeared and Madbrain Sands is now just a name on the map. A few, like Greenaleigh Pool, just survive. The idea developed in Norman times or earlier and was common practise on the Exmoor coast between the thirteenth and seventeenth centuries. The fisheries were valuable and usually brought rent for the various Lords of the Manor, who owned the rights of use of the foreshore. After that time it became more common to string lines of nets on poles, although weirs continued in use into the twentieth century, particularly for whitebait. One, the salmon weir at Lynmouth, is still in use, the rights belonging to the owner of the Bath Hotel.

By the fifteenth century larger boats were travelling across the Atlantic and bringing home catches of salted fish. Improvements to Minehead and Ilfracombe harbours over the next three centuries meant that larger vessels could operate from those ports and fish further afield but the natural limitations of these harbours meant that vessels could never compete with the larger vessels and fleets from ports of national significance. Fishing, although important locally, was generally confined to the local area and market.

Towards the end of the nineteenth century, when the fishing industry was declining, pleasure fishing became more important locally. Hotels arranged fishing trips for their guests. At Lynmouth in the 1890s

William Bevan owned three hotels. His son, Cecil, managed his Lyn Valley Hotel and took guests out on his boat, the Kingfisher. Cecil became renowned for helping them to find the biggest fish, which were advertised as 'monsters of the deep'. Congers of over 50 lbs each and skate of over 100 lbs were regularly caught and, occasionally, skate of nearly 200 lbs. In 1908 he set up a record catch for a day's line fishing from Lynmouth. Weighing 675 lbs, it included 35 congers, 2 skate, 4 cod and a pollack. He fished with a spiller. This consisted of a thick, strong line 400 yards long, carrying at each fathom a length of cod line with a strong brass swivel and one inch hook baited with herring. The spiller dropped across the tidal flow and was anchored at each end, which was marked with a cork float. It would be dropped on a rising tide and when the tide ebbed the corks showed on the surface and the line was hauled in.

The only fishing boats which were being built were small open boats for line fishing. Much of this took place outside the tourist season between October and April, but the boats could be put to good use in season. Line fishing from shore, first with hand lines and later with rods, became popular after the First World War, when lower classes of visitors started to arrive in the area. Bass, pollack, grey mullet and whiting were commonly taken in summer months. Charter boats now operate from Combe Martin, Lynmouth and Minehead to fish the Bristol Channel marks. Conger, huss, skate, tope, pouting, whiting, bass, mackerel, wrasse and pollack are commonly taken from such small boats, usually operating no more than ½ mile offshore.

FISH STEW

This was the usual method of using up any trimmings of fish and fish which is normally rather tough and meaty such as conger eel, huss and tope.

Old recipe:

1½ pts cider
1½ lbs mixed close textured fish
1 onion
4 ozs mushrooms
1 oz butter
1 oz flour
Chopped herbs
Seasoning
2 ozs clotted cream

Brian Pearce

Peel and chop the onion and fry it lightly in the butter. Prepare the fish, dice the flesh coarsely and add to the pan. Add the flour and stir well. Add the cider, herbs and seasoning and bring to the boil whilst stirring. Add the sliced mushrooms and transfer to a casserole dish. Bake in a moderate oven for half an hour. Stir in the cream just before serving.

FISH PIE

Traditional method:

Make a white sauce by cooking together an ounce of butter with an ounce of flour and gradually stirring in ¼ pint milk and ½ pint fish stock until it thickens. In a greased pie dish put in layers of cooked, flaked fish with layers of cooked, sliced potatoes, with roughly twice as much potato as fish and a few slices of hard boiled egg mixed in. Cover with the sauce and add a few more sliced potatoes on top. Dot with butter and bake in a moderate oven until the top is browned.

FISHCAKES

Fishcakes were a method of eking out a meagre supply of fish with potatoes and, often, onions. They are best made with fresh fish rather than leftovers. Usually they were a mixture of white fish and kipper. Sometimes they were served with apple chutney.

SPEEDY SCOOPED FISHCAKES

Recipe from Jackie Edwards of Exford:

This is a version of fishcakes updated with the use of smoked cod or haddock. Jackie says: 'These are a great success and I do them time and time again. The fish comes from Frank Houlding, who tours Exmoor and comes to our house with his van'.

One fillet of smoked cod or haddock
½ lb potatoes
1 egg
1 oz margarine
1 oz crushed cornflakes or browned breadcrumbs
Pepper
Cooking oil

Peel, boil and then mash the potatoes. Bring the fish to boiling point and drain off water. Tip the fish onto a board and remove the skin. Mix the fish and potatoes together with a fork, adding pepper and the egg. Heat the oil in a frying pan. Place the breadcrumbs or cornflakes into a bowl. With an ice cream scoop, take individual scoopfuls of the fish mixture and place in the crumbs. Turn to coat by hand and place in the hot oil. When all the fish is coated and frying, flatten the fishcakes. Turn when brown on one side.

FISH POT

Fish was often pot roasted like meat. This method was used for odd pieces and trimmings of fish. An earthenware dish was greased and chopped onions were thrown in with the fish. A close fitting lid was put on the dish and the whole was baked, cooking the fish in the steam arising from it. When cooked, the bones were extracted from the fish. The fish was flaked, seasoned and mixed with an equal quantity of mashed potato. The mixture was then returned to the pot and baked, without lid, until browned.

BASS

This is one of the most sought after fish along the Exmoor coast and fetches high prices. Small shoals arrive all along the coast in mid summer, but particularly to the west, from Lynmouth to Combe Martin. They come in close to shore and can even be found in Lynmouth harbour. These shoaling bass are known as school bass. The larger bass follow on later and are often known as salmon bass from their similarity in form to salmon, although they are not related. Duty Point is a renowned place where bass of up to 12 lbs can be caught. The local record is one of over 17½ lbs caught from Minehead harbour. They can be caught by bottom or float fishing or with spinners. Each fisherman seems to have his own favourite bait but almost any kind of fish bait, plus worms, crab or prawns can be used.

SEA BASS IN PASTRY WITH CHIVE SAUCE

Recipe from Bob Deville of Martinhoe:

1 4-6 lbs bass, skinned, boned and filleted: keep all the trimmings for stock
4 ozs sharp tasting cooking apple, peeled, cored, diced and cooked in a little butter
1 lb cooked mashed potato
1½ lbs puff pastry
2 tablespoons chopped parsley
2 tablespoons chopped chives
2 tablespoons cider vinegar
½ pt dry cider
½ pt double cream
2 eggs, beaten
1 small onion, chopped
Salt, sugar and pepper to taste
Parsley stalks and a few sprigs fresh thyme

First make the fish stock: put the fish head and trimmings into a saucepan with the parsley stalks, onion and thyme, cover with water and simmer gently for about 45 minutes. Let it cool and then strain through muslin. Boil the stock until it is reduced by two thirds. Cut the pastry into two pieces, one piece about twice as big as the other. Roll both out as thinly as possible into oblongs. Fold up, cover and reserve the larger piece. Lay the smaller piece onto a baking tray, prick all over to prevent it rising and bake until golden. Allow it to cool. Place one bass fillet skin side down onto the cooked pastry and season. Mix together the mashed potato, apple and parsley with two thirds of the egg and spread over the fish. Place the other fillet on top skin side up and head to tail so that the whole becomes even in thickness and season. Brush the visible edges of the pastry with egg, place the raw pastry on top and press firmly on the bottom pastry. Trim unsightly edges. Paint all with the remaining egg and bake in a moderate oven for 30 minutes. Remove to a warm place for another 15 minutes. With a very sharp knife, cut across into portions and serve with sauce. It could be served cold.

For the sauce: put the cider vinegar in a small stainless steel saucepan and heat until it is nearly evaporated. Immediately add the cider and fish stock and boil rapidly until you have about a half cupful of dubious looking liquid in the saucepan. Don't despair: add the cream and boil gently until it begins to thicken. Add the chives and taste for the addition of salt and sugar. If too strong, add a little more cream.

CODLING

These are usually caught by beach casting, using crab or lugworm as bait. Anglers tend to catch their bait in the summer and freeze it for year round fishing. Heavyweight gear is required, but the cod rarely exceeds lbs in weight. Cods' heads were popular in the nineteenth century and considered a delicacy. They were poached, then grilled and served with chopped lobster meat.

FISH SOUP

Traditional method:

Boil a cod's head in sufficient water for the soup required, with salt and pepper. Next day strain and reheat, with a little grated lemon rind added. Just before serving add a teacupful of cream or milk, in which has been beaten sufficient flour to thicken. Beat up the yolk of one or two eggs, pour soup into yolks, stirring all the time. Serve at once, in a heated tureen with a little chopped parsley.

SOMERSET CASSEROLE

Old recipe:

2 lbs cod fillets
1 lb potatoes
4 ozs mushrooms
4 ozs tomatoes
2½ ozs butter
½ pt cider
1½ ozs plain flour
Grated cheese

Brian Pearce

Dice the cod into cubes, place in a buttered baking dish and season. Skin and dice the tomatoes, dice the mushrooms and add to the dish with the cider. Cover and bake for 25 minutes at 375°F\190°C\ Gas Mark 5 for 25 minutes. Meanwhile peel, boil, mash and cream the potatoes. Strain the liquid from the fish, make a roux with the butter and flour and stir in the liquid, gradually heating until it thickens. Pour the sauce back over the fish, pipe mashed potato around the edge, cover with grated cheese and brown in a hot oven at 425°F\220°C\Gas Mark 7 for 10 minutes.

CONGER EEL

Congers live in rocky gullies and crevices and as such are classic fish of Exmoor's rocky coast. They are especially noted at Woody Bay, where 25 pounders are common. In the autumn they leave their crevices and swim to sandy areas to feed and build themselves up for the winter. They are most easily caught at this time, as they tend to put up a fight and keep a firm grip in rocky places. They are also quite vicious and can weigh up to 40 lbs, so heavyweight gear including a gaff is required. Fishing for conger is not a lone sport but congers do tend to turn up when not wanted. The record was a 56 pounder caught by the well-known local fisherman, Cecil Bevan, off Lynmouth in 1907. The larger ones are best caught at night, using fish bait. They are often caught with a flapper – a mackerel with the backbone and tail removed, leaving the sides attached to the head. Sometimes they are simply gaffed from their crevices at very low tides. On the Quantock coast was the sport of glatting, where dogs of various breeds were trained to sniff out congers hiding under boulders on the shore.

They are not commonly eaten and often end up as cat food, but make a welcome addition to fish soups and stews in that they add a more meaty texture. Almost all conger recipes seem to have originated in Cornwall, which once exported boned and dried conger. Such recipes, if not the fish, will have inevitably filtered up the coast to Exmoor.

CONGER STEW

Old recipe:

3 lbs conger eel
½ lb onions
2 pts cider
2 ozs butter
2 ozs plain flour
Seasoning

Clean and skin the eel and cut it into a few large pieces. Chop and fry the onions in the butter until soft but not brown. Add the eel pieces and keep turning until slightly browned all over. Stir in the flour and add the cider gradually, stirring until it thickens. Place in an ovenproof dish, cover and bake at 350°F\180°C\Gas Mark 4 for one hour.

CONGER PIE

Traditional method:

Clean, skin and bone the eel and cut into one inch slices. Place in a buttered ovenproof dish in layers with onion rings in between and each layer seasoned and sprinkled with chopped herbs. Just cover with milk into which eggs have been beaten. Cover with breadcrumbs and dot with butter. Bake for one hour at 350°F\180°C\Gas Mark 4.

DOGFISH AND BULL HUSS

These are sometimes respectively known as lesser and greater spotted dogfish. They are very similar in appearance, with the bull huss growing slightly larger – up to about 12lbs. They are common all along the Exmoor coast. The dogfish are found all the year round and are so common that they are usually discarded by commercial fishermen. Netted dogfish are often just dumped overboard. As they will readily take any bait they are regarded as a nuisance to rod and line fishermen after other catches. When they come inshore they often appear fearless and will approach and touch people, so can easily be caught by hand.

Bull huss, being larger, tend to be slightly more marketable. They are caught mostly in autumn and winter months when they come inshore to attach their eggs to kelp and are thus mainly caught by beach casting, using fish bait. They occasionally end up on fishmongers slabs as one of a number of fish euphemistically termed 'rock salmon'. They are not prized eating and, being cheap, often end up as cat food. However, they are a useful addition to fish soups and stews, their fleshy texture adding variety. They should be cooked slightly longer than most fish.

FLAT FISH

Known as 'flats', these are not common off the Exmoor coast, being fish of sandy shores and estuaries. Dab are probably the most common, with small runs in winter and spring. They are sweet tasting and worth cooking, even though they look very small when filleted. The traditional method of cooking them was not to fillet them but to cut the heads, tails and fins off, dip them in seasoned flour and fry them quickly in butter.

Small flounder and plaice are caught, usually by beach casting with worm or crab bait. Turbot are common in season, the largest being no more than 2 lbs in weight. More scarce are brill, halibut, plaice and Dover sole.

Brian Pearce

FLAT FISH IN CREAM

Traditional method:

This works best with sole, but any flat fish can be used. The traditional method is to skin the fish without filleting them. This could prove difficult for the inexperienced cook and the recipe works just as well with fillets of fish. Dust each fish with ground mace, ground nutmeg, salt and pepper, then spread the top with clotted cream. Place them in a fireproof dish and scatter them with chopped chives. Cook in a moderate oven for about 15 minutes. The cream melting into the fish and spices makes a good sauce. Serve with lemon.

BAKED FLAT FISH

Traditional method:

This works best with brill and turbot. Clean the fish and score it across the white side. Chop some onions and mushrooms and spread them across the bottom of a baking dish. Cover with fish stock and a little sherry or Madeira. Lay the fish on this, white side up. Season and sprinkle with breadcrumbs and chopped herbs. Dot with butter and bake in a moderate oven for about 30 minutes.

HERRINGS

According to local saying: 'Herrings and Bread go the Bells of Minehead'.

Herrings were considered to be a local speciality, but their appearance on the Exmoor menu was relatively brief and erratic. There is a suggestion that they were first fished at Lynmouth in the sixteenth century by Dutch fishermen who were Protestants escaping religious persecution in Holland. The local surnames of Litson and Vellacot are reputed to be derived from such people. Cooper, in his guide of 1853, suggested that there was a trade with Scotland in cured herrings and many locals married into the families of Scottish people who came for the herrings.

Herrings appeared in large numbers in the Bristol Channel early in the seventeenth century. In an account of a flood at Lynmouth in 1607 it was mentioned that red herring houses were destroyed. Lynmouth was mentioned in Risdons *Survey of Devon*, finished in 1630, as being 'notable for the marvellous plenty of herrings there taken, a kind of fish, which in our forefathers' days, kept, as it were, their station about Norway; but in our time, not without divine providence, take their course round about this isle of Great Britain, by shoals, in great numbers. And from September until Christide offer themselves to the fishers' nets.' By that time large fleets of fishing vessels were following the shoals as they migrated from the North Sea around Scotland and down the Irish Sea, arriving in the Bristol Channel in late autumn. It was probably such intensive fishing which drove them into the Channel in the first place and later finished them off. The small local vessels could not compete with such competition but for a while they prospered from the welcome influx of fish.

Westcote, in a retrospective view of the same period, tells of Lynmouth as a 'little inlet, which in these last times God hath plentifully stored with herrings (the king of fishes), which, shunning their ancient place of repair in Ireland, come hither abundantly in shoals, offering themselves to the fishers' nets.' He says fishermen 'soon resorted thither with divers merchants, and so for five or six years continued (to the great benefit and good of the country) until the parson vexed the poor fishermen for extraordinary unusual tithes, and then the fish suddenly left the coast, unwilling, as may be supposed, by losing their lives, to cause contention. But (God be thanked), they began to resort hither again, though not, as yet, in such multitudes as heretofore.'

At Lynmouth, Porlock Weir and Minehead red herring houses were erected for drying the fish. Hostels grew up at these places for traders coming to buy the fish and fishermen from other areas landing their catch in local ports. Lynmouth specialised in red herrings, which were like bloaters. The fish were salted and oak smoked in red houses, which left them with a reddish colour. Manorial records show large numbers of these in the early eighteenth century but they appear to have disappeared by the end of the century. Continuing, however, were a few fish cellars where white herrings were produced. These were herrings pickled in barrels of salt. Boatloads of red and white herrings were taken to Bristol, from whence they were exported to the West Indies and southern Europe.

All prospered until 1753, when it was reported: 'The herring fail, no fish caught.' However, the cartographer Bowen said of the trade of Minehead port on his map of 1760: 'tis improved by the catching of Herrings, which come up the Severn about Michaelmas, in great Shoals, which being cured, and sent to divers parts in the Mediterranean, where they come to a good Market.' For the rest of the century the herring behaved erratically, with occasional large summer catches and years in between with nothing. Shoals reappeared in 1787 and the last big catches were made in the following decade. In 1797 the shoals did not return and regular catches were gone for good. A story goes that there was such a glut of herrings at Lynmouth that they were used as fertiliser by the Lord of the Manor and they left as God's retribution to the locals for wasting the bounty he had given them. Superstitious locals said it was an 'insult offered to the fish by using them as manure.' There are also stories of surplus fish from Porlock Weir being spread on the land at Bossington.

From the early nineteenth century large catches of herrings were infrequent enough to be big news locally. On Christmas Day in 1811 the church service at Lynton was interrupted when it was announced that a shoal of herrings had entered the bay. There was another such shoal in 1823. In 1895 the West Somerset Free Press reported: 'Minehead herrings were uncommonly plentiful this season, local fishermen having some very large takes. The largest quantity taken by any one boat was six maze or thirty hundred. These big catches caused prices to drop and at one time herrings were being hawked in the town at two shillings per hundred.'

The herrings were sold in long hundreds, or 120s. At the quay they were counted out into boxes or maunds (two handled wicker baskets) in front of the buyers. Two men would pack them counting in threes. After 120 they would warp and tail, which involved placing an extra two herrings in the box and one on the ground to mark each long hundred. The extra herrings were supposed to be for paying any turnpike tolls or harbour dues on the dealer's journey.

Herrings became much regarded a poor man's food. They would be sold straight from the boat or from the fish quay at Porlock Weir and joulers (dealers) would take them around the villages. It was not uncommon to see joulers taking the fish around town with a handcart. In Ilfracombe they shouted 'Combe 'errings' and locals seemed to prize fish landed locally, as they did at Porlock Weir. They were no different from any other herrings but the assumption was that they were better, presumably because they were fresher than those landed further afield.

The truth was that from the nineteenth century onwards there were never enough herrings to warrant an export trade and they were only sold for local consumption, even when salted. In the 1870s the last salting house at Lynmouth was cleared of two tons of salt and local herring curing ended. There were no specialist herring fishing boats in the twentieth century. The last of the old boats were converted for carrying cargoes such as bark and hides to other Bristol Channel ports. By the 1930s there were no sailing boats and only a handful of local fishing boats of any sort operating on the Exmoor coast. It became uneconomic to purchase herring fishing gear, although some boats fished on and occasional catches of up to a thousand herrings per tide were had up to the 1940s. They were fished mainly by small boats which would carry tourists in the summer and be stripped out at the end of season for the October herring fishing. Herrings are caught by drift netting. The boats would no go far, just dropping down Channel on the ebb tide to shut their nets and returning on the flood. You can still purchase local herrings, but catches and fish are small and the future of stocks does not seem to be assured. Throughout the twentieth century the same reasons have been used – pollution, operation of foreign fleets, overfishing of breeding grounds, bigger boats taking smaller fish. It is interesting to reflect that it was probably overfishing that caused their first arrival in the Bristol Channel in the seventeenth century and it has taken until now to introduce quotas.

Herrings were mostly fried with their roes and served with laver. However, there were many methods of cooking and preserving them. Red herrings were salty and needed soaking to remove the salt before they were cooked. Often they were soaked in beer, which was then discarded before baking with butter.

HERRING PIE

Traditional method:

Herrings were often baked in a pie with apple and onion slices rather like a fish version of squab pie. The herrings were filleted as well as possible although, inevitably, small bones would remain. The fillets were put in a pie dish, dotted with butter and seasoned with salt, pepper and mace. On top were put thin slices of apple and onion and a little water. This was topped with a pastry crust and baked well.

BAKED HERRING

Traditional method:

The fish were filleted and the fillets seasoned and rolled up with a bay leaf in each. They were then placed in an ovenproof dish and sprinkled with brown sugar. They were then just covered with a mixture of half vinegar and half water. The dish was then covered with onion rings and baked for about 30 minutes in a moderate oven. Cider could be substituted for the vinegar and water.

MACKEREL

Shoals of mackerel are common off the Exmoor coast in summer months and are amongst the easiest and best fishing. Trips are laid on for tourists, with catches being almost guaranteed. The easiest method – so easy as to be considered unsporting by many anglers – is by feathering. This consists of sinking a weighted line sporting brightly coloured feathered hooks and drawing it up again so that the feathers spin. Spinning is the commonest method of catching them but baited lines – surprisingly using mackerel strips as bait – are also used. Local boatmen drag lines with spinners behind their boats. The lines have small wooden boards attached to them in such a way that the movement of the boat keeps them under water until a mackerel is caught, at which time the board bobs to the surface, indicating a catch. There are many local variations of this method.

Mackerel

Mackerel does not keep well but, served the day it is caught, there is little to equal it and it is very underrated. It is a rich fish and is generally paired with a tart, fruity sauce, such as apple, gooseberry or rhubarb and cooked in cider or vinegar. Gooseberry sauce for mackerel is reputed to have been introduced by the Normans.

PICKLED MACKEREL

Traditional method:

Fillet the mackerel and dust the fillets with seasoned flour. Fry until golden brown and leave to cool. Place a layer of fillets in the storage pot and sprinkle with salt and sugar. Build up the mackerel in layers like this and on top add pepper and some onion slices. Then fill the pot to the top with vinegar.

Steve Guscott

MACKEREL WITH FRUIT SAUCE

Old recipe:

4 mackerel
3 tablespoons dry cider
1 oz butter
Bay leaves and seasoning

For the sauce:
½ lb peeled and cored apple, diced rhubarb
or gooseberries
4 tablespoons cider
Juice of ½ lemon
2 tablespoons brown sugar

Clean and gut the mackerel. Place with the bay leaves in a buttered ovenproof dish, dot with butter and season. Pour over the cider and place a lid on the dish. Bake at 350°F\180°C\ Gas Mark 4 for 20-30 minutes. Meanwhile, put all the ingredients for the sauce together in a pan and cook gently until the fruit is soft. Remove the mackerel and, when slightly cool, fillet them carefully. Serve with the sauce and new potatoes.

MULLET

Grey mullet are the ones caught along the Exmoor coast and there are three species: thick-lipped, thin-lipped and golden. They are more common in estuaries, but occasional shoals come near the small river mouths of Exmoor. Combe Martin is locally renowned for mullet fishing, especially from the Camel's Head rock at the northern end of the bay. They are usually caught by spinning and early and late in the day are the most productive times. They are not to be confused with the red mullet more frequently found on fishmongers' slabs. Red mullet are smaller but better eating. The grey mullet tend to have the slightly earthy taste of a freshwater fish. They are good simply baked on a bed of onion and fennel or in white wine.

MULLET PIE

Traditional method:

Fillet and skin the fish and cut into pieces. Poach the fish lightly in milk and remove. Thicken the milk with a little mixed butter and flour. Mix fish and milk with chopped parsley and seasoning and place in a pie dish. Cover with short crust pastry and bake in a moderate oven for ½ to ¾ hour.

POLLACK

These are abundant off the rocky parts of the Exmoor coast in summer months. They are fished in a similar manner to mackerel – on spinners or feathers or float tackle, especially after dark. They mostly weigh up to about 3 lbs, although they can be larger. They are excellent simply grilled over a summer barbecue.

RAYS

Several species of ray are caught off the Exmoor coast, the most common being the small-eyed or painted ray. Other species include blonde, spotted, thornback and undulate rays. Skate are now rare. They can come in close to the shore on beaches from April to September and are generally caught by beach casting, using fresh bait. They are generally caught at night. Sillery Sands is a well-known site for a variety of rays. They average about 7 lbs in weight but specimens of up to 20 lbs or more can be caught.

As they are large fish, they are usually sold in pieces, the backs and wings separately. They have a slimy coating which is best removed by soaking the fish in cold water for at least 12 hours. The flesh appears to contain many small bones, which are actually cartilage and rays are best served with the flesh pulled from the

cartilage, which can easily be done before cooking. After cooking, this generally means flaking it. Skate is good cooked in cider and served cold with a vinaigrette made with cider vinegar. As such it suits a green salad with chopped apple and crisply cooked bacon pieces.

SKATE WITH BLACK BUTTER

Old recipe, which seems universal, not confined to Exmoor:

3 lbs skate wing
2 pts fish stock
2 tablespoons cider vinegar
Juice of 1 lemon
4 ozs butter
2 ozs capers
Chopped parsley

Soak the fish overnight in cold water. Cut into portions adequate for each person and simmer in the fish stock for 15 minutes. Skin the fish and keep warm. Garnish with chopped capers and sprinkle with lemon juice. Cook the butter in a pan until nut brown, stir in the vinegar and parsley and pour over the fish.

WHITING

These are common off the Exmoor coast, particularly to the west, and are usually taken in winter months and after dark. They are fished from boat or shore using a weighted line with fish bait. The traditional way to prepare whiting is to cut off their heads and tails and skin them but leave the flesh on the bone to cook.

STEWED WHITING

Old recipe:

Take off skins, heads and tails, lay fish in stew pan, season each with ¼ teaspoonful salt, 1 grain white pepper, ¼ salt spoonful mixed herbs in powder; and for the whole (4 or 6) the grated rind of half a lemon: pour in ¼ lb dissolved butter and simmer ten minutes, add large wineglassful Marsala and strained juice of a lemon, simmer again five minutes, but on no account more. Place fish neatly on dish and pour sauce over.

EXMOOR WHITING

Old recipe:

2 medium sized whiting, about 1 lb each
1 onion
4 ozs mushrooms
3 teaspoons cornflour
1 tablespoon chopped parsley
2 tablespoons clotted or double cream
½ pt cider

Chop the onion coarsely, slice the mushrooms and put them with the cider in a large pan with the whiting. Bring the cider to the boil, reduce to a simmer and cover the pan. Cook for 10-15 minutes, until the whiting is cooked but not flaking. Remove the fish and keep warm. The cider can continue simmering if necessary until the onion is tender. Mix the cornflour with a little cold water and add to the cider mixture, stirring until thickened. Season if necessary, stir in the parsley and cream and remove from the heat immediately. Serve the whiting with the sauce poured over on the plate.

SHELLFISH

CRAB

Fresh local crab is one of those memories which go with the seemingly longer, sunnier days of childhood summer. Crab was relatively cheap and plentiful a few decades ago and, in those days when dinner was at lunchtime, it was a frequent morning task for us children on summer holidays to dress the crab for dinner. I can't imagine many children doing this nowadays but I believe that preparing fresh meat, fish and shellfish is best learnt young, as it is not thought about in the squeamish terms which we tend to apply in later life.

Extracting the meat from the crab was a tedious job and the incentive was to be allowed to eat the meat from the legs as we went along. There is little meat in the legs and extracting it is a fiddly job which was done armed with nutcrackers and a pointed knife. My favourite part was the meat from the tips of the pincers, which has a different texture from the rest.

Summer holidays were usually spent on the beach poking about in rock pools. I often accompanied adults trying to pull lobsters and crabs from rock crevices with gaffs. Crabs should not be gaffed unless you can clearly see what you are doing. The crabs are often in the crevices whilst they are waiting for their new shells to harden after moulting and you cannot eat them at this stage but can easily damage them with a gaff. The best way of getting them out is to put your hand in and try to pull them out by the base of a pincer. A large crab can give a nasty nip and, unlike a lobster, it is difficult to release the claw, so this is definitely a skilled job. I preferred to turn over large stones in rock pools. This made it easier to grab the crabs but they were invariably too small to eat. To be edible they should be at least 8 inches across the carapace (the top part of the shell) and if I could hold them across the breadth of the shell with one childish hand I knew they had to be put back.

Some North Devonians were renowned for being able to lie down in the surf along the rocky ridges of Croyde, Baggy and Morte Points and just pull up crabs by the pincers. They would spit in the face of a crab to make it tuck its claws in enough for them to put it into a hessian bag. I longed to be able to do this but no amount of snorkelling about on the beach resulted in the proverbial crab the size of a dinner plate. The larger crabs are, as one might expect, caught in deeper water, usually where there is a mixture of sand and boulders on the bottom.

Local fishermen assert that crabs are clean feeders and the pots are baited with fresh fish, unlike the refuse often used for lobsters. Often, conger eels caught in the pots are returned as bait. In the old days, however, Lundy fishermen used to swear by puffins' gizzards.

Shellfish counter at Ocean Catch, Minehead

Steve Guscott

Steve Guscott

Edible crab

Kind fishermen may stun the crabs with a mallet when they are caught. They are, however, cooked alive; plunged into a pan of boiling salted water and cooked for 15 to 20 minutes. Contrary to old wives' tales, they do not scream but sometimes you can hear bubbles escaping from the expanding air under their shells.

Crabs are sold by weight. It is best to hold one before you buy it. It should feel heavy for its size and not sound hollow when tapped. It is best to dress it yourself. Some unscrupulous commercial establishments put the meat into large, standard sized shells and, in doing so, eke it out with other ingredients. Breadcrumbs are added to the dark meat and flavourless fish to the white meat. Crab has a strong flavour and a little goes a long way.

To dress a crab start by wrenching off the legs and claws. Break their shells carefully with a hammer or nutcracker so that there are not too many small fragments of shell. Extract the white meat with a knife. Then with a knife prise apart the top and bottom parts of the body shell. Underneath the top shell will be the dark meat or 'cream' as it is locally known. It is mostly liver and not strictly meat. This is carefully scraped out, discarding the small piece of plating and stomach sac found behind the eyes. The main part of the body, from which the legs were removed, contains more white meat. Discard the soft, feathery parts, which are the gills, known as 'dead man's fingers'. I usually break the rest of the shell with a heavy knife and poke out the remaining white meat with a skewer. The main shell is then washed and used to serve the white meat and cream, which are kept separate. The cream is often

runny and breadcrumbs (preferably fresh) are added to give a drier texture. Sometimes clotted cream was added at the same time. It was usual to add cider vinegar as well but I prefer lemon juice if anything. Also added to the cream was often something to 'devil' it, such as mustard, cayenne pepper or Worcestershire sauce. I prefer a little mustard but feel that the less added the better.

The dressed crab was garnished with the sieved yolks and chopped whites of hardboiled eggs. The usual manner of displaying a crab was to line the sides of the shell with white meat and have the cream running in a band in the middle. The bands were then pushed apart with a knife and, starting from the cream, was inserted a band of egg white, a band of egg yolk and a band of parsley. If coral was available from the crab, this was mixed with butter and piped around the edge of the shell. The crab was displayed on lettuce leaves garnished with tomato slices and served with brown bread and butter.

Brian Pearce

Dressed crab

CRAB MOUSSE

Modern recipe adapted by Heather Burnett-Wells:

Ingredients to serve six persons:
*1 large crab (over 1 lb. in weight) or at
least 8 ozs prepared crabmeat
4 fluid ozs double cream
6 fluid ozs aspic jelly
2 egg whites
juice of half a lemon
1 tablespoon grated Parmesan cheese
salt, pepper and a pinch of cayenne pepper to season*

Aspic jelly comes as a powder like gelatine and is made up in a similar way, stirring it into warm water and heating without boiling until it is dissolved. Make up the jelly and leave it to cool but not set. Meanwhile, mix the brown and white crabmeat with the Parmesan cheese and then thoroughly mix with the cream. This can be done in a liquidiser or food processor. Season with the salt, pepper and cayenne pepper, add the lemon juice and mix with the aspic jelly. Leave the mixture to cool until almost set. Whisk the egg whites until frothy but not too firm and fold gently into the crab mixture. Turn the mixture into a greased mould or soufflé dish. Leave in the refrigerator to set. This will usually take about two hours. If the mousse will not turn out easily, it can be loosened by dipping the mould briefly in hot water. Turn onto a plate and garnish with cucumber. The mousse can be served with a green salad.

CRAB SOUP

Old recipe:

*8 ozs crabmeat
1 onion
1 stick celery
1 pt milk
1 pt fish stock
¼ pt double cream
2 tablespoons sherry
2 teaspoons anchovy essence
½ oz butter
Pinch cayenne pepper and seasoning*

Peel the onion and chop finely with the celery. Cook in the butter over a low heat until soft but not brown. Process or blend (sieved originally) with the crabmeat and return to the pan with the milk and stock. Season and simmer for ten minutes. Add the anchovy essence and cayenne, stir in the sherry and cream and serve.

LIMPETS

Limpets are one of the easiest wild foods to gather and are present all year round, so must have been a fall-back for Exmoor people in times of hardship. However, there is no great written tradition of eating limpets. Almost any mussel recipe can be adapted for limpets, although the 'foot' of the limpet is tough and needs special treatment. Some people are known to eat limpets raw, as in this account of Frederick Brock, a once well-known North Devon character, by his friend, B. R. Faunthorpe:

> Limpets are very good to eat. To collect them you either slip a stout knife-blade under the shell, or tap them with a light hammer when they are not expecting it. They are normally cooked twice. First Sinelled and boiled for ten minutes when they fall out of the shell. Then you grasp the head, where two little horns stick out, and pull. The head comes away followed by two inches of twisty tube. Brocky used to kick limpets off and eat them raw without any horning. After being boiled, the limpets are minced and fried with whatever you fancy. Real seafood they are. Potted salt-wind, spume and sunshine!

By 'Sinelling' he was referring to marine biologist Joseph Sinel, who recommended that the most humane way to kill all shellfish was not to drop them into boiling water but to place them in cold water and raise the temperature gradually.

FRIED LIMPETS

Old recipe:

Limpets, brown bread crumbs, salt, pepper, cayenne, lard

Collect about 2 dozen limpets per person. Put the limpets into boiling water. Remove the shell, cut off and discard the tough feet, wash the humps well to remove sand. Roll them in seasoned breadcrumbs and fry in hot fat.

Steve Guscott

LOBSTER

Like crabs, lobsters were often caught by gaffing from crevices on the shore as well as in lobster pots. Gaffing was a considerable skill as it was easy to tear a lobster apart when it held tightly to its crevice. Lobsters shed their claws as a defensive mechanism and it is necessary to hook them by the body. Gaffs were home made with hazel twigs and sharp conger hooks. They had to be flexible and sensitive to the movement of the lobster. Some skilled gaffers could turn a lobster around in its crevice so that it could be hooked and pulled out backwards, which made it more difficult for the creature to hold on. Good lobster crevices were well known enough to be given names. Many were only accessible at extreme low tides.

Like crabs, a lobster should feel heavy for its size. It is best to choose a lobster with barnacles on its shell, as this means that it will not have shed its shell for some time and the shell will be well filled with flesh. Apart from this, young lobsters are considered better eating than older ones, unlike crabs. It is also best to buy lobsters live and cook your own to ensure freshness, although those kept alive in tanks of sea water are not necessarily any better and, to avoid cruelty, it is best to have them cooked as soon as possible after being caught. Traditionally all shellfish are cooked by boiling for 20 minutes in salted water, but twice that time may be necessary for a large lobster. The eggs of hen lobsters, known as 'coral', are often used in cookery and served with the lobster. Traditionally the coral was pounded in a mortar with an equal amount of butter and lobster meat, seasoned with cayenne, mace and clove and used to decorate a mould of lobster or salad.

After cooking a lobster it is best to keep it moist until cool. To serve a lobster, usually the claws, legs and head are pulled off and the body cut in half lengthwise. The stomach and intestine are discarded and the body served with the claws and garnished with the meat picked from the head and legs and the coral, if present.

LOBSTER SAUCE

Old recipe:

Stir together over the fire 3 tablespoonsful of butter, 3 dessertspoonsful of flour seasoned with a good pinch of salt, the same of pepper and 2 or 3 drops of Tabasco sauce. When this is all perfectly blended, add gradually ½ pt new milk or cream and let the sauce thicken. Stir in a cupful each of flaked lobster and cold cooked green peas or asparagus tops. Mix together and let it cook gently for about 6 or 8 minutes. Serve very hot, and, if possible, in the dish it was cooked in.

SAVOURY CREAM

Old recipe from Mrs M H Toller of Barnstaple:

A small lobster
½ pt cream
1 gill aspic jelly
1 tablespoon mayonnaise
½ oz gelatine powder
1 gill tomato juice
Tarragon and chervil

Decorate a border mould with tarragon and chervil leaves and some nice pieces of lobster. Melt the gelatine in the tomato juice. Whip the cream and the aspic jelly. Mix these together, stir in the mayonnaise and the melted gelatine, also some small pieces of lobster. Fill the mould carefully and set. When cold, turn out and fill the centre with small salad.

LOBSTER STEW

Recipe from Bob Deville of Martinhoe: Bob says: 'Lobsters are always expensive and if you compare the weight of meat you can extract from them to the price you paid you will find that the cost per pound will be about twice the price of smoked salmon! Hence you need to make it go a long way to be affordable. Here is a main course soup that will extract every bit of flavour from your lobster. You will need to plan ahead and reserve some pre-cooked vegetables.'

Ingredients for 6 persons:
1 1¼ – 1½ lb cooked lobster (the tastiest size, I think)
or the same lobster alive (if you have
the courage, plunge it into boiling water and
simmer for 15 minutes)
6 ozs diced leeks – the pale green part is the best for this
6 ozs diced raw potato
6 ozs pre-cooked mixed vegetables such as cauliflower,
carrots, broccoli, sprouts, cabbage –
avoid strong tasting ones such as parsnip
6 ozs cooked potatoes – left overs will be fine
Half an onion
Parsley, thyme, salt and pepper to taste

Cut the lobster in half by inserting a sharp knife below the head and slicing down to the tail, then the other way through the head. Pick out all the white meat and pink coral and dice up carefully. Break up the claws with a hammer or rolling pin, extract the meat and dice. Discard the soft gills and anything not white or pink. Break up the remaining shell, place in a saucepan and just cover with water. Simmer gently for an hour. Add half a chopped onion and some sprigs of parsley and thyme for the last half hour. Sieve and then boil the liquor down by about a half. Meanwhile, cook the diced leeks in butter until soft. Cook the diced potato until just soft and add to the leeks. Put the lobster liquor, pre-cooked vegetables and pre-cooked potatoes into a liquidiser or processor and process until smooth. Combine with the leek and potato mixture and stir. You can refrigerate it at this point until later. Put everything except the lobster meat into a saucepan, add milk until you have a creamy consistency and heat up to nearly boiling. Serve into six bowls, then add lobster meat into the centres. Sprinkle chopped parsley over and serve with very crusty bread. This recipe will go further by adding more mixed vegetables and potato.

NB For crusty bread: using a brush, paint water over a Vienna type loaf, sprinkle with a little salt and bake in a hot oven for ten minutes.

MUSSELS

Although mussels are plentiful locally, not many are now eaten because of the way they concentrate pollutants from the water. Even when waters were comparatively clean, most of the mussels collected were for fishing bait rather than human consumption. Traditionally the mussels were fed on oatmeal in fresh water for a day before being cooked. Nowadays they are washed thoroughly and then put in tanks of sterilised water to cleanse themselves whilst still alive. When out of this water they hold their shells tightly shut and remain clean inside. They were normally, like all shellfish, boiled in salted water for 20 minutes. Nowadays they tend to be cooked in a shallow pan and eaten when their shells open.

BOILED MUSSELS

Traditional method:

Make a roux by melting a knob of butter with a dessertspoonful of flour in a pan and gradually add to it a pint of milk which has been simmered with a chopped onion, pinch of mace and a bunch of herbs. Stir over a gentle heat until thickened. Shell and wash about three dozen mussels and put them in the hot liquid for about 10 minutes. Keep hot, but not boiling. They can be served on toast or used to fill bread rolls and garnished with lemon or watercress.

MUSSEL PIE

Traditional method:

In a greased casserole put a layer of shelled mussels with a dash of white wine or cider. Scatter the mussels with finely chopped onion and parsley, seasoning and a thin layer of breadcrumbs. Dampen the breadcrumbs with liquor from the mussel shells and dot with butter. Cook in a moderate oven for 20 minutes, until the top is just browned. Serve with toast.

MUSSELS WITH SAFFRON

Old recipe:

2 dozen mussels
2 onions
2 leeks
4 tomatoes
2 ozs butter
1 glass cider
Juice of ½ lemon
Seasoning
Thyme, bay leaf and a pinch of saffron

Peel and chop the onions, wash and finely slice the leek and cook both gently in the butter until soft. Peel and chop the tomatoes and add to the pan with cider, lemon juice and seasoning. Cook all until thickened. Add the cleaned mussels and cook for about 5 minutes until all are opened. Arrange mussels on a plate and pour the sauce over.

Steve Guscott

OYSTERS

Until the late nineteenth century oysters were a common poor man's food throughout much of Britain and were literally three a penny in London in the 1850s. About that time Exmoor fishermen responded to the demand and started to exploit the oyster beds between Lynmouth and Blue Anchor. They had fished oysters for local consumption for centuries. Piles of oyster shells are still frequently uncovered in Porlock gardens. An early eighteenth century map of Porlock Bay indicates oyster beds and harbour dues at Porlock Weir for 1723 show that 6d was due to the Lord of the Manor for each boat load of oysters landed.

A press account from Minehead for the 1860s mentions stealing of oysters from beds rented by James Smith from Henry Luttrell. Oysters were already becoming scarce and the Pollard family, who had been fishing oysters off Porlock went to try their luck off Swansea. Having exhausted the beds there they returned home to seek new beds off Porlock Bay. These they discovered about 1870 and for a few years there was an oyster boom, with catches of 1200 being common. Boats would dredge them from the sea bed between Hurlstone and Foreland Points. A dozen sailing boats would be employed, each crewed by three or four men. They would average about 300 oysters per boat per day and they sold the oysters at about 10d per hundred. Lynmouth oysters were sold by the long hundred, which was 120, and purchased in shops for about 2 shillings per hundred. The oysters were stored in bags of 600 in a perch, a small, walled pond uncovered at low tide. They remained there until they could fill enough barrels to send to Bristol or where required. The perch at Porlock Weir can still be seen opposite the cottage called Oyster Perch.

Oyster dredgers distinctive to the local area were built at Porlock Weir. They dredged with an oyster plough. This was shaped like a triangular draw-bar with a cutting edge about a metre long known as a sword, which had to be sharpened by a blacksmith. Trailing behind was a chain link bag to collect the oysters after they had been cut from the sea bed by the sword. The plough weighed about a hundredweight and was dragged along in several fathoms of water. The oyster beds were overfished within about ten years. An arrangement was made between Lynmouth and Porlock fishermen to keep to their own grounds either side of the county boundary and they allowed the beds to recover for spawning, but it is said that fishermen from Colchester and Whitstable came to replenish their own dwindling stocks. The last local dredger of its type was built in 1906 and refitted during the First World War in an attempt to locate new oyster beds, but the enterprise failed.

OYSTER SOUP

Old recipe:

2 pts milk
1 oz butter
1 oz flour
1-2 pts shelled oysters
1 small onion
2 egg yolks
2 tablespoons single cream
1 teaspoon chopped parsley
1 teaspoon lemon juice
Salt, pepper and mace to season

Chop the onion finely and simmer in a pan with the milk, parsley, mace and seasonings for 20 minutes. Melt the butter in another pan and stir in the flour. Strain the milk mixture over this and bring to the boil, stirring constantly. Simmer for 10 minutes. Mix the egg yolks with the cream and add to the pan, stirring briskly. Stir in the lemon juice and oysters and continue to cook for a few minutes, but do not allow the soup to boil or it may curdle.

OYSTER SCOLLOPS

Old recipe:

Butter scollop tins, put in a layer of bread crumbs, a few oysters, little bits of butter, a few drops of oyster liquor or milk, then more bread crumbs and butter. Brown nicely in oven.

WINKLES

Several types of winkle live on Exmoor shores but only the largest, the edible periwinkle, is eaten. As with the eating of most seashore molluscs, there is little written tradition in the form of recipes. There is only one way they have been eaten traditionally. Many people can tell you how to cook them but nobody has bothered to write it down.

Steve Guscott

Winkles

Traditional method:

As with all shellfish, boil for 20 minutes in salted water. About a tablespoon of salt to a pint of water is normal. When cool, pull the winkles from their shells with a pin. Discard the scab – the hard plate which forms a seal with the shell. Put in a jar and cover with vinegar. Cover the jar lightly with paper.

❊ Meat ❊

POULTRY

Ducks, geese and chickens have been birds of the Exmoor farmyard from the earliest days. Most Exmoor farmers and cottagers would keep hens but its is only recently with battery farming that chicken has become a cheap and common dish. Occasionally capons, which were cockerels not needed for breeding and castrated, were fatted up for the tables of the wealthy, but hens were for laying rather than eating. From the seventeenth century chickens and geese for eating became status symbols for the wealthy or for the special occasion such as Christmas. Occasionally a hen which passed its laying days or was not a good layer would be killed for the pot and boiled or made into pies and puddings but, again, it is mainly in recent times that hens have been bred to maximise egg production in their first couple of years and then be discarded. Now, because of salmonella infection, they tend to be discarded even earlier from commercial flocks. Exmoor hens have tended to be hardy stock which may not be prolific layers but continue to lay throughout their lives. As a result, most chicken dishes are of recent origin and traditional Exmoor chicken dishes are hard to find.

Ducks in an Exmoor cottage garden

There does not seem to be a traditional Exmoor hen breed: most Exmoor hens have been crossbred, often nowadays with a mix of Light Sussex, Rhode Island Red, Warren and bantam breeds. They tend to be free range, which means that they do not fatten well for the pot. Whereas enclosed birds are given a high protein diet, heat and light and breed all year round, the free range farmyard hens tend to be hatched in the spring and it will be well into the autumn before any are ready for the pot.

Now seen as game birds, pigeons were originally included as poultry and frequently reared in the farmyard, where dovecots became fashionable in the sixteenth and seventeenth centuries. For the wealthy lords, however, they had been around on Exmoor since Norman times at least. Guinea fowl, however, were once considered game and are now commonly bred as poultry on Exmoor smallholdings.

Bert Verney remembers keeping poultry on his farm near Landkey in the 1940s. There were no battery birds then and compared with today they were extremely expensive and a considerable luxury, reserved for special occasions:

> Keeping about 200 hens free-range and fattening turkeys and geese for the Christmas trade. Also, Indian game crosses for chicken at Christmas. This meant that the farm kitchen came into use once again. I used to stun, kill and bleed the birds, pull out the large wing and tail feathers outside on a line, and then bring them into the kitchen where three or four people would finish the plucking. My wife and another lady would do the `drawing' (removing the innards from the birds), dressing them off with liver, hearts, gizzards and fat from the insides of the birds. They then had the job of weighing, and then labelling with people's names who had ordered for their Christmas dinners. They were a real treat to look at, lined up on the slate slabs in the old dairy to set and keep cool. The food on plucking days was usually cups of tea and sandwiches and other cold snacks. There were too many feathers flying around to have a sit-down meal, and the old kitchen table was being used for drawing and dressing the birds. I suppose a chicken took 15 to 20 minutes, a turkey 20 minutes and a goose up to half or three quarters of an hour, to pluck. So, depending on the number of birds and the number of pluckers, it took either one or two days. A turkey would weigh 10 to 20 lbs, the price 25 shillings a pound. The geese 10 to 14 lbs and 27 shillings and 6 pence per pound. A chicken 6 to 8 lbs at £1 per pound. This was always regarded as a farmer's wife's perks, to help buy a Christmas present and the goodies for Christmas.

Brian Pearce

Poultry feeding at Porte Farm, Kentisbury c1930   Exmoor Photographic Archive

Most poultry were once cooked baked in pastry. A seventeenth century recipe for chicken suggests stuffing the bird with breadcrumbs mixed with butter and herbs, wrapping it in a good shortcrust pastry and baking in a bread oven. It was served with a white wine sauce, thickened with egg yolks and seasoned with salt, pepper, cinnamon, sugar and rosewater.

EXMOOR CHICKEN

Old recipe:

> *1 prepared chicken*
> *3 ozs butter*
> *½ lb dessert apples*
> *½ pt cider*
> *1 large onion*
> *4 fl ozs chicken stock*
> *2 ozs clotted cream*
> *1 oz flour*
> *Seasoning*

Quarter the chicken and dust the joints with seasoned flour. Fry the joints in 2 ozs butter in a large pan until browned. Remove the joints from the pan, placing them in an ovenproof dish. Peel, core and chop the apples. Chop the onions and fry with half the apple in the pan for a few minutes without browning. Add the remaining flour to the pan and stir. Add the cider and

stock and bring to the boil whilst stirring. Pour the contents of the pan onto the chicken, place a lid on the dish and bake for 15 minutes at 350°F\180°C\ Gas Mark 4. Place the chicken on a serving dish. Brown the remaining apple with the remaining butter in the frying pan and arrange the slices on the chicken. Add the liquid, apple and onion from the baking dish to the pan and stir in the cream. Heat through without boiling and pour the sauce over the chicken.

HONEYED CHICKEN

Recipe from Ina Gage of Withypool:

> *2½ lb chicken cut into joints*
> *4-6 shallots, chopped*
> *2 oz butter*
> *2 oz Exmoor heather honey*
> *Teaspoonful of strong English mustard*
> *¼ pt dry cider*
> *Herbs: parsley and rosemary chopped fine*
> *Seasoning: salt and pepper*

Fry the shallots in the butter until soft and add the chicken pieces, browning on each side. Blend the honey, mustard, herbs and seasoning. Remove the chicken pieces from the pan and brush with this mixture. Transfer to an oven to table dish with the shallots. Cover with cider. Bake uncovered at

350°F\180°C\Gas Mark 4 until crisp and golden. Serve with any remaining liquid as sauce and accompany with sauté potatoes and salad.

Brian Pearce

CHICKEN BREAST WITH REDCURRANTS AND CREAM

Adapted from a recipe by Suzie Neate of Wheddon Cross:

Ingredients to serve four persons:
1 lb skinless chicken breasts
1 oz butter
1 tablespoon plain flour
4 ozs redcurrants
¼ pt dry white wine
¼ pt single cream
4 spring onions
Salt and pepper for seasoning

Cut the chicken breasts into scallops no more than ½ inch thick. It is best to do this against the grain of the meat. Dust them with seasoned flour. Cut the spring onions lengthwise into thin strips and fry briskly in the butter for just two minutes. Add the chicken pieces to the frying pan and cook on each side for two minutes. Add the white wine and allow to boil for one minute. Add the redcurrants and cream, stirring all the time whilst they heat through, but do not boil. Serve immediately.

The dish looks well when garnished with sprigs of redcurrants and a few redcurrant leaves. It can be served with fresh green vegetables and new potatoes or with a cold summer ratatouille.

ROAST DUCK WITH GOOSEBERRY SAUCE

Old recipe:

1 duck
1 lemon
2 ozs butter
2 ozs plain flour
½ pt stock
¼ pt cider
Seasoning

For the sauce:
8 ozs gooseberries
¼ pt cider
2 tablespoons caster sugar
1 oz butter
½ teaspoon mace

Rub the cut lemon all over the duck, then rub the butter into the breast and legs. Place on a trivet in a roasting pan and bake in an oven at 400°F\200°C\ Gas Mark 6 for 20 minutes per lb and an extra 20 minutes. Baste occasionally and during cooking sprinkle the breast with flour and seasoning. The stock can be made with the giblets, if any, and the juices from the cooking pan after the fat has been drained. The remaining flour is added to the juices in the pan and heated on a stove, stirring until thickened. The stock and cider is added to the pan, stirring whilst heating through. This makes the gravy. The sauce is made by heating the gooseberries in a pan with the sugar, cider and mace. When they are reduced to a pulp the butter is stirred in and the sauce is ready to serve with the duck.

Steve Guscott

GOOSE

Lonely farms have always been difficult to police and many Exmoor farms had a goose house, rather like a kennel, near the back door for a gander to warn of strangers approaching. Goose was naturally the usual Christmas dinner and at Michaelmas, a tradition dating from Tudor times. Michaelmas Day is 29th September and was well known in country areas as the end of a years' service for hired farmworkers and the day on which they kept or lost their jobs. It was also a time when tenants paid their rents and went to their landlord's house to do so. They would often dress for the occasion and the landlord would provide them with a meal. Goose was traditional at this time as the geese were fattened on the gleanings from the corn harvest. Markets would be full of geese and 'goosey fairs' were held in some areas, although not on Exmoor.

Christmas roast goose

Roast goose was traditionally stuffed with prunes and apples and served with apple, bread or gooseberry sauce. In other areas the fruit stuffing was turned into a sauce with the addition of wine. As it was a luxury dish and there is little meat for its size, the goose was sometimes stuffed with rabbit joints to give to the children whilst the adults feasted on the poultry. From medieval times it was also common to bake it in a pastry crust.

MICHAELMAS GOOSE

Old recipe:

1 goose
Juice of ½ lemon
Butter
Seasoning

For the stuffing:
8 ozs breadcrumbs
2 cooking apples
2 ozs prunes
1 teaspoon sage
1 onion
1 oz butter
Seasoning

Remove any accessible fat from the goose. Weigh the goose. Rub with lemon juice and season. Peel, core and dice the apple. Soak and stone the prunes if necessary and chop. Mix all the stuffing ingredients together, binding with the melted butter. Place the stuffing in the cavity of the goose. Put the goose in a roasting dish and dot with butter. Cover and roast in an oven at 350°F\180°C\ Gas Mark 4 for 20 minutes per lb and an extra 20 minutes. Take the lid off for the last 30 minutes of cooking. The goose can be served with gravy made with stock from the giblets, if any, and the cooking juices from which the fat has been drained.

BEEF

Cattle have been around on Exmoor for thousands of years. It has been suggested that the local Devon breed is descended from the Longrifons race introduced with the advent of farming in Neolithic times. This is combined with traces of the Urus breed, introduced later, and the native British cattle. The Saxons certainly brought cattle with them and these will have interbred with the local cattle. Red cattle seem to have been in the Exmoor area for centuries but before the nineteenth century accounts of cattle on the moor are mainly of small, almost wild black cattle. There were reputed to have been a thousand summered in the Royal Forest in the early seventeenth century. However, more reliable accounts put numbers at there at little more than a hundred until the late eighteenth century, when they were no longer given summer grazing.

Beef traditionally comes from beeves, which are castrated males. Breeding them on the poorer hill pasture of Exmoor was supposed to give them a strong constitution and firm bone, so that they would eat well and fatten up quickly when brought on to richer, lowland pasture. In the nineteenth century the Knight family experimented with introducing hardy Scottish breeds which could be fattened on their estate but returned to local breeds until the Fortescues introduced Galloways in the early twentieth century. Today Scottish breeds of cattle predominate on the higher parts of the moor.

Local breeds of cattle are now uncommon on Exmoor generally. The continental breeds tend to grow faster and produce heavier, leaner carcasses. The cattle eat more feed but produce more meat in the same amount of time. The EU grading system also seems to discriminate against the local breeds. Less production means steady supplies to supermarkets cannot be guaranteed and so the downward spiral continues. However, the traditional Devon cattle produce superb quality meat and their efficiency of grazing, ease of calving and mothering ability are traits of great value to breeders.

Steve Guscott

Red Ruby Devon cattle, Langleigh Farm, Cadleigh

Brian Pearce

Great Champson, Molland

A few Exmoor farmers still rear the traditional Red Ruby Devon cattle for beef. Devons have been around from at least the sixteenth century and are thought to be the ancestor of breeds such as the Sussex and Hereford. The modern Devon was bred in the late eighteenth century by Francis Quartly and his brothers at Champson, Molland. It was bred to suit their particular needs: to graze land at over 1000ft above sea level, particularly to withstand the exposed conditions on Exmoor, and to mature early from grass. They also sought docility, ease of calving, ample milk to rear calves and a high quality carcass. Some of the older steers used to be kept for plough oxen at between three and six years old, after which they were sold for meat.

Currently 18 of the 170 pedigree herds nationwide are in the Exmoor area. Also known, incorrectly, as the Red or North Devon cattle, they are smaller and finer boned than their South Devon and Somerset counterparts and have traditionally been crossed with the latter to produce more meat without reducing their hardy and thrifty qualities suited to Exmoor. They are dual purpose cattle but have not been used for dairying since the 1950s and on the moor are run as suckler herds. Generally the cattle mature early when brought down off the moor. Often they are raised on the moor for about 18 months and brought down to lowland farms for fattening for another 12 months.

The fact that the Devons are traditionally reared purely on grass meant a revival in their local popularity during the BSE crisis and many local butchers have since been specifying the breed of the beef and the method of production. However, carcass quality is more important than breed and the Devon Cattle Breeders Society has been concentrating on this quality aspect to increase interest in the meat. They run a Devon-friendly butcher scheme to link producers with butchers. West Country Quality Meat branding grew out of the success of Aberdeen Angus marketing schemes and is now being applied to Devon beef. The West Country Cooking Campaign has also inspired many local hotels and restaurants to serve and specify that they use Devon beef.

Breeders feel that new measures to ensure the traceability of meat from farmer to butcher will help the discriminating customer. They also feel that they must act co-operatively to ensure regular supplies to the big supermarkets. A group of local farmers have formed themselves into Exmoor Quality Beef Producers. In a European funded project, they have been experimenting with electronic tagging of cattle. The tags are produced locally at Cutcombe and inserted into one of the cow's stomachs. It can only be removed at slaughtering and ensures full traceability of the meat. Local butchers like Gerald David are at present the main suppliers of the meat. Gerald kills at Porlock to supply his shops at Minehead, Taunton, Dulverton, Lynton, Topsham and Ipplepen. The animals are all local and under minimum stress from travel. The meat is hung for a minimum of two weeks to give tenderness and flavour. His business, started in 1969, has grown as his three sons have taken up the trade.

Peter Greig of Cullompton won an award as Butcher of the Year for 1995, partly for the quality of his Red Devon beef. Much of the flavour of meat depends on what the animals eat, how old they are and how the meat is treated. Peter recommends hanging the meat for about four weeks:

> We chose the Devons as an early maturing, traditional grass breed, designed to live on grass, which would mature in two to three years. It has a natural bark of fat, so you can hang it and there is natural marbling. People are looking for texture and flavour and I think both are achieved by having an animal reach maturity and through hanging. It then doesn't simply fall apart; you have to bite a piece and you get the reward of fullness of flavour.

Nearly half of the Devon herds have been established in the 1990s and these have mostly been linked with organic farming. Whilst continental breeds may put on weight faster, Devons still compete well against others when organically fed. Their ability to convert rough forage into beef has resulted in the Devon being used for a number of conservation grazing schemes, where the animals still put on weight when they are required to graze areas with limited growth potential for other breeds.

The method of cutting up beef varied from region to region and the standard method of jointing shown in many old cookery books was that used in London and the Home Counties. Now that beef on the bone is suspect and much imported beef is already boned the joints of beef seem irrelevant, let alone the local ways of jointing. Tag end of rump, for instance, was a choice local joint which can still be cut to order in Exmoor butchers, but the meat is now usually cut into steaks.

Despite the fact that the English are renowned for their roast beef, few poorer people ate beef. Locally, the bread ovens were not best suited to roasting joints of beef on their own. Often a large joint would be sent to the village baker's for roasting and would be made to last a week. Pot roasting on open fires was common and suited to the more commonly eaten, cheaper cuts of meat, such as brisket. The pot was an iron pan with a tight lid and short handles. The meat was put in the pot with plenty of dripping for basting and the pot placed in the hottest part of the fire and covered with embers. The meat would baste itself in the steam inside. Often the whole meal was cooked in the same pot and this tradition was carried on to regular ovens, where the meat was placed on top of the vegetables and gravy in a roasting tray, alongside the suet pudding. The method was even applied when cheap cuts of meat, as opposed to joints, were cooked. Often braising steak or skirt would be cut up and mixed with offal and onions and baked like a roast.

Spiced beef

Brian Pearce

DEAKINS ROAST DEVON BRISKET

Recipe from Chloe Deakin of Cadleigh, Tiverton:

Ask your butcher to bone out a fresh (unsalted) brisket of beef. Remove any excess fat. Score the fat on the outside and sprinkle the inside with the desired seasoning. Spread sausage meat or sage and onion stuffing on the inside, roll up and tie. Brush the outside with this mixture:

> *1 tablespoon black treacle*
> *1 dessertspoon salt*
> *1 tablespoon wine vinegar*

Put the meat in a roasting pan into a hot oven for 20 minutes, the moderate to slow cooking for about 2-3 hours. Baste occasionally and, if it is getting too dark, cover with tin foil. Pour off excess fat and make gravy with the juices and red wine to your taste. Serve with baked potatoes. This is also delicious when cold.

BEEF OLIVES

Old recipe:

2 lbs Devon rump steak
½ lb onions
2 ozs beef dripping
1 pt beef stock
½ pt red wine
seasoning
1 oz butter mixed with 1 oz flour

To make stuffing:
½ lb breadcrumbs
2 ozs bacon
2 ozs onions
1 lemon

Steve Guscott

Cut the steak into eight thin slices. Make the stuffing by chopping the onions and bacon and mixing well with the breadcrumbs and grated rind and juice of the lemon. Spread the stuffing on each slice of steak, which is then rolled and held with string. Slice the onions and fry in the dripping. Add the meat to the pan and brown lightly. Add the stock, wine and seasoning and bring to the boil, then reduce to a simmer for 1½ hours. Near the end of cooking, thicken the stock by stirring in the flour and butter mix. To serve, remove the string from the olives and strain the reduced stock over them.

BEEF IN CIDER

Recipe from Mrs H Messenger of Cutcombe:

Ingredients for 6 persons:
2 lbs\900 gms cubed chuck steak
8 ozs\225 gms streaky bacon
12 ozs\300 gms whole, small onions
4 ozs\100 gms sliced mushrooms
¾ pt\450 mls dry cider
1 medium onion
2 cloves garlic
1 tablespoon plain flour
Bay leaf, thyme, beef dripping

Fry the sliced onion for 5 minutes in beef dripping, then add meat and brown quickly on all sides. Sprinkle with flour to absorb juices, then gradually add cider, stirring all the time. Add garlic and herbs, season well, transfer to casserole, cover and cook for 2 hours at 325°F\170°C\Gas Mark 3. Lightly brown the whole onions and chopped bacon in a little more dripping, add to casserole with the sliced mushrooms and cook for a further hour.

EXMOOR STEAK AND KIDNEY PIE

Often, if there was not enough kidney, beef melt was added to this. The melt is attached to the inner side of the ribs and makes a tasty, kidney flavoured gravy. Sometimes the gravy was made on its own with a little onion for invalids.

Old recipe:

1½ lbs Devon stewing steak
½ lb ox kidney
4 ozs onions
1 oz beef dripping
¾ pint beef stock
¾ lb shortcrust pastry
flour
seasoning and herbs such as parsley
2 ozs clotted cream

Dice the steak and kidney and dust with the seasoned flour. Chop the onions and fry with the meat in the dripping until lightly browned. Transfer to a large pan, cover with the stock and add herbs and seasoning. Put a lid on the pan and simmer for 1½ hours. Make the pastry with beef dripping, put the meat in a pie dish and cover with the pastry. Bake at 400°F\200°C\ Gas Mark 6 for about 1 hour until the pastry is golden brown. Just before serving lift the pastry lid and put clotted cream on top of the meat.

Steve Guscott

EXMOOR FARMHOUSE PIE

Recipe from Miss L Halsey and Mr M Bassett of South Molton:

Ingredients for 6 persons:
2 lbs\1 kg beef
6 ozs\150 gms ham
1 tablespoon butter
1 lb\450 gms carrots
2 tablespoons flour
8 ozs\225 gms mushrooms
2 large onions
1 swede\turnip\parsnip
7 ozs\175 gms tomato purée
¼ pt\150 mls water
1 garlic clove
1 stock cube
Paprika, tarragon

For the pastry:
12 ozs\300 gms lard
12 ozs\300 gms butter
1 teaspoon lemon juice
2 lbs\1 kg flour
Salt, pepper and water

Dice the beef finely, sprinkle with salt, pepper and herbs and brown in a frying pan. Add the chopped onions, cook for a few minutes, then add the diced carrot, cruched garlic, chopped ham and the swede, turnip or parsnip. Stir in the flour, then add the boiling water, stock cube and tomato purée. Simmer for 45 minutes until meat is tender and stew is rich and thick. Place in a large pie dish, cover with the pastry and cook in a moderate oven for 35-40 minutes.

BEEF AND EGG PIE

This old recipe is for a raised crust pie. In the past the crust would have been raised by hand. This required much practice: raise the pastry too quickly and it collapses, too slowly and it dries and cracks. Even raising around a mould takes some skill.

2 lbs Devon braising steak, chuck steak or skirt
4 ozs beef suet
3 hard-boiled eggs
5 fluid ozs beef stock or aspic jelly
seasoning
1½ lbs hot water crust pastry

Mince the beef and mix with the shredded suet and seasoning. Take three quarters of the pastry and raise it around a mould. Remove from the mould and fill with the meat and suet, pushing it around the eggs. Cover the pie with a lid made from the remaining pastry and glaze with milk or beaten egg. Bake in a preheated oven at 425°F\220°C\Gas Mark 7 for 30 minutes, then reduce the heat to 325°F\170°C\ Gas Mark 3 for two hours. When the pie has cooled, pour the stock or aspic through a hole made in the lid and leave to cool and set. Serve cold.

ORGANIC BEEF PASTIES

Recipe from Jo Budden of Burrington:

1 lb short crust pastry
1 lb of organic beef: any part can be used
e.g. flank, braising steak or any joint,
chopped very small or put through a food processor
2 lbs potatoes
1 lb swede
1 small onion
Seasoning

Steve Guscott

Make up the short crust pastry. Peel and finely chop the vegetables, mix with the chopped meat and season generously. Roll out the pastry and cut circles using a saucer or small plate. Place generous amounts of the mixture in the centre of each round, draw up the sides and pinch them together. Glaze with beaten egg. Cook at 375°F\190°C\Gas Mark 5 for 50-60 minutes. Reduce the heat if they are cooking too fast, but not the cooking time as the inside must be thoroughly cooked.

MINCEMEAT

This was so named as it originally contained minced meat. As such it was not used as a preserve, although the spices were often used to disguise meat which had gone off. It could be used in main course or pudding dishes according to the proportions of meat and sweet ingredients. Mincemeats are particularly good containing lamb, but pork or beef will do.

Brian Pearce

An old recipe from Brian Pearce's great grandmother, Sara Ann Smith who was the wife of an Ilfracombe butcher and farmer:

2 lbs suet
1 lb minced beef
2 lbs raisins
1 lb sultanas
1½ lbs currants
2 lbs chopped cored apples
2½ lbs sugar
12 ozs candied lemon peel
Juice and grated rind of 2 boiled lemons
2 grated nutmegs
1 teaspoon mace
1 teaspoon ginger
½ oz salt
½ pt ginger wine

Mix ingredients thoroughly and leave overnight to swell the fruit, but then use the mixture immediately as the beef does not keep.

MUTTON AND LAMB

Despite thousands of years of sheep farming on Exmoor, mutton or lamb did not form a large part of the local diet until the days of the Agricultural Revolution in the late eighteenth century. Until then the sheep were seen as wool producers and were not selected for their meat. If mutton was eaten it was

usually from broken mouthed old ewes whose useful breeding life had come to an end. It was not usual for mutton to be salted and was usually eaten fresh at the end of summer, when the lambs had been weaned. The only other time it may have been eaten is when the poor were starving and forced to steal sheep for food, usually in the hard winter months. Records of sheep stealing are common throughout Exmoors long history and shepherds kept a close watch on their flocks. Steal the sheep and sell the wool, Say the bells of Withypool was an apt saying.

Traditionally sheep were agisted or pastured on the moors in the summer. Ewes and lambs were brought down in late autumn, but wethers were left until winter weather set in or left out all year for three or four winters until they were fat. The meat produced was very lean, close grained and full of flavour, so moorland wether mutton was much prized. Unfortunately it has long since disappeared as all lambs have been sold for stores or kept for breeding. The practice of rotating grass with oats and turnips meant that wethers were fattened on turnips and cake over winter and sold off as early as possible.

The traditional ancient sheep breed of Exmoor is the Exmoor Horn. More recently it has been crossed with the Devon Longwool to produce the Devon Closewool, also very common on the moor. In the nineteenth century there was also the Bampton Nott, so called because it had no horns. In fact locally the sheep were simply divided into horns or notts. The horned sheep did not fatten well in lowland areas and frequently broke out of fields, so were usually put to Bampton or Leicester rams to produce more easily fatted and manageable lambs. It was found that the crossbred sheep were equally hardy and had started replacing the horned sheep when Frederic Knight introduced even hardier northern English and Scottish breeds to the area. He found that the lambs fattened well on rape crops used to improve the soil after breaking up moorland. Such lambs could be sold fat between August and November without having to be finished off elsewhere. Knight then made use of the new railway connection at South Molton. The lambs were killed in South Molton and the carcasses hung in special meat vans provided by the Great Western Railway. The meat could then arrive in London as fresh as any in the country.

In the surrounding parts of Exmoor the horned sheep still survive, although blackface and Cheviot sheep are prevalent in the former Forest. Maud Harding of Winsford speaks of her childhood at Torr Farm:

> It was mainly Exmoor Horns you see when we were children – it was like the Exmoor Horn Sheep Breeders Society that was held at Winsford. But Closewools were also kept on some of the farms. We kept a few but since then

Judging of Exmoor Horn sheep at Winsford Fair c1923

there's a number of breeds as you know come in. At Winsford there was a Sheep Sale, once a year – the others were at Exford for mainly the breeding ewes, rams at Winsford you see. A registered flock. Everyone wasn't registered in those days. They weren't all registered so they had the sales, which is done away with now a few years at Exford. The dealers came from a ways-away you see.

Crossing has long been practised as the local ewes are mated with rams of heavier breeds such as a Suffolk to produce store lambs for sale for fattening elsewhere.

The sheep were traditionally pastured on the moor in summer to free the in-bye land for hay making and other animals and keep them away from flies. This was either done free through commoners' rights or by renting grazing on the Royal Forest. Moormen employed by the Forest Warden would 'cry the moor' in villages in the spring to announce the opening of the grazing and the prices for the year. They would also count the sheep in 'telling houses' as they were drifted up onto the moor and check that each had the owner's mark – usually a raddle mark and an ear cut. Shepherds would live with their flocks on the moor for the summer and jealously guarded the best grazings.

As pastry for meat was normally made with the fat from the meat, the pastry for mutton pies and pasties

was made with mutton fat. To make traditional Exmoor pies, therefore, you will have to make your own mutton suet. To do this you should melt pieces of chopped fat with hot water and strain it off through a fine sieve into a clean, cold basin. A little vinegar mixed with the water helps to take away some of the sickly flavour. When cold and set, the fat should be carefully scraped from the gravy underneath. Hard mutton fat can be shredded or warmed over a basin of hot water and creamed with lemon juice before using. It was also creamed by whipping with a little cider. It was used this way in piecrusts and in cake making and makes good apple dumplings and gingerbread.

Mutton and lamb has a delicate flavour and sauces should bring out the subtleties of its flavour, not drown them. Sauces for mutton were supposed to reflect what the animals had eaten. Therefore, hot laver sauce was prized for marsh mutton, which was supposed to taste of the salt grasses and seaweeds of the estuaries where the sheep fed. Mountain mutton was accompanied by the wild thyme which flavoured that meat and mutton from orchards had fruit sauces such as apple or redcurrant jelly. In the same way rowan jelly was used for much Exmoor mutton. Lamb, which was traditionally reared on wet lowland meadows, was usually flavoured with the mint which grew on the banks of the streams flowing through the meadows.

CROCKY

This is basically a local version of hot pot. The same recipes as for squab pie made with mutton are used, but sliced potatoes are substituted for the pastry top. Sometimes pastry is added on top of the potatoes when the pie is mostly cooked and timed to finish cooking when the pastry is baked.

EXMOOR LAMB MEDALLIONS WITH SWEET CIDER, TOMATO, THYME AND ROSEMARY

Recipe from Ian Hamilton of Allerford:

To serve 4 persons:
2 best ends of lamb, filleted and cut
into medallions ¾" thick
½ pt of sweet or medium sweet cider
4 skinned tomatoes, roughly chopped
Fresh thyme and rosemary to taste
2 ozs butter

Steve Guscott

Heat 1 oz butter in a heavy frying pan. Add medallions and brown both sides for a few minutes until just cooked. Transfer to heated serving dish. Add tomatoes and herbs to pan and cook. Add cider and bring to the boil. Season and add 1 oz butter to thicken the sauce. Pour over medallions. Serve with Parmesan potatoes and a green vegetable.

EXMOOR LAMB STEW

Old recipe:

8 lamb chops
1½ lbs potatoes
4 ozs button onions
½ lb mushrooms
6 fl ozs cider
½ pt mutton stock (made by boiling bones and
trimmings of mutton joints with a few root vegetables)
2 ozs butter
2 ozs clotted cream
Seasoning and herbs: thyme and parsley are recommended

Gently brown the chops in the butter in a large pan. Remove the chops and to the pan add the potatoes, cut into large pieces, onions and mushrooms, cooking for about 5 minutes. Add the cider, stock and seasoning to the pan with the chops. Cover and simmer gently for about an hour until tender. Stir in the cream just before serving.

FLANK OR BREAST OF LAMB

Traditional method:

Bone the flank and use the bones to make a stock. Season and spice the flank well, rubbing the mixture with about a tablespoon of salt into the spaces. Leave for a day. Dice or slice turnips, parsnips and onion and spread on one side of the flank. Roll up and tie with string. Simmer with vegetable trimmings in the bone stock until the vegetables are cooked. Shred a cabbage finely and cook it like spinach: packed into a pan with a little butter and milk. Cook gently for about 15 minutes with the lid on, tossing and stirring occasionally. Serve the meat on a dish with the cabbage around and a gravy made from the cooking liquid from the cabbage and a little of the strained stock.

ANSTEY HONEYED LAMB

Recipe from Alison Milton of West Anstey:

Ingredients for 4 persons:
4 trimmed chump chops
¾ pt\450 mls farmhouse cider
1 large chopped onion
1 oz\25 gms butter
1½ tablespoons cooking oil
1½ tablespoons flour
¾ teaspoon mustard powder
4 teaspoons honey
2-3 large carrots
4 ozs\100 gms sliced mushrooms
1 beef stock cube
Salt and pepper

Fry the onion in the butter and oil and transfer to a casserole. Sift the flour, mustard powder, salt and pepper together and coat the chops. Fry to seal all over, then place in the casserole. Stir any surplus flour into the pan and let it brown gently. Add the cider, honey and stock cube, then pour into the dish with the mushrooms and sliced carrots. Bake for an hour and a quarter at 350°F\180°C\Gas Mark 4.

LAMB AND WHORTLEBERRY HERB PANCAKES

Recipe from Miss S. Wardell of Monksilver:

Ingredients for 4 persons:
For the pancake batter:
3 eggs
2 ozs\50 gms flour
8 fluid ozs\200 mls milk
3 tablespoons vegetable oil
1 tablespoon chopped parsley and thyme

For the filling:
2 leeks
2 carrots
2 ozs\50 gms butter
3 lamb noisettes
Salt and pepper

For the sauce:
8 ozs\225 gms whortleberries
10 fluid ozs\300 mls stock
2 ozs\50 gms butter
6 fluid ozs\175 mls red wine

Brian Pearce

Make four 8" diameter pancakes, mixing the eggs, flour, milk, oil and a pinch of salt, adding the herbs and leaving to stand for an hour before cooking. Cut carrots and leeks into fine julienne strips, blanch for a minute in boiling water, refresh and set aside. Seal the noisettes in the butter and cook until brown on the outside but still pink in the middle. Set aside and deglaze the pan with red wine. Reduce, add the stock, pureed whortleberries, salt and pepper, and simmer until a syrupy consistency is achieved. Whisk in the butter, divide into small pieces. Slice the noisettes and divide between the pancakes, placing the meat in the centre. Top with blanched vegetables and a little of the sauce. Fold over the edges to enclose the filling, brush with melted butter, reheat, then flash under the grill before serving with the remaining sauce.

EXMOOR LAMB WITH WORT SAUCE

Old recipe:

1 rack of lamb (can use chops), roasted but pink
8 oz whortleberries
2 glasses red wine

Simmer together the wine and whortleberries until reduced by half. Serve the lamb carved into individual portions (usually two chops together) and pour over the sauce. Decorate with paper frill on the end of each chop and serve with vegetables in season.

ORGANIC LAMB WITH HONEY AND CIDER

Recipe from Jo Budden of Burrington:

1 shoulder or leg joint of organic lamb
2 teaspoons ground ginger
4 tablespoons clear Exmoor honey
2 teaspoons rosemary
¾ pt local cider
Seasoning

Rub the joint with the ginger and seasoning. Pour over the honey and sprinkle with rosemary. Put in a roasting tin with the cider. Cook in a roasting oven at 375°F\190°C\Gas Mark 5 for 1½-2 hours depending on the size of the joint and how you like it: usually 20 minutes per pound plus 20 minutes. The meat juices can be used for gravy: boil to reduce them if desired.

TENDER LAMB IN A MINT AND SORREL SAUCE

Recipe from Susan Samuel of South Molton:

Ingredients for 4 persons:
4 leg of Exmoor lamb chops
½ pt\300 mls stock
5 fluid ozs\125 mls white wine
5 fluid ozs\125 mls double cream
2 tablespoons oil
1 garlic clove
6 young sorrel leaves
6 sprigs mint

Heat the oil in a frying pan, crush the garlic clove and add it with the lamb chops, browning them on both sides. Add the stock and white wine and reduce to a simmer. Roll up the mint in the sorrel leaves, chop finely and sprinkle over the chops. Shake the pan and mix them in and simmer for 5 minutes. Turn into a heated ovenproof dish, cover and cook in a moderate oven until tender. Skim off excess fat before adding cream and heating through for another 5 minutes. Serve with creamed spinach, boiled onions and boiled or creamed potatoes.

MUTTON PASTY

Steve Guscott

'But now, at Dulverton, we dined on the rarest and choicest victuals that I ever did taste. Even now, at my time of life, to think of it gives me appetite, as once and awhile to think of my first love makes me love all goodness. Hot mutton pasty was a thing I had often heard of from very wealthy boys and men, who made a dessert of dinner; and to hear them talk of it made my lips smack, and my ribs come inwards.

And now John Fry strode into the hostel, with the air and grace of a short-legged man, and shouted as loud as if he was calling sheep on Exmoor – "Hot mooton pasty for twoo trarv'lers, at number vaive, in vaive minnits! Dish un up in the tin with the grahvy, zame as I hardered last Tuesday." 'so related Jan Ridd in *Lorna Doone*.

The Cornish claim pasties as their own and locals call them tatieoggies. Oggie is the local term for a for a Cornish or Welsh man but in this case the reference may be to a 'hoggan', which is a pasty without potato. However, they were common fare throughout the West Country. Basically they were a way of packaging a meaty lunch for anyone working outside during the day, be it Cornish miner, fisherman or Exmoor farmworker. The pastry was seen as the method of

packaging and, when made to be portable, was baked hard and dry so that it was occasionally discarded when the contents were eaten. However, the tastiest pasties were cooked long and slowly so that the meat juices were absorbed by the pastry. Some enterprising housewives managed to pack a savoury main course at one end and a fruit dessert at the other.

A pasty was usually the width of a plate and made for an individual, sometimes with their initials made in pastry, but some were later made longer for family meals. There is a modern tradition that a Cornish pasty has the pastry joined at the edge and a Devon pasty has it joined across the top, also that a Cornish pasty must contain swede. Some say that the meat and vegetables should be diced, others that the meat should be minced and the vegetables grated. The truth is that there was probably more variation from family to family and season to season than county to county and that ingredients varied according to what was available at the time. In poor times pasties may only have contained potatoes and onions, or culinary weeds and offal. In his book *The Way 'Twas* Walter Isaac recalls his packed lunches at Chittlehampton School:

> All food and drink for the day had to be carried, even by the youngest. Pasties of potato, turnip, apple, eggs, bacon, even kidney at pig killing time, sustained us for the day.

On Exmoor, naturally, it was most common to make pasties with mutton.

Old recipe:

> 2 lbs mutton
> ½ lb potatoes
> ½ lb onions
> 2 lbs short crust pastry
> seasoning and herbs such as thyme

If lamb is substituted for the mutton it will not be necessary to cook it first but the mutton is best at least partly cooked and it is usual to be the left-overs from a previous meal. Mince or dice the mutton and dice the potatoes and onions. Mix together with the herbs and seasoning. The pastry is traditionally made with mutton suet. Roll out the pastry about ¼ inch thick and cut it into rounds of about 9 inches diameter. Divide the filling equally by placing in the middle of the pastry rounds. Wet the edge of the pastry and draw it up to meet over the top of the filling. Crimp the edges together with your fingertips. You can brush the pastry with beaten egg or milk and bake at 350°F\180°C\Gas Mark 4 for about an hour, until the pastry is golden brown.

A variation was to make squab pasty, where apple was substituted for the potato.

Old recipe:

For the pastry:
6 ozs plain flour
1½ ozs lard
1½ ozs butter
Water

For the filling:
8 ozs cooked mutton
1 onion
1 apple
Seasoning

Rub the fats into the flour and mix to a stiff dough with a little water. Dice the mutton finely, also the apple and onion. Roll out the pastry and cut into rounds. Place meat in the centre of each round, followed by onion and apple. Season and crimp up edges of the pastry around the filling. Bake in a moderate oven for about 45 minutes to an hour, until the pastry is golden brown.

ROWAN GLAZED EXMOOR LAMB

Recipe from Anne Boldry of Oakford:

2 lbs\900 gms boned loin of Exmoor lamb
3 ozs\75 gms brown breadcrumbs
1 oz\25 gms shredded suet
¼ pt\150 mls cider
1 egg
½ teaspoon dried rosemary
½ teaspoon dried thyme
2 teaspoons grated orange rind
Rowanberry jelly, seasoning

Preheat the oven to 400°F\200°C\Gas Mark 6. Mix together the breadcrumbs, suet, herbs, orange rind, egg and seasoning to form a stuffing. Place it in the loin and tie up with string. Roast for an hour, pour off excess fat, spread the joint with rowan jelly and pour cider into roasting tin. Return to oven for 20 minutes. Serve with gravy made from pan juices.

LAMB'S TAIL PIE

This is traditional on Exmoor, but not peculiar to the area. It was best known from the Cotswolds, where the local breed of sheep have much fatter and meatier tails. It was made at Easter, when the lambs' tails were docked. A docker was a bit like a large chisel and nowadays this rather primitive method has been replaced by placing a restricting ribber ring around the base of the tail. The tail gradually withers and drops off, making it useless for eating. The tails were skinned and cut up like oxtail. They were very fatty, so they were boiled and the fat skimmed off before putting them in a pie.

Traditional method:

About ten lambs tails were skinned and cut into lengths of 1-2 inches. They were simmered in water for about an hour with a chopped onion and pieces of fat bacon. The fat was skimmed off and the meat and stock put in a pie dish with a couple of sliced apples. The dish was covered with pastry and baked until the pastry was cooked.

SQUAB PIE

This is the version which evolved from a pigeon pie to a mutton pie. Some say that it had nothing to do with squabs but came from squabble – the master demanding meat and the mistress wanting apple. Any cheap cuts or off cuts of meat were used and the same recipe was applied to beef, particularly skirt. With mutton, this was a recipe for the proverbial scrag end. Neck chops were frequently used, boned or on the bone, but any chops or offcuts would do.

Old recipe:

Ingredients for four persons:
4 four neck chops of mutton
4 medium sized potatoes
4 medium sized onions
2 cooking apples
¾ cup of water
1 teaspoon sugar
Short crust pastry

Brian Pearce

Peel the potatoes and onions. Peel and core the apples and cut all into a ¼ inch dice. Place a layer of potatoes in an ovenproof dish. Add a layer of onions, then a layer of apples, seasoning as you go and sugaring the apple if necessary. Add the chops in one layer and cover with another layer of potato, onion and apple. Pour in the water, cover with pastry and cook at 400°F\200°c\Gas Mark 6 for ¾ hour, then reduce the temperature to 300°F\150°C\Gas Mark 2 for ½ hour. This can be served with clotted cream placed under the pastry just before serving.

DUNKERY HILL LAMB

Recipe from Peter Fuller of Barnstaple:

Ingredients for 4 persons:
4 X 5 ozs\125 gms leg of lamb chops
1 lb\450 gms puff pastry
4 ozs\100 gms mushrooms
2 ozs\50 gms butter
½ medium onion
1 egg
4 sprigs rosemary

For the whortleberry sauce:
8 ozs\225 gms whortleberries
8 ozs\225 gms sugar
¼ pt\150 mls water
2 tablespoons port

For the white wine sauce:
½ oz\15 gms butter
½ onion
½ pt\300 mls demi-glace
¼ pt\150 mls Pilton Manor white wine

Make the whortleberry sauce by placing all ingredients in a pan, bringing to the boil and simmering for 10 minutes. Leave to cool. Melt most of the butter in a large frying pan set over a high heat, season the lamb, brown on both sides and reserve. Roughly chop half the onion and slice the mushrooms, place in the pan with the rest of the butter and fry until the onion is translucent. Deglaze with a little white wine and place to one side.

Divide the pastry into four and roll it out. On each piece place a sprig of rosemary, a quarter of the mushroom mixture, two dessertspoons of whortleberry sauce and a lamb chop. Fold over the edges and seal, brush with beaten egg and make a small incision in the top of each parcel, set on a greased baking sheet and cook in a hot oven until the pastry is golden brown (15-20 minutes). Meanwhile make the white wine sauce by sweating the chopped onion in a little butter in a saucepan, adding the white wine and reducing it until syrupy. Add the demi-glace, bring to the boil, season to taste, pour around the pastry parcels and serve.

MARINER'S LAMB

Recipe from Suzanne Powell of Lynton:

Ingredients for 8 persons:
3 lbs\1.5 kgs boned lamb fillet
12 oysters
1 tablespoon rum
2 medium onions
4 ozs\100 gms chopped mushrooms
2 ozs\50 gms butter
12 ozs\300 gms puff pastry
1 egg
1 pt\600 mls vegetable stock
1 tablespoon chopped parsley
1 teaspoon thyme
1 teaspoon rosemary
Salt and pepper

Wipe the meat clean, then spread out, skin side down. Place the shelled oysters at one end and roll up, securing with string. Place in a roasting tin, pour the rum over, and cook in an oven pre-heated to 375°F\190°C\ Gas Mark 5 for an hour. Remove and cool. Soften the onions and mushrooms in the butter, season well, add the herbs and allow to cool. Roll out the pastry to quarter inch thickness and spread the onion mixture to within an inch of the edge. Place the lamb in the centre, moisten the edges and fold over, sealing into a parcel. Turn it over and replace in roasting tin, baking for 30 minutes at 425°F\220°C\Gas Mark 7. Turn down heat to 300°F\150°C\ Gas Mark 2, brush pastry with the beaten egg and cook for a further 30 minutes. Keep the parcel warm while adding a little flour to the pan juices and making up to a thick gravy with the vegetable stock.

EXMOOR LAMB COBBLER

Recipe from Theresa Sampson of Bishops Nympton:

Ingredients for 6 persons:
2 lbs\900 gms shoulder of lamb
2 ozs\50 gms dripping
4 large carrots
2 medium onions
1 small swede
4 sticks celery
2 pts\1.2 litres stock
1 tablespoon concentrated mint sauce
6 ozs\150 gms plain flour
3 ozs\75 gms suet
Salt, beaten egg

Bone and cube the lamb and brown all over in the dripping. Add the vegetables and cook for a further 10 minutes, stirring once or twice. Add stock, seasoning and mint sauce and cook on a low heat for 2½ hours. Preheat oven to 350°F\180°C\ Gas Mark 4, transfer meat and vegetables to a casserole, adding more stock, if necessary, to cover.

Brian Pearce

Make a soft dough with the flour, suet, salt and a little water and form into scones to cover the top of the casserole. Brush with beaten egg and bake in the centre of the oven until brown on top (about 25 minutes).

SAVOURY LAMB CRUMBLE

Recipe from Joyce Fulcher of Dunster:

Ingredients for 4 persons:
4 lamb chump chops
1 tablespoon oil
1 small onion
1 tablespoon paprika
¼ pt\150 mls beef stock
1 orange

For the topping:
4 ozs\100 gms plain flour
2 ozs\50 gms butter
2 ozs\50 gms grated cheese
1 teaspoon dried mixed herbs

Rub the butter into the flour until it resembles fine breadcrumbs, the stir in the grated cheese (preferably Exmoor, otherwise Cheddar), the herbs and a little salt and pepper. Trim the chops and season well and brown in the oil on both sides. Transfer to casserole or pie dish. Fry the chopped onion in the remaining oil until softened, add the juice of the orange, the stock and the paprika. Simmer for 2 minutes or until the mixture thickens slightly, then pour over chops. Spoon the crumble mixture over the meat and press down lightly. Bake in a moderate oven for 40 minutes.

LAMB AND CIDER PIE

Recipe from Mrs J. D. Boulding of Minehead:

Ingredients for 4 persons:
1 lb\450 gms cooked lamb
½ lb\225 gms cooked ham
1 large onion
3 cooking apples
1 lamb stock cube
2 tablespoons tomato puree
½ pt\300 mls dry cider
1 lb\450 gms rich shortcrust pastry
1 egg
Dried mint, rosemary, pepper, garlic salt

Brian Pearce

Mince the lamb and ham and mix together. Arrange in layers with the thinly sliced apples and onion in a 8"-10" pie dish, sprinkling each layer with the garlic salt, herbs and freshly ground black pepper and ending with a layer of meat. Heat the cider to dissolve the stock cube, add the tomato purée, stir and pour in. Cover with the pastry, brush with beaten egg and bake in the centre of a hot oven for 10 minutes, lowering the temperature to moderate for a further 25-30 minutes.

LAMB AND LEEK PIE

Traditional recipe

For the pastry:
4 ozs plain flour,
2 ozs lard,
Pinch salt

For the filling:
3 large leeks
1 lb lamb mince
Salt and pepper
Water

Boil the lamb until tender in just enough water to cover it. Season well. Season leeks and cut into ¾ inch pieces.

Add to mince and simmer until leeks are almost cooked. Make pastry in usual way and roll out to size of pie dish. Turn filling into pie dish and cover with pastry. Bake at 400°F\200°C\ Gas Mark 6 for about 20 minutes until pastry is browned.

EXMOOR LAMB'S LIVER PATÉ

Recipe from Rosemary Pile of Countisbury:

1¼ lbs\550 gms lean belly pork
12 ozs\350 gms lamb's liver
4 ozs\100 gms bacon
4 ozs\100 gms chopped onion
1 garlic clove
1 teaspoon salt
Freshly ground black pepper

Skin and de-bone the belly pork and dice finely. Rinse the liver under cold water, then dry and cut into large pieces. Mince pork, liver, bacon, onion and garlic together three times, working in the seasoning. Turn into a 2 pint terrine or small casserole, stand in a roasting tin of water and cook at 300°F\150°C\Gas Mark 2 for 1½ hours. Cover with foil and place a 2 lb weight on top until cool. Cover with a little melted butter and chill.

MUTTON SAUSAGES

Old recipe:

1 lb mutton
½ lb bacon from a boiled joint suck as a hock
½ lb mutton suet
½ lb breadcrumbs
Seasoning and herbs such as thyme, or a little laver
sausage skins

Mince the mutton, bacon and suet finely. Mix in a bowl with the breadcrumbs, seasoning and herbs or laver. Press the mixture into the sausage skins. The sausages are traditionally cooked by boiling for about 15 minutes, but can be baked in the oven. Like other mutton, they can be served with laver sauce.

PORK

'Makk zuch ado about un, wi hogs-puddens, and hock bits, and lambs-mate, and whaten bradd indade, and brewers ale avore dinner-time...' said Betty Muxworthy in *Lorna Doone*.

Most Exmoor farmers and cottagers would keep a pig for their own consumption, although there were never many pig farmers in the area. A law forbidding the keeping of pigs near the house, designed with urban areas in mind, eventually confined pig keeping to

Organic pig rearing enterprise, Hindon Farm, Minehead
Penny Webber

farms. A piglet, usually a Large Black or, more recently, a Saddleback, although the native breed was long, thin and white, would be purchased and kept in a pen in the garden or left to run with the cattle until it was ready for fattening. It would then be penned or closely confined in a 'loose' or pig house and fed on barley meal or grist corn (roughly ground oats, barley and maize), potatoes and scraps. It was allowed little movement and had to wallow in its own dung, which kept it cool. Treated in this way it produced much prized fat bacon, with little lean.

A pig was usually killed by the owner or an experienced neighbour – against regulations nowadays. Killing was either by sticking or poleaxing. With skill a pig could be killed by sticking a long knife through the throat and down into the heart, but this was could be a hit and miss affair and often a skilled neighbour would lend a hand. Usually a slip rope would be pulled around its nose and pulled over a beam to hold the animal steady whilst its throat was cut. The pig normally bled to death and was held over a bucket to collect the blood for black pudding. The blood letting usually took 2-3 minutes, during which time the pig was kept on its feet. It was thought that the more relaxed the pig was the longer it would bleed and the better the resulting meat would be. Poleaxing was a slightly more humane way of killing a pig and the common method with butchers or those with several pigs to kill. Humane killers, which fired a bolt into the brain, were introduced in the 1930s.

Maud Harding of Winsford remembers her childhood at Torr Farm, where her mother used to salt the pigs:

> We used to slaughter our own pigs for our own consumption. We were allowed to do it on the premises. It was lovely. Now of course they dont know the difference – because of the deep freeze. I've done it since I've been married. 'Tis then making the sausages. Chitlings it was really an

art. Making the brawns with half a pig's head and his trotters with a rabbit with it. Yes, two rabbits and pigs trotters made a nice brawn. I left Torr when I was young. I expect it would have been 1963 was the latest we would have killed our own pig.

The carcass was put on a pig stock and carried to where it would be scalded with water from the copper boiler and its hair scraped off. This was done with a special tool shaped like a candlestick with a blade at one end and a candle at the other end for singeing off stubborn bristles. Whatever the original colour of the pig it usually ended up an off white colour. The carcass was hung up on what was known as a 'gammer' to spread the legs and cut open the belly. The entrails were removed and washed and their preparation usually took a couple of days. Large quantities of water were required for this and the process often took place in the outside pump trough. The stomach and intestines were scraped of fat, which was then rendered down for lard. The intestines were turned inside out to clean them. This was often children's work and they pulled the intestines over sticks to aid the process. The result was chitterlings, which were common children's food, and skins for sausages and puddings.

After a day, when the carcass had become stiff, it was sawn lengthwise and then brought down onto a slab and cut up. Fred Rawle of Parracombe remembers working with neighbours to ensure supplies of fresh meat. As soon as there was an r in the month (the meat would not keep in warm summer months), one would kill their pig and distribute the joints amongst neighbours. There was a rota and after a couple of weeks another would kill their own pig and distribute the joints and so on. The head went to make brawn. The feet and ears were salted to make souse and the hams treated in a special pickle. The remaining joints not eaten fresh were salted in a large wooden trough or barrel called a salter. Recent versions tended to be about three feet high and wide but some older versions looked like small dugout canoes and were used for salting whole sides of pork

Earthenware salter at Allerford Rural Life Museum

Brian Pearce

to make gammon joints. The joints were rubbed with salt and in the salter it drew out the meat juices to form a brine in which the meat would pickle itself. Fred Rawle remembers using two large oval salters for each pig: 'They were a big pig then, you see – 27 to 30 score. You wouldnt kill 'em until they was 20 score – twas a big pig.'

The meat would normally be salted for about five weeks, then wrapped in newspaper and hung in the chimney to dry. The dried joints would then be hung from ceiling hooks and were preserved for about six months in this way. The salt would crystallise on the outside, making the joint 'rusty'. Before cooking, the meat was soaked in cold water for about 48 hours to draw out some of the salt and then it was usually boiled in water which was later discarded.

Pig killing was usually an autumn job. Pigs were not all slaughtered at once and there was a supply of fresh pork from September to Christmas, when the boar was finally killed. Boar's head, of course was a traditional Christmas meal. The heart, kidneys and liver of a pig could not be preserved, so it was the offal which was generally consumed in autumn. The chitterlings could, however, be hung up to dry or bottled for later consumption. From Christmas onwards the salted meat was consumed in the form of pies, boiled pork, ham, bacon and lard. Fried bacon and potato or eggs became the standard breakfast for many country people. Often it was just the farmworkers who had the bacon and the women and children had bread dipped in the dripping. Often the bacon fat substituted for butter in the winter.

Exmoor has never been known for pig farms, although there were some in lower lying areas such as Braunton and Barnstaple. However, most pork sold in Britain is home produced. Pork can now be purchased all year round. Pigs are killed younger and are generally leaner. The older, fatter carcasses are used in the meat processing and canning industry and do not often turn up at the butcher's. Pork has more flavour on the bone and a loin joint is considered to be the tastiest. However, many joints are now sold boned and sometimes ready rolled and stuffed. The tenderloin is usually the most expensive boneless joint as it is lean and tender. It is the muscle underneath the backbone in the hind loin and is reserved from bacon pigs when their carcasses are cut up for curing. Such joints are very popular with modern Exmoor caterers as they require little preparation.

BACON

Fat bacon was commonly fed by farmers to their labourers. It was usually so fat that there was only about 15% lean. Curing was a skilled job, and often

Roast Loin of Pork

Steve Guscott

the bacon went off. 'Risty' or 'rusty' bacon was streaked brown from an uneven or incomplete cure. Although it would not be to modern tastes, its calorific value was important for the heavy and long labour involved in work such as ploughing and hedging.

In the days of open fireplaces it was common to cook bacon in the bottom of a cauldron. It would be wrapped in a huff or pastry crust made of pork fat and flour and then in cloth. It would be placed under the board at the bottom of the cauldron, brought to the boil slowly and allowed to cool slowly when the other cooking had been removed from the cauldron.

SMOKED HAM

Traditional method:

A ham of 18-20 lbs was taken and covered with salt for a few days to let the blood run out into the salt. A basic pickle consisted of 1½ lbs treacle, 1 lb of bay salt, ½ lb of rock salt, 2 ozs saltpetre and 1 oz pepper. Bay salt was sea salt from the Biscay coast. Sometimes brown sugar was substituted for the treacle and beer and juniper berries could be added. The pickle was heated in a pan and the hot mixture worked into the ham and then the ham was left to lie in it for about a month, in a great earthenware pot, glazed inside and known as a salting 'trye' or 'keeve'. The ham was turned daily and rubbed with the pickle. It was then hung in a chimney over a smoky wood fire for about three weeks. Some farmhouses had special curing chambers, burning oak sawdust, but these were unusual. Others rubbed it in

'essence of smoke' which was wood vinegar or pyroligneous acid and was bought at a chemists. It could then be wrapped in muslin and hung in a dry place for up to a year before using.

Sal prunella was a form of saltpetre which could be bought in balls from a chemists. Like saltpetre, it is potassium nitrate, but also contains some nitrites which quicken the curing process. In old wooden and earthenware salters, bacteria would work on the salts absorbed into the vessels to form nitrites which meant that the more use the salter had, the better it would become.

Old recipe from Brian Pearce's great grandmother, Sara Ann Smith, wife of an Ilfracombe butcher and farmer

Proportions for a ham of 16 lbs:
First sprinkle with ½ lb of plain salt. Let it remain for two days, then mix well together the following ingredients:
1 lb raw sugar
½ lb common salt
2 ozs salt petre
2/3 ozs sal prunella
2 ozs black pepper
Blade of mace
A few cloves

Lay the ham in a large dish and put the pickle on it. In a few days, when in a liquid state, bathe it well several times a day and continue doing so for about three weeks, or more if a large ham. It should be slightly smoked. This can be done with Cambrian Spence of Smoke.

HAM AND ASPARAGUS

Old recipe:

12 slices ham
12 asparagus spears
6 hard boiled eggs
6 tomatoes
1 pt cheese sauce
seasoning

Brian Pearce

Wrap each asparagus spear in a slice of ham and arrange in a buttered ovenproof dish with slices of the egg in between. Season and cover with the cheese sauce. Slice the tomatoes and arrange the slices on top. Bake for about 20 minutes at 325°F\170°C\Gas Mark 3.

CREAM HAM

This is a traditional way of cooking sliced gammon. The sliced meat is rubbed with dry mustard and fried in butter. The gammon is sprinkled with herbs such as tarragon and cream is poured into the pan. The cream is gently warmed but not allowed to boil and served with the ham.

CIDER HAM

Ham was traditionally served at Easter. The ham would be put aside throughout Lent and brought out again on Easter Sunday. In many areas it was traditional to boil or bake ham with hay, which was supposed to improve the flavour. This is not an Exmoor peculiarity and is common in France.

Traditional method:

Soak a whole ham overnight in cold water to remove some salt. Dry and put in a pan with enough cider to cover. Add pepper, herbs, a few diced carrots and onions and a small bunch of fresh, clean hay. Bring to the boil, then simmer for about 3 hours. The ham is then removed from the stock, skinned and finished off by baking in a moderate oven for half an hour. It is often glazed before baking and served hot or cold with an apple sauce.

WESTERMILL CIDER HAM

Recipe from Jackie Edwards of Exford:

Half a gammon
½ pt\300 mls cider
2 ozs\50 gms soft brown sugar
16 cloves
Water

Weigh gammon and soak in water. Discard water, place ham in a large saucepan and cover with fresh water. Calculate cooking time allowing a quarter of an hour per lb\450 gms plus quarter of an hour. Bring ham to the boil and simmer for about two thirds of the time. Lift ham from water onto a board and remove skin with a knife. Place the ham in a baking tin and pour over the cider. Press the sugar all over the fat surface and push cloves into the sugar. Bake the ham for the remainder of the time in the top oven of an Aga or top oven. Baste and turn tin from time to time until surface has baked brown all over. Remove to dish up hot with the cider juice and parsley white sauce served separately or cool to serve with salad.

BRAWN

Originally made from a wild boar's head and shoulders, this was richer and fattier than ham and regarded as a delicacy for feasts, especially at Christmas. In medieval times it was seasoned with galingale, a spicy root similar to ginger, and from this is derived the modern galantine. Other seasonings included grated lemon rind, mace, allspice, cloves and cayenne pepper. This is the basic recipe. Often a rabbit was added to the pork half way through the cooking and two trotters could be substituted for the half head. Sometimes the brawn was wrapped in a large piece of tripe and pressed.

Old recipe:

½ pig's head
1 onion
6 peppercorns
Blade of mace
Sprig of parsley
salt and pepper

Wash the head thoroughly and put in a large pan of cold water. Bring to the boil and simmer until the flesh begins to part from the bones – 3 to 4 hours. Lift out the head and leave to cool slightly. Remove and discard the skin. Remove the flesh, cutting it into small pieces. Take 1½ pints of the remaining liquid and boil with the onion, spice and seasoning for ½ hour. Strain this liquid over the meat in a pan and boil for 5 minutes. Pour into a wetted mould. When cold skim off the surplus fat, turn out and garnish with the parsley.

POTTEN PUDDING

This is a classic Exmoor dish and is a variation of a medieval recipe. It is not clear whether potten pudding and hogs pudding is the same thing. Both can be found in skins or without, like sausagemeat. Potten could, therefore, refer to it being cooked in an earthenware pot or in pots: the local name for intestines or sausage skins. Fred Rawle of Parracombe suggests that potten pudding is the local name and hogs pudding a more general term, possibly of Scottish origin.

Traditional method:

Strip the flesh from a pig's head as for brawn. Mince with the skinned tongue and 2lbs cooked beef. Mix with 1lb breadcrumbs, a little liquid from boiling. Season with pepper, cayenne and nutmeg. Bake in a covered pudding basin.

HOGS PUDDINGS

Traditional method:

There are many variations but, basically, these are sausage skins stuffed with minced pig's head, cereals and seasonings. This type of pudding seems to date back to the sixteenth century. An Elizabethan recipe has them gently fried then boiled with shallots in beer and wine. They can be simply fried like sausages but they are generally larger than sausages and need to be cooked gently, to prevent the skin splitting, and thoroughly to swell the grain and cook right through. They are better boiled or baked and particularly good when baked until slightly crispy.

The classic recipe is to use the Potten Pudding mixture but substituting groats (crushed grain) for the breadcrumbs. The groats are soaked overnight in the stock from the boiling of the pig's head. Scalded pig's intestines known locally as `pots' are used for the pudding strings (sausage skins). Sometimes other odd bits of the pig – trotters and parts of the belly – were minced and added to the mixture. Variations are found including pearl barley or fine oatmeal, pig's liver, substituting mutton for beef, using different spices, or adding pig's blood and suet to make a black pudding. The blood must be drawn from the pig immediately it is killed and stirred to remove the fibres which cause it to clot. The sausage skins are brushed over with blood to make them black. Although black pudding is eaten in the Exmoor area, traditional black pudding and white pudding (without the blood) comes from the north of England and Scotland.

To suit modern cooking it is possible to use any minced pork or pork and offal mixture in the proportion of 3 lbs pork to ½ lb groats and to bake in a basin like Potten Pudding. Anne Petch of Heal Farm meats and country foods at Kings Nympton says:

> Today they are more commonly made from the same meat that is used for sausage making, which at Heal Farm is prime shoulder meat. The key ingredient is groats (the kernel of an oat which has been heat treated to stop it sprouting) which are pre-soaked and cooked to make a thick, coarse type of porridge. To this is mixed the minced pork with a liberal seasoning of salt and pepper. The mixture is filled into large hog casings and tied off in rings which are then simmered in water until cooked through. To serve you bake or fry the puddings, either whole or cut into slices. Either way they tend to burst open and when properly cooked produce a gloriously crunchy, peppery feast.

EXMOOR BREAKFAST

Recipe from Anne Petch of Kings Nympton:

Quantity per serving:
4 tablespoons cooked laver
2-3 tablespoons fine oatmeal
2 twists of freshly ground black pepper
Bacon fat for frying
Bacon
Hogs pudding

Mix the laver, oatmeal and pepper together so that it is firm enough to form into little cakes about 5 cms (2 inches) across. Fry gently in hot bacon fat until the oatmeal is cooked and lightly browned.

For a variation, make a light batter with 120 gms (4 ozs) plain flour, 1 large egg, just over 300 mls (½ pt) milk and a pinch of salt. Stir in 6 tablespoons of laver and cook in bacon fat as small pancakes.

Serve with crisp bacon and a sizzling hogs pudding.

Steve Guscott

BREAKFAST GROATS

Traditional method:

An alternative to hogs pudding was simply to fry up some groats with some bacon. The groats were boiled until soft but not puddingy. They were seasoned and spiced and fried together with diced fat green bacon over a low heat until they were browned and had absorbed the bacon fat.

CHITTERLINGS

These are pigs' intestines. Sometimes known as pig's fry, as they were usually cut into small pieces and fried with onions, breadcrumbs and seasoning. Pigs fry, however, usually meant internal organs such as heart, liver and kidney. Nattlings or knotlings can be any intestines but usually pig's. The name refers to the fact that they were knotted or plaited before cooking.

CHITTERLING DUMPLINGS

Old recipe:

1½ lbs chitterlings
6 ozs onions
2 ozs bacon fat
2 lbs potatoes
3 ozs grated cheese
2 ozs breadcrumbs
seasoning

Boil, mash and season the potatoes. Chop the chitterlings and onions and fry in the bacon fat until browned. Mould the potato into balls with the chitterling and onion mixture in the middle. Roll the balls in the grated cheese mixed with the breadcrumbs. Place in a baking dish and bake at 350°F\180°C\Gas mark 4 for about 20 minutes until the cheese is melted and browning.

FAGGOTS

These are not confined to Exmoor or the West Country, but some claim that they originated in Somerset and are still popular in the area. They are baked meat balls made of pork offal and wrapped in pigs caul – the inner membrane around the pigs stomach and organs and containing the flead lard. Pigs offal could not be preserved and faggots were a way of using it up quickly. The offal meat and fat were minced with onions and made into bundles – hence the name faggot – with breadcrumbs soaked in milk. In some areas soaked oatmeal, wheat or barley or a mixture of 'girts' replaced the bread.

They are usually served warmed with gravy and vegetables. Cider and apple can be incorporated into the gravy, or they can be served with apple sauce. In the absence of the caul the mixture can be baked in a tin like a meat loaf and, when cold, sliced and fried as a breakfast dish or served cold with salad. In this form it is known elsewhere as savoury duck. The mixture can be used like mince to form the basis of a cottage pie or served with a pastry or scone top.

Old recipe:

1 lb pig's liver
4 ozs fat bacon
3 ozs fresh breadcrumbs
2 onions
1 egg
Teaspoon mixed herbs
Salt, pepper and mace to season

Mince together the liver, bacon and onions. Add the breadcrumbs, herbs and seasoning and bind with beaten egg. Add a little milk to moisten if necessary. Cut pig's caul into 4" squares. Roll faggot mix into balls abut 2" diameter and wrap in the caul. Bake in a covered tin or pot in a hot oven at 400°F\200°C\Gas Mark 6 for about ¾ hour.

SWEET HOGS PUDDINGS

(Main course) – Old recipe:

1 lb minced meat from boiled pig's head
½ lb minced suet
½ lb currants
2 ozs flour
2 ozs sugar
1 teaspoon mixed spice

Mix all ingredients well and stuff into sausage skins to make sausages about the size of eggs. The sausages are boiled.

SWEET POTTEN PUDDING

(Pudding course) – Old recipe:

1 lb of the mixture from the
Potten Pudding recipe, but omit
the pepper and cayenne.
1 lb of mixed dried fruit
4 ozs chopped almonds
6 ozs sugar
2 teaspoons of mixed spice
Mixed herbs to season
½ pt sherry
2 eggs

Mix well and leave for at least 2 hours to swell the fruit. Place in a pudding basin, cover and bake for 2 hours in a moderate oven. Serve with cream.

SOMERSET PORK IN CIDER

Recipe from L W J Pluck of Allerford:

Ingredients for 6 persons:
1½ lbs\750 gms pork leg
1 onion
1 clove garlic
4 tablespoons double cream
8 ozs\225 gms mushrooms
¼ pt\150 mls cider
1 oz\25 gms butter
1 stock cube
1 tablespoon chopped parsley

Roast the pork in the normal way, then slice off meat and reserve. Heat all the other ingredients except mushrooms and cream until a slightly thick sauce is formed, then add the mushrooms and pork. Brown the top lightly in the oven and add cream before serving.

EXMOOR HOTPOT

Recipe from Mrs S Wright of Lynton:

Ingredients for 4 persons:
1½ lbs\700 gms stewing pork
2 lbs\900 gms potatoes
1 oz\25 gms lard
½ oz\12 gms butter
2 medium onions
2 medium cooking apples
2 ozs\50 gms Cheddar cheese
¼ pt\150 mls cider
1 clove garlic
Salt and pepper

Brown the cubed pork thoroughly in the fat and place in a shallow dish. Add the sliced onions, crushed garlic clove, chopped apples and salt and pepper, spreading evenly over the meat. Pour in the cider, then cover with an overlapping layer of potatoes. Dot with butter and cover with foil. Cook in a pre-heated oven at 325°F\170°C\Gas Mark 3 for 1½ hours. Remove foil, sprinkle grated cheese over the potatoes and cook for a further 30 minutes to brown the topping.

SPARE RIBS OF PORK IN CIDER

The spare rib joint is the part of the neck end of the pig which remains when the blade is removed. It has little fat and skin and is suited to a variety of pork dishes using meat on or off the bone. This recipe calls for chops from the joint. The ribs from the joint can also be cut separately. They are not to be confused with the spare ribs from the belly commonly associated with barbecuing, although they can be barbecued.

Old recipe:

Ingredients for four persons:
4 spare rib pork chops
6 ozs peeled and stalked field mushrooms
1 onion
2 ozs butter
About ⅓ pt dry cider
4 ozs Cheddar cheese
2 ozs dried breadcrumbs
Salt, pepper and parsley to season

Steve Guscott

Slice half the mushrooms. Grease a shallow, ovenproof dish and arrange the mushroom slices over the base. Chop the onion and parsley and scatter over the mushrooms in the dish. Arrange the chops on top of this with the remaining mushroom caps. Pour over enough cider to reach just below the top of the chops. Grate the cheese, mix it with the breadcrumbs and scatter the mixture over the chops and mushrooms. Dot the surface with the butter. Bake for about 45 minutes at 400°F \200°C\Gas Mark 6, until the chops are tender and the topping browned. Garnish with chopped parsley.

PORK CASSEROLE
(VARMER'S VAVRIT)

An old Devonshire recipe from Mary Hawksford of Wootton Courtenay:

1 large onion
1 lb lean, cubed pork
8 ozs tomatoes
1 small cabbage
½ pt stock
½ teaspoon sage
Salt and pepper

Chop and fry the onion and place in a casserole. Fry the pork and add to the onions. Slice the tomatoes and cabbage. Quickly fry these together until the cabbage is limp and add to the casserole. Stir together with the stock, sage, salt and pepper. Cover and cook for 2 hrs at 200°F\100°C\Gas Mark ½. Serve with mashed potatoes.

SAVOURY PASTIES

Old recipe:

12 ozs chopped cooked pork
½ lb damsons
1 onion, finely chopped
2 tablespoons water
½ teaspoon nutmeg
Seasoning

For the pastry:
8 ozs plain flour
2 ozs margarine
2 ozs lard
Water to mix
1 egg, beaten

Wash and stone the damsons and stew with the water and nutmeg. Mix the pork with the onion and seasoning. Drain the plums and mix with the pork and onion. Sift the flour, rub in the fats and mix to a smooth dough with water. Roll the pastry and cut into 6 inch rounds. Put the pork and damson filling in the centre of each round, dampen the edges of the pastry, fold up and seal. Brush with beaten egg. Bake in a moderate oven for 30 minutes.

WESTCOUNTRY PORK PIE

Recipe from Mrs J Cavanagh of Ilfracombe:

Ingredients for 6 persons:
1 lb\450 gms minced belly or shoulder pork
4 ozs\100 gms finely chopped onion
8 ozs\200 gms cooking apple, peeled, cored and chopped
¼ pt\125 mls dry cider
½ pt\250 mls stock
1 oz\25 gms dry stuffing mix
2 ozs\50 gms wholemeal breadcrumbs
8" hot water crust pastry case

Steve Guscott

Sweat the onion in a little water for 2 minutes, add pork and fry in its own fat to seal. Add apple, cider and stock and simmer for an hour. When the meat is cooked add dry stuffing mix and enough breadcrumbs to bind to a firm consistency. Cool, pack into pastry case, top with pastry lid, seal and glaze. Cook for 15 minutes at 400°F\200°C\Gas Mark 6, then reduce heat to 350°F\180°C\Gas Mark 4 and cook for a further 30 minutes.

GAME

The hunting and shooting of game has been a part of the Exmoor way of life from prehistoric times, but the game have varied over the years. Claude Wade said of Exmoor in 1903:

> Shooting, of course, there is of various kinds. Grouse, as most people know, have been tried several times, but they refuse to take to Exmoor, though everything would seem to suit them there. Blackcock and grey hen thrive, and give excellent sport, but they are not nearly as plentiful as they were twenty or thirty years ago, or at all events I know the bags are not as large as they used to be, in spite of the landowners doing all they can to spare the hens. Hares are very few and far between, but rabbits, in some parts swarm on the moor itself and in the fields and hedgerows; and there a good many coveys of partridges about if you know where to look for them. Pheasants can hardly be said to exist on the moor or in its close neighbourhood, but this year I have heard of a brave doctor who is trying what he can do in rearing them.

Today the black grouse, once found in their thousands, are extinct on Exmoor. Blackcock is dry meat and the birds need to be hung for some time. They were traditionally roasted and basted with bacon fat, then served on a slice of fried bread and accompanied by bread sauce. Pheasants are now the main target for shooters. Pheasant shooting is popular on estates around the wooded fringes of Exmoor and on the Brendon Hills, where striped plantings of game crops are a modern landscape feature. Farmers, however, have traditionally engaged in rough shooting as one of their pastimes. Bert Verney remembers in his *Reflections*:

> I preferred a day of rough shooting (wild birds) mallard, teal, woodcock, snipe, pheasant, rabbits, hare and pigeons. Perhaps five or six guns would bag 20-25 head of game and would have walked five to six miles in doing so.
>
> Later on in life, I belonged to two small syndicates where we put down about 800 birds, of which we shot in the region of 350 to 400. Where the rest disappeared, I do not know, but these figures were regarded as good. In this type of shooting you, and the guns, stood at the pegs

numbered one to eight, the number of guns in the shoot. A team of beaters were employed to go in the wood or field of roots, kale, swedes, rape, at the far end, to drive the birds over the guns which were waiting near the end of the beat. You were often waiting doing nothing for very long periods using this system. The bag was somewhere in the region of 45 to 60 for the day. To me rough shooting will always be my favourite way of shooting. One wild bird is worth ten keeper-reared birds. As for the syndicates who put down thousands of birds (where anything between 400 to 600 birds are shot in a day), I consider this to be mass murder, not sport, killing just for the sake of killing.

It is very easy to become embroiled in the arguments for hunting and shooting on Exmoor. Everyone has a different view but clearly more local people are in favour of such sports than against, as opposed to the national view. It can be argued that field sports are responsible for the survival of some species on Exmoor and the demise of others but many factors other than sport need to be considered. Rough shooting seems to have finished off the black grouse, Exmoor's indigenous game bird, which were once extremely plentiful but farming methods, disease and habitat changes are probably more responsible for their decline. On the other hand, the lack of intensive game rearing and keepering in the past has led to the survival of birds of prey and mammals considered as pests in other areas.

Keepering on Exmoor has long been associated with protection against poaching. In *Within Living Memory* by Margaret Bate a farmer recalled night poaching at North Molton:

> Well, there used to be a lot of poaching in those days, the pheasants and the fish. It wasn't big business but a challenge. Really if you didnt go poaching, you werent worthy of living in the area. But you werent really supposed to get caught.

The pheasants belonged to Lord Poltimore and another local, who admits poaching in hard times, was caught:

> Of course, if you were caught you had the option of coming before Lord Poltimore, on the carpet, as the chaps used to call it. You would get a severe ticking off and be sent away. Or, you could choose to come before the Chairman of the Magistrates – Lord Poltimore. He then had the power to fine and imprison you. The lesser of two evils was the usual choice.

Some pheasants were caught by poachers in long net rabbit traps. Fine nets a hundred yards or more long were laid out across fields. These were set on dark windy nights when the rabbits were out feeding. The poachers would then drive the rabbits towards the nets by clapping and lights. They would become entangled and were picked out of the nets by the poachers and killed by a blow to the head or a quick shake like cracking a whip to break the neck.

Today's poachers tend to go out at night, often with powerful lights. Rabbits in particular are mesmerised by the lights and make easy pickings. Sometimes it is viewed as a pastime and poachers may shoot almost anything that moves. Often, however, it is big business where valuable creatures such as deer and salmon are involved. Game dealers now have to be licensed. This involves keeping records of where the game comes from and checking that the game is shot by persons both licensed for firearms and the taking of game by the landowners. Poachers methods are often more cruel than those used in country sports and also more threatening to the survival of some species than such sports. There is now much demand for more scientific management of stocks of wild animals used for food but poaching will probably always be a problem in this respect.

The association of game with poaching and hunting has made many of today's customers wary of game and animal welfare and food scares have added confusion. Many are very fussy about what they will or will not eat and fashion prevails as with other foods. Many supermarkets and butchers now sell venison and wild boar sausages and patés. Go to a local country show and you are likely to be able to buy venison burgers or to farmers' markets and buy a range of game and game products such as smoked venison and duck.

DUCK

The main place for wildfowling on Exmoor has been on Porlock Marsh, at least until its recent flooding by the sea. There the remains of decoys, where dogs were used to drive ducks into funnel-shaped traps, can be seen. The area is currently part of the Porlock Manor Estate.

WEST COUNTRY CASSEROLE OF DUCK

Recipe from Suzanne Powell of Lynton:

Ingredients for 2 persons:
1 wild duckling
2 small onions
3 dessert apples
¼ pt \ 150 mls stock
1 bouquet garni
2 ozs \ 50 gms butter
2 stalks celery
½ oz \ 12 gms flour
¼ pt \ 150 mls Exe Valley cider
4 fluid ozs \ 120 mls double cream
Garnish: fried apple slices

Pre-heat oven to 400°F\200°C\Gas Mark 6. Prick duck skin well all over, rub with salt, seal in the oven for 20 minutes, then reduce heat to 300°F\150°C\Gas Mark 2. Put one peeled apple inside the bird and place, breast down, in a casserole. Gently cook the chopped onions in the butter until soft, add the celery and the two remaining apples, chopped. Blend in the flour, add stock and cider and bring to the boil, stirring well. Cook until the sauce is smooth. Pour over the bird and cook for 1½ hours in the oven. Transfer duck to serving dish, pour sauce into a clean pan, adjust seasoning, heat the cream without boiling and serve with the quartered duck, garnished with the fried apple slices.

PARTRIDGE

Both types of partridge – the grey and the red-legged – are resident on Exmoor. Both are reared as game birds, but more commonly the introduced red-legged species. As they are small birds, one per person is necessary. Young partridges are usually roasted and served whole and tougher, older birds are usually jointed and casseroled.

STUFFED ROAST PARTRIDGE

Old recipe:

1 partridge per person
per partridge:
2 rashers streaky bacon
1 cooking apple
¼ pt dry cider
2 ozs clotted cream

Liver stuffing for 6 partridges:
8 ozs partridge livers, supplemented with
chicken livers if necessary
1 lb chopped onions
4 ozs butter
8 ozs fresh white breadcrumbs
2 teaspoons chopped fresh sage
2 eggs
¼ pt dry cider
Nutmeg, salt, pepper and sugar for seasoning, to taste

Boil the livers for a few minutes, then chop or mince finely. Cook the onions in the butter gently until soft but not brown. Mix the liver with the onions, breadcrumbs and seasoning, stir in the cider and bind with the beaten eggs.

Stuff the partridges as fully as possible from the tail end. Cover each bird with the bacon. Place each bird in a roasting pan on top of a layer of sliced apple. Cook in a moderate oven (400°F\200°C\ Gas Mark 6) for about half an hour, basting occasionally with the cider. Remove the partridges and keep warm. Heat the

contents of the roasting pan over a low flame, stirring in the cream and any remaining cider. Mix well and do not boil. Use this as a sauce to pour over the partridges.

PHEASANT

There is a world of difference between fresh pheasant and pheasant which has been hung like game. When fresh it should be treated like chicken. The meat is dry and needs to be basted with bacon fat or stuffed with fat ham or bacon. Pheasant which has been hung for some time is usually stuffed with fruit or served with a fruity sauce.

EXMOOR PHEASANT WITH SOMERSET CIDER, APPLES AND CREAM

Recipe from A J Rhodes of Williton:

Ingredients for 4 persons:
2 oven-ready pheasants
3-4 English eating apples, peeled and sliced
(Cox's, Spartan or similar)
5 ozs\125 gms fresh cream
6 fluid ozs\150 mls medium cider
2 ozs\50 gms butter or margarine
Salt and freshly-ground pepper

Steve Guscott

Brown the pheasants all over in a large sauté pan using the butter or margarine. Set aside and in the same pan sauté the apples until they turn golden brown. Pour in enough cider to cover them and de-glaze the pan. Season with salt and pepper. Pour the mixture into a roasting dish, place the pheasants on top, cover with buttered paper and roast at 400°F\200°C\Gas Mark 6 for 45 minutes or until they are tender, removing the paper for the last 10 minutes. Place the pheasants on a serving dish and complete the sauce with the remainder of the cider and cream. Serve the pheasants, either split in half with the backbone removed or carved, on a bed of the sauce with a watercress garnish.

EXMOOR PHEASANT CASSEROLE

Recipe from Daphne Criddle of Lower Vellow:

Ingredients for 2 persons:
1 large plump pheasant
2 ozs\50 gms Somerset butter
1 tablespoon tomato purée
3 pts\1.5 litres home-made stock
2 ozs\50 gms plain flour
12 ozs\325 gms mushrooms
8 ozs\225 gms small onions
2 sliced carrots
1 sliced onion
1 shredded leek
1 small grated swede

For the marinade:
2 glasses red wine
1 crushed garlic clove
1 sliced onion
2 sliced carrots
Bay leaves, juniper berries, seasoning

Hang the pheasant in a cool place for 3-10 days, depending on your taste. Pluck and dress, marinade for a day or two in the refrigerator, turning frequently. Drain, dry and brown all over in butter, then transfer to casserole with stock, tomato purée, onions, carrots, leeks and swede. Cover and cook for an hour at 375°F\190°C\ Gas Mark 5. Remove bird from liquid and cool. Strain and cool liquid and skim off solid fat. Heat this in a pan, stir in 2 ozs\50 gms flour and make up to 2 pints\ 1 litre of sauce with the stock. Add meat, fried mushrooms and onions and reheat. Serve with piped, creamed potatoes.

SCRUMPY PHEASANT

Recipe from Messrs C Steven and D Sampson of Winsford:

Ingredients for 4 persons:
4/6 ozs\150 gms pheasant breasts
4 ozs\100 gms sliced button mushrooms
8 ozs\225 gms vegetable mirepoix
4 rashers back bacon
½ pt\300 mls cider
1 teaspoon brown sugar
1 teaspoon chopped parsley
½ pt\300 mls double cream
3 ozs\75 gms butter
1 medium cooking apple
Bread for croutons

Make an incision on the underside of pheasant breasts and fill with four slices of apple. Wrap each breast in bacon. Sauté the mushrooms and mirepoix in butter for 5 minutes, then add the pheasant and cook for 5 minutes each side. Add cider, parsley stalks and the remainder of the apple. Season with black pepper. Cover with greaseproof paper and a well-fitting lid and cook in a moderate oven for an hour. Remove parsley stalks, place pheasant breasts on a warmed serving dish, add cream and brown sugar to the sauce and reduce slightly. Serve breasts on heart-shaped croutons topped with the sauce and garnished with parsley.

PIGEON

Although woodpigeons are seen as a pest, they were never common food on Exmoor. Woodpigeon can be very tough and usually only the breasts are used in cookery, and then they are usually casseroled and cooked long and slow. The remainder of the bird makes good stock. Pigeon pie usually mixed steak, bacon and pigeon breasts under a double layer of pastry and was cooked very slowly. Squabs are young pigeons and usually were only eaten by those who could afford to have a dovecote, although many farm buildings had a

Medieval dovecote at Dunster Priory

Brian Pearce

few 'culver holes' for pigeons to nest. In medieval times this was usually the lord of the manor and his pigeons would plunder his tenants crops whilst they would be under severe penalties for killing or interfering with the pigeons. It was said that a dovecote should have a nest for each acre of the estate. The early medieval dovecote Luttrells at Dunster still exists. It is a circular building with hundreds of nest holes covering the inside wall. The nests were reached by means of a revolving ladder known as a 'potence'. Up to five hundred squabs would be eaten at banquets at the castle. Even squabs could be quite tough and boiling or casseroling was the usual method of cooking.

PIGEON CASSEROLE

Recipe from Stephanie Cudmore of Allerford:

Ingredients for 4 persons:
1½ lbs\70 gms pigeon breasts
8 ozs streaky bacon
4 ozs\100 gms field mushrooms
1 lb\450 gms carrots
1 green pepper
½ teaspoon coriander
1 lemon
1 pt\600 mls stock
Salt and pepper and a little top of the milk

Cut the pigeon breasts into small wedge-shaped pieces, toss in seasoned flour and fry in butter. When browned, add coriander and transfer to casserole. Fry diced carrots, bacon and pepper and add to the meat. Stir about a pint of stock into the pan, add the mushrooms and transfer to casserole. Cook in a moderate oven for 2½ hours. Remove, adjust seasoning and add juice of one lemon and the tops of 2 pints of milk.

PIGEON BRAWN

Traditional method:

Prepare pigeons and boil up with an onion in seasoned water for at least three hours. When cool, remove the breast and thigh meat and dice it. Season well. Make a jelly by dissolving ½ oz gelatine in ½ pint of the stock in which the pigeons were boiled. Mix with the meat and pour into a mould to set in a cool place. The brawn can be sliced and served cold with salad.

SQUAB PIE

'Squab pie, junket and cider brew' are the traditional Devon fare according to the song *Glorious Devon*. Squabs, however, were not usually used in this dish, at least after the eighteenth century. As squabs were rich man's fare, they were substituted by almost any meat, game or poultry. One old Cornish recipe is for 4 lbs

meat and a cormorant in a large pie dish, with sliced apple and onion rammed into every conceivable crevice. Near the coast they often added fish to the meat. On Exmoor mutton was the usual substitute for squab. However, veal and bacon were often added to the mutton and anything that was in season, including rooks and mushrooms. Most recipes include apples, but those were also a seasonal variation. A recipe for squab pie is included under mutton.

Old recipe:

4 squabs
1 lb mutton
1 lb onions
2 lbs cooking apples
½ lb prunes
2 ozs dark brown sugar
cinnamon
mutton stock
¾ lb short crust pastry

Dice the mutton and simmer in the stock for about an hour. Cut the squabs in half and put a layer of squab and mutton in the bottom of a deep pie dish. Peel, core and slice the apples, stone the prunes and slice the onions. Put a layer of fruit and onion on top of the meat and scatter with sugar and cinnamon. Put another layer of meat on this and another of fruit, onion, sugar and cinnamon. Pour on mutton stock to just below the top layer. Make the pastry with mutton suet. Cover the pie with the pastry, glaze with milk or beaten egg and bake at 350°F\180°C\Gas Mark 4 for two hours.

WILD PIGEON PATÉ

Recipe from Jackie Kingdon of Umberleigh:

12 pigeon breast fillets
½ pt\300 mls red wine
8 crushed juniper berries
8 crushed black peppercorns
1 medium onion
1 carrot
1 garlic clove
1 teaspoon rock salt
3 ozs\75 gms butter
2 ozs\50 gms dried bread
4 ozs\100 gms streaky bacon or back fat
Bay leaf

Place the pigeon fillets in a bowl with the wine, berries, peppercorns, half the onion, carrot, garlic and salt and marinade for 24 hours, turning at least four times. Remove the fillets and reserve the strained liquid. Soften the onion in the butter in a frying pan and reserve. Toss the fillets briefly in the butter and remove. Then add the marinade, heat gently and leave to cool. Mince the pigeon, onions and bread (twice if a fine paté is preferred), add the marinade and season well. Line an ovenproof dish with the bacon or back fat and spoon in the mixture until about three-quarters full. Stand in a baking tin in enough water to reach half way up the dish and cook for 45 minutes in a moderate oven. Mature for 24 hours before serving.

ROOK

Rooks are common on Exmoor but not as plentiful as they used to be and rookeries are much smaller. They are a pest on the arable land around the fringes of the moor and as such were and still are shot. They are rarely eaten nowadays but were a common poor mans food in the past. Like pigeons, they can be surprisingly tough and generally it is only the tiny breast and thigh parts which are eaten. The remaining meat and skin is black and bitter and not just tough but inedible. Also, like pigeons, it was the young ones which were used for food. May was the usual shooting time, when the young birds were fledged.

In *Within Living Memory* by Margaret Bate is an account of rooks at North Molton and an old poacher called Arthur:

The largest rookery in North Devon was in Bampfylde Clump. The whole ring of trees was full – as a lad I used to go there rook shooting. The year that the Lord of the Manor left, the rooks left and have never been back.

> A neighbour of ours, further up the road, was having a lot of trouble with rooks. He'd planted some corn and the rooks were coming in an picking it out of the ground. So he had a word with Arthur who was handy with a gun and said: Scare em off, Arthur. So Arthur went up with his gun. Later in the pub, he told the tale of what happened. I went up and had a look – black with rooks, so I put my gun over the top of the fence, didn't bother to aim. I pulled both barrels. Then I went in and picked up ninety nine rooks. There was an old chap in the corner who said: Arthur, may as well say a hundred, mightn't you? Do you think I would tell a b… lie for the sake of one rook?

ROOK PIE

Traditional method:

Usually about twelve rooks were baked in a pie, as only the breast and thigh meat was used. The other parts of the rook carcasses were used to make the stock, which was made thick. The rook meat was supplemented with fat bacon and sometimes rabbit or other meats. It could be made with a suet crust and steamed as a pudding, or a pastry crust and baked. Sometimes it was covered with figgy pastry and steamed. Figgy pastry presumably at one time contained figs but, like figgy pudding, these were later substituted by mixed fruit. A frequent sauce to go with rook pie was gooseberry jelly.

To make figgy pastry:
8 oz self raising flour
4 oz margarine
2 oz currants
2 oz raisins
Salt and pepper
Water to mix

Mix all dry ingredients in a bowl, first rubbing the fat well into the flour, and gradually mix in water to make a stiff but pliable dough. Roll out fairly thick and place over the pie dish, overlapping the sides. Cover with a layer of greaseproof paper and wrap all in muslin. Boil for three hours, making sure that the water does not cover the pastry.

To make gooseberry jelly:
Top and tail gooseberries and simmer them in a pan with a little water until soft. Strain the juice through coarse muslin or a sieve. Return the juice to a pan and for every pint of juice add 1 lb of preserving sugar. Boil the juice and sugar together for several minutes – half an hour or so, depending on quantities – until a drop of the mixture sets on a cold plate. Cool slightly, pour into jars and seal.

Traditional method:

In *Within Living Memory* an old lady called Mary recalls her mother making rook pie:
> First you had to skin the rooks, using only the breasts and thighs of young rooks. This left a lot of little bits of black feather, then you washed them well in salted water. Belly bacon and hard boiled eggs cut in half went in and a good pastry crust on top. This was cooked then eaten cold. A lovely thick jelly formed inside.

MIXED GAME

POACHER'S POCKETS

Recipe from Penny Webber of Minehead:

8 ozs\225 gms venison
3 pigeons
1 rabbit
8 ozs\225 gms lean Exmoor lamb
2X 8 ozs\225 gms packets frozen puff pastry
1 egg
½ pt\300 mls Taunton cider
4 ozs\100 gms wholemeal breadcrumbs
3 cooking apples
1 pt\600 mls stock
Bay leaf, parsley and seasoning

Preparation time: 20 minutes. Serves 4

Cube all the meat and casserole with the stock, cider, bay leaf and parsley very slowly (preferably in an Aga) overnight. Drain off most of the liquid and reserve. Add the breadcrumbs, beaten egg, chopped apples and seasoning. Divide the pastry into four, roll out into rectangles, divide the meat mixture between each and fold over to form an envelope. Seal the edges, brush with beaten egg to glaze and bake in a hot oven until crisp and brown. Use a little flour to thicken the remainder of the liquid to form a rich gravy.

RED DEER AND RABBIT FILLET TERRINE

Recipe from David Johnson of Minehead:

1½ lbs\700 gms saddle of rabbit
1½ lbs\700 gms venison (loin)
½ pt\300 mls double cream
3 eggs
8 rashers of bacon or back fat
2 tablespoons port
Salt, pepper, nutmeg, cayenne pepper

For the jelly:
3 oranges
4 heaped tablespoons redcurrant jelly
2 tablespoons white wine vinegar
½ pt\300 mls mead
Gelatine

Steve Guscott

Heat the oven to 350°F\180°C\Gas Mark 5. Remove bone and sinews from rabbit, season and pan fry until pink. Drain and leave to cool. Purée the venison in a food processor with the egg whites and pass through a fine sieve. Place in bowl over ice and chill for 30 minutes. Slowly add port and seasoning to cream, then very slowly add the double cream to the purée. Line a terrine with bacon or back fat, then pour in half the mixture. Place the rabbit fillets in a line down the middle then add the remainder of the venison. Cover

with more back fat or bacon and cook in a bain-marie for 1½ hours. Press while cooking and chill overnight before turning out.

Boil the freshly squeezed juice of the oranges with the jelly, vinegar and mead until reduced by half, then add three pre-soaked gelatine leaves. Pour into a shallow receptacle and chill. Serve thinly sliced terrine on a bed of the chopped jelly.

GAME GALANTINE

Recipe from Penny Wright of Allerford:

¾ pt\550 mls aspic jelly
1 pheasant
8 ozs\225 gms venison
8 ozs\225 gms chicken in strips
4 tablespoons cream
Pork fat
Salt, pepper and nutmeg
Truffle paste

For the chaud-froid sauce:
4 ozs\100 gms margarine
4 ozs\100 gms flour
1/3 pt\200 mls cream
2 ozs\50 gms gelatine
1½ pts\1 litre stock

Remove the skin from the pheasant, as near as possible in one piece, and place in cold water. Remove all meat from the bones and place in a liquidiser with the venison, nutmeg, seasoning and a little pork fat. Liquidise for a few seconds and add the cream. Boil the pheasant bones with a few vegetables and a good bunch of herbs to make a stock. Place the skin on a tea cloth and add a layer of the meat mixture. Lay the chicken strips, marinated overnight in cider, on the top and finish off with the rest of the mixture. Roll up into a sausage shape, then roll up tightly in the cloth and tie with string. Poach in the stock for 2 hours, then remove cloth and string and chill in a refrigerator.

Melt the margarine in a saucepan, add the flour and cook for a minute. The gradually add the stock and sprinkle in the gelatine, stirring until dissolved. Remove from the heat and add cream. When almost at setting point, pour a third of the sauce over the roll. Return roll to a cool place and gently re-heat the sauce and repeat the process twice. Finally, decorate the roll with a stag's head formed with truffle paste and glaze with two coats of aspic.

GAME PIE

Pat Wright of the Moorland Larder game dealers at South Molton sells literally hundreds of pies and pasties each day, all made from the finest ingredients. Her sole complaint was from an old lady who could not manage the amount of meat in one. For years she has collected recipes and has a considerable library of cook books. She produces about 22 varieties of pies and 9 varieties of pasties. I say 'about' because she is always experimenting and specials can be cooked to order. The pies include combinations such as rabbit, bacon and leek; rabbit, prune and cider or venison and mushroom. Fitchet pie is a hot pot of bacon, onion, apple and stock with sliced potatoes on top and hunters pie is like a cottage pie only with minced venison. The venison pasties include mixed vegetables and cranberries. Less traditional pasties include buffalo and ostrich (all local) but such exotic meats are not strictly game.

Moorland Larder Game Pie

Recipe from Ian Baker of Filleigh:

Ingredients for 8 persons:
For the pastry:
1 lb\450 gms plain flour
4 ozs\125 gms lard
1/3 pt\120 mls water

For the filling:
1 pheasant
1 partridge
1 grouse or whatever game is in season
1 lb\450 gms sausage meat
1 onion
1 bacon rasher
1 egg to glaze
Salt, bouquet garni

Sieve the flour and salt. Bring the lard and water to the boil in a pan, add the flour and mix to a dough. Place on a board and knead well, then line a greased loaf tin with two thirds of it. Line the pie with three quarters of the sausage meat, remove meat from bones, chop and add with chopped onion and bacon. Cover with remaining sausage meat, roll the remaining pastry to form lid, cover

and seal. Brush with egg glaze and form a small vent. Cook for 30 minutes in an oven pre-heated to 400°F\200°C\Gas Mark 6, then reduce heat to 350°F\180°C\ Gas Mark 4 for a further 2 hours. Meanwhile, make a good stock by placing bones and bouquet garni in enough water to cover and simmering for 3 hours. Fill the cooked pie by pouring strained stock through the vent. Refrigerate for 24 hours before serving.

RABBIT

No one is sure when rabbits were introduced to Britain. Some say the first were brought by the Normans and that the oldest colony is on Lundy Island or, perhaps, the Scillies. They were originally kept on islands to save fencing them in, then in warrens. The de Mohuns at Dunster had established a warren on Conygar Hill by the thirteenth century and probably as early as the eleventh century. The name 'Conygar' means rabbit enclosure. The rabbits at Conygar seem to have grown out of hand by the thirteenth century and in 1266 a new warren was established between the marshes and the sea on the Minehead side of Dunster. This continued in use until the nineteenth century and a warrener was employed to create the best possible breeding conditions for the rabbits and keep away predators. Medieval warreners were paid well and in the thirteenth century the price of a rabbit was more than a craftsman's daily wage. Catching the rabbits in nets seems to have been womens' work. The Aclands kept them much later at Warren during their wardenship of the Royal Forest in the eighteenth century. The pillow mounds, built to make burrowing easier for the rabbits, can still be seen and may date from as early as the sixteenth century, although they are more likely to have been established by James Boevey during his ownership of the Forest in the seventeenth century.

The rabbits were largely food for wealthy landowners, providing them with some fresh meat in winter. Rabbits stayed largely confined to warrens until the eighteenth century, when they first started to become a pest. However, in the mid thirteenth century the rabbits at Conygar seem to have escaped into Dunster and were causing such a nuisance that the de Mohuns allowed the burgesses of Dunster to kill them and eat them if they were causing nuisance on their property, as long as they handed in the valuable pelts to the castle. Generally, it was not until the end of the nineteenth century that they became plentiful and cheap enough to become part of the diet of ordinary Exmoor folk.

Rabbits were not only food, but a source of income. In some cases they paid the rents of farmers. This happened for the Westcott family on the former Royal Forest at Picked Stones and Wintershead Farms. Records kept by Mr F.J. Westcott show that he trapped 3932 rabbits during the winters between 1932 and 1935. The skins were sold for making felt hats and some

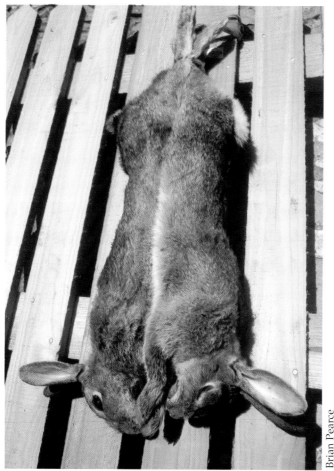

Brian Pearce

Rabbits , once common Exmoor food

Trapping was a specialist job involving the use of gin traps or snares, now illegal. One professional could work several hundred traps. He would be called for by a farmer and sleep at the farm so that he could set traps last thing at night and inspect them first thing in the morning. Otherwise rabbits may struggle free, leaving dismembered limbs in the traps. The trapper was paid per rabbit. Some would be collected by dealers, whilst others were crated and sent up to Smithfield by the rabbit train, picking up at South Molton and Dulverton. In war years the rabbits became an important source of meat and during the early 1940s three trains a week each took five wagon loads of rabbits from Dulverton station.

Maud Harding of Winsford remembers her childhood evenings at Torr Farm:

> We used to go to bed between half past nine and ten. Father would make spars for thatching the ricks, in front of the fire – hazel sticks you see – making all the spars, or spinning a rope and making nets for rabbiting. That was a great thing done, making rabbit nets. There were rabbiting parties that became like sheep shearing parties. Not the same people. They cleared the wires and traps during the day and then they'd come in and there's something to eat at 5 oclock. Then they'd stop and play a game of draughts. I used to play with Walter Stephens. Then they'd go out and see the traps and wires before they went home.

Rabbits were often considered the property of those who caught them, although legally they belong to the landowner. On arable land, harvest time was a great time for catching rabbits. After the introduction of mechanical reapers and binders corn was cut around the field first and the rabbits became concentrated in the patch in the middle as more and more corn was cut. Those cutting the corn would shout 'Loo!Loo!loo!' to startle and confuse the rabbits, and hares, which would bolt for cover under the cut sheathes, from where they could easily be grabbed by dogs or boys or shot by the men.

Ferreting was a winter activity. It was particularly popular around Christmas and New Year and was a social event. The ferret would be carried in an old hessian seed bag inside the poacher's pocket of the handler's coat to keep it warm. As well as nets to catch the rabbits, the ferreters would also carry traps for the ferrets. Sometimes a ferret would eat part of a rabbit in a hole or become exhausted and lie up for a while. The trap would be pushed into the hole and baited with a little rabbit liver to retrieve the ferret later. Bert Verney remembers rabbiting in the 1940s:

> We had a lot of rabbiting and card parties at this time of the year. The men used to go early in the morning, armed with ferrets and guns. They

landowners even farmed them for skins or sporting activities. However, this was short lived as rabbits became such a pest that they could not be encouraged. Skins were imported from Australia, where there was an even bigger problem, and by the late 1930s the local market had been almost wiped out, whilst rabbit numbers kept increasing. Fred Rawle of Parracombe remembers skinning the rabbits, stuffing the skins with newspaper and drying them in the chimney. A Mr Potter, who lived at New Invention, Dulverton, would come round with his horse and trap to purchase them.

In *Within Living Memory* by Margaret Bate a farmer named Herbert recalls his childhood at Coombeshead Farm, North Molton:

> There were so many rabbits around at that time that there were some farms where they paid their rent with the money made on rabbits. I used to catch the rabbits to sell. The money I made was my spending money. Sometimes there were as many as two thousand rabbits on our farm. We had the professional trappers in. They caught a hundred a night. We then used to go in with the ferrets. It went on for weeks and weeks. There was a special train from South Molton (it may have started from Barnstaple) to London, known as the rabbit train. They all went to Smithfield Market.

usually went into the house for coffee, when arriving at their destination. Lunch was usually carried, and a short stay in operations would take place about 1pm. This was quite good fun, with a bag of some twenty five rabbits per pair (you always went in twos to cover each side of the Devon hedges). The day usually ended about half an hour before dark.

Before the last war it was not unusual to have 30 rabbits per acre on Exmoor farms. As ten rabbits eat about the same as one sheep, it is a wonder that there was any grass at all for the sheep. They would generally reduce the grazing area of a field by about 20 yds either side of a hedgebank, so small fields became ineffective. They also caused considerable damage to hedgebanks, which were time consuming to repair, and many internal banks on farms were left to disintegrate. It took the introduction of myxomatosis to Britain in 1953 to have any significant effect on numbers. Nationally the numbers were reduced by about 95%. The disease took hold on Exmoor two or three years later but many of its colonies were isolated enough to remain intact and today rabbits are still numerous, although different strains of the disease recur. A large psychological effect was, however, to follow in that people hesitated to eat rabbit in case it was diseased. Some preferred to breed their own rabbits in runs in their gardens, others to buy imported rabbit at greatly inflated prices. Many cooks would now not know how to prepare a rabbit or find it a gruesome and smelly job. Ferreting still continues as a traditional pastime, but it is becoming rare to see wild rabbit in local shops.

STEWED RABBIT

Old recipe from Mrs H E Hussell of Ilfracombe:

Cut up rabbit with ½ lb pickled pork; add little pepper (no salt), large Spanish onion cut fine, and 2 tablespoonsful Worcester sauce; cover with water, boil up, simmer gently 1½ hours, and thicken with a tablespoonful cornflour. Dough-boys can be added if liked.

RABBIT SOUP

Old recipe:

1 rabbit
1 small head of celery
4 ozs carrot
1 onion
1 turnip
3 pts stock

Peel and dice the vegetables. Prepare and joint the rabbit. Boil all ingredients together until the meat is in rags, then pass through a sieve. Put back the pulp into a saucepan with 2 teaspoonsful of salt, 1 saltspoonful of pepper and a pinch of mace or cinnamon. Bring to the boil and serve.

RABBIT STIR FRY

Recipe from Jim Webber of Porlock:

There is no reason why rabbit should not suit modern tastes. It is lean and healthy eating and not strongly flavoured like some game: rabbit is not hung like hare. The fact that it is normally jointed and served on the bone puts some people off, so we decided to try a bone-free recipe. Rabbit does not immediately spring to mind as a meat for stir frying as it tends to be tough and requires slow cooking. This is, therefore, a recipe for cooked or leftover rabbit. There are various ways in which you can cook it first. After skinning and cleaning, wild rabbit is best cut into joints and marinated for several hours. I marinate mine in cider but salted water will do. Do not use anything expensive as the marinade should be discarded afterwards. The rabbit can then be boiled, potroasted or casseroled.

Steve Guscott

Take cold, cooked rabbit, cut the meat from the bone and dice it. You do not need much for stir fry: 4 to 6 ounces per person should be adequate, depending on what is served with it. Jim soaks the meat in whisky for a few hours before using. A little cider could be used instead. Only a small quantity is needed as it is not to tenderise the meat, just to flavour and add moisture. I like to add a dash of Worcestershire sauce. The meat then only needs to be reheated in a pan with stir fried vegetables. Due to the high temperature of stir frying you cannot cook in traditional butter or fat and special stir fry oil is required. The vegetables should be stirred in the hot oil and cooked al dente with the meat added last just to heat it through. You can use any vegetables in season, finely sliced – we used carrot, cauliflower, calabrese, mangetout, celery, leek, shallots and different coloured peppers and served all with a baked potato.

JUGGED RABBIT

Old recipe from Mrs Hayter of West Down:

1 rabbit
1 onion
1 pt stock
1 oz dripping
1 teaspoonful flour
Herbs: parsley, bay leaf
Salt and pepper

Cut rabbit into small joints, wash, dry and sprinkle with flour; make dripping hot in frying pan; fry rabbit quickly and place in a jar; add stock, first warmed, then onion, herbs and seasoning; bring to the boil and simmer 1½ hours. Just before serving mix flour with little cold water, pour into jar; boil up again and serve on hot dish. Garnish with forcemeat balls.

EXMOOR RABBIT PIE

This was once a mainstay dish of the poorer folk in Exmoor villages.

Old recipe:

1 rabbit
¼ lb ham
2 hard-boiled eggs
2 tablespoons flour
1 teaspoon salt
½ teaspoon pepper
Stock
½ lb short crust or rough puff pastry dough

Skin, gut and wash the rabbit and cut it into small joints. Roll the joints in the flour mixed with salt and pepper. Place the joints with the sliced ham in a pie dish and half cover with stock. Cover with greased paper and cook in a moderate oven for 1½ hours. Lift out and cool slightly. Add the eggs, cut into quarters, and cover with the pastry dough. Bake in a hot oven for ¾ hour, reducing the heat after the first 20 minutes.

RABBIT AND ASPARAGUS PIE

A modern variation on the rabbit pie recipe from Jackie Payne West Buckland:

For the filling:
1 rabbit, prepared
1 carrot, chopped into 4 pieces
1 potato, chopped into 4 pieces
1 onion, chopped into 4 pieces
4 spears of asparagus
2 ozs\50 gms margarine
1 oz\25 gms plain flour
½ pt\300 mls milk
2 pts\1.1 litres water
Salt and pepper

For the pastry:
8 ozs\225 gms plain flour
4 ozs\100 gms margarine
3 ozs\75 gms lard
3 tablespoons cold water
Pinch of salt
1 egg, beaten

Place the rabbit, potato, carrot and onion in a large pan with the water. Simmer for 1 hour until the meat begins to fall off the bones. Remove the meat from the bones. The stock can be kept and used in a rabbit casserole. Melt the margarine in a saucepan and lightly fry the onion until soft but not brown. Add the flour to make an onion roux. Heating gently and stirring all the time, gradually add the milk to make an onion sauce. Season to taste. Remove from the heat and allow to cool before stirring in the rabbit meat. Meanwhile, make the pastry. Put the flour, salt, margarine and lard into a bowl. Rub together until it resembles breadcrumbs. Mix in the water to form a dough. Roll out half the pastry and line a pie dish. Prick with a fork. Half cook the lining in a hot oven for 10 minutes. Fill the pie with the rabbit mixture and arrange the asparagus on top. Using the remaining pastry, make a pie lid and garnish with pastry leaves. Make a X in the middle of the pastry lid and brush with beaten egg. Bake at 400°F\200°C\Gas Mark 6 for 20 minutes or until golden brown.

RABBIT PIE

Recipe from Miss C M Routier of the Royal Huntsman, Williton:

Ingredients for 4 persons:
1 large rabbit
2 tablespoons oil
2 ozs\50 gms butter
4 ozs\100 gms flour
1 egg yolk
1 pt\600 mls dry cider
8 ozs\225 gms puff pastry
8 ozs\225 gms cooking apples
1 tablespoon tomato puree
1 lb\450 gms chopped tomatoes
4 ozs\100 gms celery
4 ozs\100 gms swede
4 ozs\100 gms carrot
4 ozs\100 gms turnip
4 ozs\100 gms potato
2 large onions
Bay leaf, parsley and bouquet garni

Cut up the rabbit, flour the joints and brown in the butter and oil before placing in a casserole. Fry the diced vegetables in the same pan for 5 minutes and add to the casserole with the rest of the ingredients. Simmer gently on the top of the cooker for 2 hours. Remove the meat from the bones and place with the drained vegetables in a pie dish. Thicken the liquid to the consistency of a béchamel sauce with a little flour, check seasoning and add to the dish. Top with puff pastry, glaze with egg and cook in a hot oven until the crust is golden brown.

HARE

Unlike rabbits, hares are hung before preparation. This is usually about 4-5 days in warm weather and up to 14 days in cold weather. Jugged hare was a traditional Boxing Day dinner on Exmoor.

EXMOOR HARE SOUP

A shortened version of the recipe given by A. C. Sandison in the *Exmoor Review* of 1971:

Take 2 lbs each of beef and veal, to include shin, meat and bone. Oven brown the bones and simmer for 4 hours in three quarts of water with the usual seasonings and vegetables. Strain, allow to cool and remove fat. Meanwhile, tie the meat pieces together and brown in a minimum of fat. Add ½ pt of stock and simmer until reduced. Add stock from bones and simmer until meat is cooked. Strain, allow to cool and remove fat. Brown joints of hare in beef dripping in a large saucepan with 2 ozs sliced ham and a sliced onion. Add the stock to the saucepan together with a stick of celery, a sliced carrot and turnip, bouquet garni, bay leaf, piece of lemon rind and seasoning. Simmer gently for four hours. Strain, leave to cool and remove fat. Add a little of the hare meat rubbed through a sieve and before serving add 2 teaspoons of browned flour mixed with a glass of port, 1 dessert spoon of redcurrant jelly and a squeeze of lemon juice. Put forcemeat balls in the tureen and cover with the very hot soup.

VENISON

Surprisingly, there is little written history of venison recipes for Exmoor and most recipes tend to be modern. In past centuries few people purchased meat and venison was only available to the wealthy and the few farmers whose land was hunted over. Today not every Exmoor butcher sells venison but it is widely available, even in supermarkets, although such venison is usually Scottish.

Venison is traditionally cut as beef but on Exmoor it was often jointed in a similar way to lamb. The saddle is considered to be the finest cut. When removed from the bone it resembles fillet steak and the price is similar. The cost is so high that it is rare to sell a large joint on the bone. This means that the usual way of butchering venison nowadays is in the French manner of stripping the flesh from the bone as complete muscles. It can then be cut as strip loins or fillets and sold as steaks. Small joints are then usually rolled from the top rump. In practice the cutting of the meat will vary according to the demands of the wholesale customers.

The meat is much prized nowadays because it is lean and perceived to be organically produced. However, wild deer are prone to disease and it is not usually possible to establish the history of wild venison in terms of what it has been feeding on. There has been a recent food scare about the amount of antibiotics in meat from deer picking up feed intended for pheasants. There is still a large trade in poached venison and that may not be the most hygienically butchered. Licensed game dealers should know exactly where the meat comes from and how it has been treated. At the Moorland Larder at South Molton

Pat Wright of the Moorland Larder, South Molton

Brian Pearce

it all comes from local suppliers – mostly farms but some comes from culling of wild deer in conserved woodlands. The meat from hunted deer is not sold but divided amongst the farmers whose land the deer have been grazing on. These animals are roughly quartered and not butchered into joints – that is a matter for the farmers. The offal, apart from the liver, is given to the hounds. You cannot buy venison liver and I cannot find a recipe for it apart from a modern use in paté but it is very much an Exmoor speciality which is usually simply fried. The umbles are other offal, such as the sweetbreads, which are also fried.

Venison is best when it has been hung for some time but five days is enough and three weeks is the limit, at which point it very much becomes an acquired taste. In the old days it was hung in a cool part of the chimney or covered with leaves to keep the flies away. Nowadays it is often bought as vacuum packed steaks and it continues to mature in the packs. It is dry meat and a venison joint was often wrapped in the skin and fat of a gammon joint to baste it. It can become dry and tough if cooked too fast. Venison is never served with a thick brown gravy: it is usually served with a thin sauce made from the meat juices and red wine or cider.

HAUNCH OF VENISON

Haunch can be almost any cut from the hind quarters of the animal. The fore quarters are generally too tough for roasting and best diced for casserole or minced for pies. Pat Wright of Moorland Larder says that technique in the roasting is very important. She tends to dry her meat first and coat it with a paste of olive oil, garlic and honey. The joint is then laid on foil in a very hot preheated oven for ten minutes to seal it. The foil is then wrapped over the joint, which is then cooked more slowly. After cooking, it is important to open the foil and let the meat rest before serving.

Old recipe:

3 lb haunch of venison
1 pt cider
2 ozs flour
2 ozs butter
8 ozs onions
4 ozs carrots
¼ pt venison stock
seasoning, herbs and spices

Steve Guscott

Marinate the venison in the cider overnight. Remove the joint, dry it and dust it with seasoned flour. Brown the joint in the butter in a large pan. Transfer to a large ovenproof dish. Chop the onions and carrots and add

to the venison with other ingredients, plus a little of the cider from the marinade. Place a lid on the dish and bake at 350°F\180°C\Gas Mark 4 for two hours. Add a little more cider during cooking if the joint dries too much. Serve garnished with mushrooms and watercress.

ROAST HAUNCH OF VENISON WITH PEAR AND RED WINE SAUCE

Recipe from Philip Leighton of Exford:

Ingredients for 6 persons:
1 haunch of venison
1 bottle red wine
2 carrots
2 onions
4 ozs\100 gms chopped celery
2 ozs\50 gms flour
1X 16 ozs\250 gms tin pears
4 ozs\100 gms mushrooms
Pepper corns, parsley stalks, mace, bay leaves and thyme

Marinade the venison overnight in half the wine with a sliced onion, celery, herbs and seasoning, turning the meat after 12 hours. Remove the joint, place in a roasting tray and cover with water paste made with the flour. Add the vegetables strained from the marinade. Cook in a slow oven for 2½ hours. When tender, remove, and add a little flour to the pan juices, brown and gradually add the marinade and the rest of the wine to form a thick sauce. Cook gently for 10 minutes. Slice the remaining onion and the mushrooms and sauté together for a few minutes without colouring. Strain the sauce over them, add the pears and simmer for a few minutes before serving with the meat.

VENISON MEDALLIONS WITH GREEN PEPPERCORN SAUCE

Recipe from Mrs J Redfern of East Down:

Ingredients for 6 persons:
6 venison medallions (cut from saddle or loin)
6 rounds wholemeal bread
2 tablespoons green peppercorns
8 ozs\225 gms mushrooms
½ pt\300 mls double cream
1 glass white wine

Heat a little oil in frying pan and brown rounds of wholemeal bread (cut to same size as medallions) on both sides. Sauté mushrooms, put aside and keep warm. Brush medallions with oil and cook for 3 minutes in a hot pan. Remove and keep warm. Add wine, cream and peppercorns to pan, heat through and season to taste. Serve medallions on a mushroom bed on the bread rounds.

FILLET OF VENISON
WITH JUNIPER BERRIES

Recipe from Peter Wilson of Wiveliscombe:

Ingredients for 4 persons:
1 lb\450 gms venison fillet
3 fluid ozs\75 mls orange juice
¼ pt\150 mls double cream
2 teaspoons clear Exmoor honey
1 oz\25 gms juniper berries
1 teaspoon chopped fresh thyme
½ teaspoon rubbed sage
2 ozs\50 gms green beans
2 ozs\50 gms carrots
2 ozs\50 gms celery
Juice of half a lemon

Cut carrots, green beans and celery into fine julienne strips and blanch for 20 seconds. Dry and leave aside. Add orange juice, lemon juice and honey to a pan, heat through and add thyme, sage black pepper and salt to taste, juniper berries and double cream. Reduce until thick enough to coat the back of a spoon. Cut the venison into 12 slices, season well and sauté in a little butter for 2 minutes until still pink. Heat the blanched vegetables in a little butter for about 2 minutes. Pour the sauce onto four individual serving plates, place three slices of venison on each and garnish the remainder with the julienne of vegetables.

EXMOOR VENISON CASSEROLE

Recipe from Jane Farthing of Lynton. Jane says: 'This is a traditional family dish which is warming and satisfies the heartiest of appetites! It incorporates lots of vegetables and pleasant seasonings.'

Shoulder is used in this recipe because it is diced and cooked long and slowly and there is no need to buy a more expensive cut.

1½ lbs\700 gms shoulder of venison
cut into ½ in (1.75 cm) cubes
6 teaspoons\6X5 ml spoons brown flour
seasoned with salt and pepper
2 ozs\50 gms lard or margarine
2 medium onions, peeled and sliced
3 garlic cloves, peeled and crushed
3 carrots, peeled and sliced
3 celery sticks, sliced
1 lb\450 gms vegetables in season, e.g. turnips,
swede, broad beans, parsnips
10 juniper berries, lightly crushed
6 black peppercorns
2 bay leaves
½ teaspoon\2.5 mls mixed herbs
¼ pt\125 mls beef stock
¼ pt\125 mls red wine
2 tablespoons\2X15 ml
spoons redcurrant jelly
Parsley to garnish

Toss the meat in the seasoned flour and fry in the fat for 8-10 minutes until well browned. Remove, drain over frying pan and place in a casserole dish. Fry onions and garlic for 2 minutes and add all other vegetables, peppercorns and herbs. Cook for about 5 minutes and add to casserole. Add any remaining flour to frying pan, fry for 1 minute then add beef stock, wine and redcurrant jelly. Stir briskly and bring to the boil until thickened. Pour over venison and vegetables in the casserole dish. Cover and cook in the oven at 325°F\170°C\Gas Mark 3 for 3 hours or until venison is tender. Garnish with chopped parsley.

Steve Guscott

VENISON WITH RED CABBAGE

Recipe from Jane Jeyes of Brayford:

Ingredients for 4 persons:
1 venison joint
1 small red cabbage, finely sliced
½ pt \ 300 mls beer
6 tablespoons oil
3 tablespoons vinegar
2 tablespoons lemon juice
Salt, pepper, bay leaves and crushed garlic clove

Make a marinade of the beer, oil, bay leaves, garlic, salt and pepper and soak the joint for 3-4 hours, or overnight, turning at least twice. Place in a covered roasting tin with the marinade and cook slowly at 325°F\170°C\ Gas Mark 3 for half an hour per pound plus half an hour extra. Use a little of the marinade juices to make the gravy. In a separate pan, brown the sliced onion lightly in a little oil, add the cabbage, sliced apples and golden syrup. Cook over a very gentle heat for 10 minutes, stirring frequently. Add the lemon juice, vinegar and salt and simmer, covered, for another hour before serving with the venison.

VENISON CASSEROLE IN CIDER AND CREAM WITH PARSLEY DUMPLINGS

Recipe from Jackie Payne of West Buckland:

For the parsley dumplings:
2 ozs \ 50 gms self raising flour
2 ozs \ 50 gms fresh bread crumbs
2 ozs \ 50 gms shredded suet
Grated rind of 1 lemon
1 tablespoon chopped parsley
Seasoning
1 beaten egg and milk

Mix all ingredients except egg and milk. Add enough egg and milk to make a consistency able to shape the mixture into small balls.

2 lbs \ 900 gms venison from haunch or hind leg
4 onions
8 ozs \ 225 gms mixed vegetables e.g. carrots,
celery, small turnips
4 Bramley apples
2 pts \ 1 litre cider
3 tablespoons plain flour
4 teaspoons mixed spices e.g. cloves, peppercorns, salt, mace
Sprig of rosemary and 3 bay leaves
½ pt \ 500 mls double cream

Cut the venison into lean cubes and chop two of the onions. Marinade together with the spices and cider for 24 hours in a cool place. Remove the venison from the marinade and dust with flour. Chop and fry the remaining two onions until golden. Fry the meat to seal it and until browned. Place in a casserole dish. Dice the vegetables and peel and slice the apples. Add them to the venison with the rosemary and bay leaves and the peppercorns from the marinade. Discard the cloves from the marinade and make a roux the rest of the marinade and the sediment left in the pan after frying the meat, with some plain flour, using enough marinade to cover the meat and vegetables when poured into the casserole dish. Cover and simmer for about 3 hours at 325°F\170°C\ Gas mark 3. Place the dumplings on top of the casserole for the last 20 minutes of cooking. Before serving, stir in the double cream. Serve with creamed potatoes, fresh vegetables, such as Devon swede boiled and creamed with parsnips, and sloe jelly.

VENISON PASTY

Although called a pasty, this is really a dish pie.

Old recipe:

2 lbs venison
½ pt venison stock
6 ozs mutton suet
2 ozs butter
5 fluid ozs port
½ lemon
1¼ lbs puff pastry
Flour
Seasoning, herbs and spices

Any cut of venison will do, but the cheaper parts are usually used for this dish. Cut the venison into thick slices, dust with seasoned flour and brown lightly in the butter. Put the meat in a pie dish with the stock, port, juice from the lemon, seasoning, herbs and spices. Place the suet on top and the pastry on top of all. The pastry can be brushed with beaten egg or milk. Bake at 350°F\180°C\ Gas Mark 4 for two hours. If dry, the pasty may be served with gravy made from venison stock.

EXMOOR VENISON PIE

Recipe from Mrs E C Powell of Brendon:

Ingredients for 4 persons:
2 lbs \ 1 kg venison, cubed
1 cup elderberry wine
1 teaspoon salt
4 slices streaky bacon
2 medium onions
4 ozs \ 100 gms mushrooms
2 ozs \ 50 gms peppers
½ pt \ 300 mls chicken stock
4 ozs \ 100 gms cooked sweetcorn
8 ozs \ 225 gms puff pastry
Black pepper, bouquet garni, bay leaf, beaten egg

Place the venison in a casserole with the bay leaf and seasoning, pour the wine over and leave in a cool place for 6-8 hours, basting two or three times. Cook the chopped bacon gently in a little fat for 3-4 minutes, add the onions and sauté for a further 2-3 minutes. Drain the venison, brown in the same pan and return to casserole. Heat the reserved marinade in another pan with the stock. When it has reached boiling point, add mushrooms, peppers and bouquet garni, pour into the casserole, stir well and cook in a slow oven for about 4 hours. When cooked, remove bouquet garni, add sweetcorn, transfer to a 9"X11" pie dish, cover with pastry, glaze with beaten egg and cook in an oven at 425°F\220°C\ Gas Mark 7 for 25-30 minutes until well risen and golden brown.

SMOKED VENISON PATÉ

Recipe from Pat Wright of South Molton:

4 ozs smoked venison
1 lb chicken livers
8 ozs butter
8 ozs onion
8 ozs mushrooms
3 tablespoons cranberry jelly
6 ozs double cream
2 ozs port
2 teaspoons ground black pepper

Cook livers very slowly in butter until mushy. Add finely sliced onions the mushrooms and cook gently, adding pepper. Allow to cool. Chop smoked venison in food processor, add liver mix, cranberry jelly, port and cream and blend until smooth. Use within three days or freeze immediately.

Pat also makes a venison liver paté, which is similar but venison liver is substituted for the chicken liver and smoked venison.

Steve Guscott

❧ Fruit and Vegetables ❧

APPLES

Most Exmoor people grew their own apples and a good SE facing, late flowering site for the orchard was sought after and sometimes even determined the siting of a farmhouse. Even where they could not grow apples they were usually able to purchase both eating and cooking apples from a neighbouring farmer, except in a poor season. Farmers' wives would often depend upon income from selling apples for much of the winter housekeeping. Each variety was carefully stored indoors according to its keeping properties, putting the long keepers at the back of the store to ensure a steady income.

Apple picking was an important annual event, involving days of hard work for farms with large orchards. The apples were hand picked, using ladders against trees which were generally taller and older than today's varieties. The pickers would have long aprons, the bottoms of which could be looped around the neck

to form a large pouch in which to carry the apples down to carts laden with every available container. Great care was taken not to bruise the apples and keep them sorted in varieties. Not so with cider apples, which were left to ripen more and drop as windfalls or were shaken from the tree.

Bert Verney in his *Reflections* remembers apple picking near Landkey during the Second World War:

It is now September, the time to start picking the apples in an orchard of 1.5 acres. This was a time consuming job, and took two or three men about two weeks to complete. They were picked, carted and stored in the apple room on shelves and in hutches. I suppose somewhere in the region of 4.5 tons would be roughly the weight harvested. The varieties included Bramley, Blenheim Long-bider, Effingham Pippin, Thin-skin Sweet-cleave and Cornish Gillyflower. I do remember the beautiful smell which greeted you when you

Local apple varieties – Cornish Gillyflower, Tom Putt, Golden Spire

Brian Pearce

opened the door and entered the apple room. These apples were sold by Mum in the market, a few to shops but a lot to customers in the Brendon area on Exmoor. No apples were grown there, so we had a very good round. They used to be taken in a large trailer towed behind our car – half a ton to 15 cwt at a time.

You can still buy Cornish Gillyflower apples occasionally at Barnstaple market. Landkey was a centre for fruit growing and varieties of culinary apples developed in the area included Johnny Voun, Limberland, Listener and Stockbearer. Other varieties popular in North Devon were Allspice, Barum Beauty, Bowdens Seedling, Devonshire Quarrenden, Grand Sultan, Lady Henniker, Michaelmas Stubbard, Sops in Wine, Sweet Cleave, Quench, Tidicombe Seedling and Oaken Pin, which was once common throughout Exmoor.

Large orchards were common in the lower lying areas around the moor, particularly in the Vale of Porlock, and most farms had small orchards for their own use. Apples are generally not very productive above about 400ft above sea level, mainly due to wind preventing pollination but, in sheltered locations, small orchards could be found up to about 1000ft on Exmoor. The orchards themselves provided shelter and were often the place to turn out newly born lambs. Such orchards are now a rarity and a glance at old maps will show that the disappearance of orchards, along with some hedgerows, was one of the greatest changes to the Exmoor landscape in the twentieth century.

Orchard at Selworthy

Brian Pearce

Dartington North Devon Trust are trying to preserve old varieties through their Save our Orchards campaign, launched in 1991. The Campaign promotes orchard regeneration and conservation; organises events such as Apple Days and wassails; provides instruction in crafts such as grafting; has established a local nursery; provides information on local apple varieties and where to buy them. Many varieties can still be purchased from nurseries. Exmoor National Park Authority provides grants for the planting of such traditional varieties.

Apple Day

Dartington North Devon Trust

BEECH LEAVES

Exmoor is renowned for beech hedgebanks, which are a characteristic part of its scenery. Beech has never been naturally common on Exmoor and there is some debate as to whether it was introduced in ancient times. The planting of hedgebanks with beech seems to have begun in the eighteenth century and reached a height with enclosure of moorland in the middle of the nineteenth century. Many dead leaves remain attached to the trees until new growth in the spring, providing much needed shelter for stock in winter. The new leaves, when pale green and downy, are edible and can be used in salads or for making wine or the potent liqueur, noyau.

BLACKBERRIES

These were even more popular locally than whortleberries, probably as they were accessible to everyone. They were usually used for tarts and jam.

CHERRIES

Cherries grow wild on Exmoor. The only native one is the gean. Others, like the sour cherry have been introduced. Few grow well on Exmoor as the mild, damp climate renders them susceptible to a variety of pests and diseases.

MAZZARDS

Mazzard is another name for the gean or wild cherry. In North Devon the name is applied to old varieties of cultivated cherry. The Huguenots are reputed to have introduced mazzards to North Devon. These Protestants left France in the late seventeenth century to avoid religious persecution and are reputed to have arrived en masse on Barnstaple quay one Sunday afternoon. Some local names such as Acland, de la Cour and D'arch are supposed to reflect these origins.

Mazzards are small, black cherries with a sweet flavour. It is reckoned that over 90% of mazzard trees have been lost since the Second World War and they are now rare, mostly confined to the Landkey and Goodleigh area. Varieties were called Dun, Small Dun, Small Black, Large Black, Green-stemmed Black, Preservers and Bottlers (so called because of the traditional method of preserving them). Walter Isaac in *The Way 'Twas* recalls:

> Mazzards, the most gorgeous black cherry ever with the unsurpassed flavour, unique to the area and now almost extinct, were still grown nearby. The Beer and Squire families had Mazzard Greens at Venn. I say families because the youngest could contribute to the din necessary to scare the birds by beating anything which would make a noise, aided sometimes by shotguns. Sadly mazzard pie is a taste most will now never know.

Although mainly grown to the south and west of Exmoor, they were readily purchased at local markets and were a common pie filling. Being small, the size of wild cherries, mazzards were difficult and tedious to stone, which is one reason why they grew unpopular when other varieties of cherries became available. The trees take 25 years before they bear fruit, which is why they were unpopular with growers. They were best suited to jams and drinks where the flesh could be pulped and the stones extracted. However, they were classically used in open plate tarts and pies, stoned or unstoned.

Mazzard trees can still be purchased, unlike the fruit, and most varieties are available. A few people are trying to revive an interest in them and there are still people with a good knowledge. The Dartington North Devon Trust, through their Save Our Orchards campaign are trying to draw up expertise to make up for the poor literature on mazzards. They then hope to revive the interest and examine the potential for re-establishing commercial mazzard orchards. At Landkey, which had a famed Mazzard Feast in the seventeenth century, a mazzard orchard has been planted as part of the Countryside Agency's Millennium Greens initiative.

CHERRY LAUREL

Often mistaken for rhododendron, this evergreen shrub is widespread in Exmoor woodlands. A native of SW Asia, it was introduced in the nineteenth century as cover for pheasants. Like rhododendron, it is invasive and is causing a considerable conservation problem in the woodlands by shading out the native plants. It is largely poisonous to animals and entomologists often put a crushed leaf in a jar with an insect to kill it. The leaves and fruit contain cyanide, which gives an almond flavour and, when used sparingly, both can be used in cookery. Some Exmoor cooks use a leaf heated with milk to flavour custard, removing the leaf before mixing. The fruit are black when ripe and resemble cherries. They can be eaten but are not particularly tasty and care must be taken to remove the stones, which can be fatal if swallowed!

FIGS

Figs are not commonly associated with Exmoor but they do grow well and ripen around the fringes of the moor, particularly in the drier parts to the north east. Watchet fig pie used figs soaked in brandy for the filling.

FUNGI

MUSHROOMS

Cultivated mushrooms are drier and more bland than wild ones. Their stems, however, are more tender and can be trimmed and eaten with the caps. As they are dry, they are generally cooked gently in butter, or under the meat or game so they can absorb the juices.

FIELD MUSHROOMS

Also known as common mushrooms, these are common throughout Exmoor but in this case the term common refers not to their frequency but to their being sought after on commons grazed by cattle and ponies. They have a characteristic musty smell but are quite variable in shape, size and colour. They have been known to grow up to two feet across and larger ones are often confused with horse mushrooms. Their gills are pinkish when young, turning brown then black with age. Do not pick any with white gills – they are likely to be an inedible species. They are traditionally picked early in the morning, as they can become maggoty as the day wears on.

Field mushroom caps are always peeled, for reasons of hygiene, texture and as a double check that they can be peeled, unlike some inedible species. The young or button mushrooms are best for cooking simply in milk, in sauces or sliced. They were often used sliced raw and sprinkled with lemon juice in beef sandwiches for lunch packs as they kept the sandwiches moist. Older ones opened flat are usually fried or grilled with strips of bacon fat. It is a myth that smaller ones are tastiest and the larger ones best for flavouring. When they have gone black and watery, however, they are only good for ketchup.

HORSE MUSHROOMS

These are related to but not the same species as field mushrooms. They are similar in smell and taste but are generally larger, thicker and less delicate. If they go yellow when cut, they should be discarded as they are likely to be an inedible species. They bake well and the cup-shaped ones are often eaten baked and stuffed with tomato, bacon or both. If they open flat they can be grilled but are not as good this way as field mushrooms. The really large ones are best chopped and added to casseroles or pies for flavouring.

To bake horse mushrooms with tomatoes, peel the tomatoes first. Stalk the mushrooms and season the insides. On a baking tray, cover each tomato with a suitably sized mushroom and lay a small piece of fat bacon over the top. Bake in a hot oven until the juices run together.

Button-shaped horse mushrooms can be cooked in milk with a little mace added. The cooked mushrooms are then baked in a white sauce made from the milk. The mushrooms and sauce are dotted with butter and a red currant or whortleberry jelly which melts on the top.

PARASOL MUSHROOMS

These mushrooms are easily distinguished by their parasol shape. The cups are attached to the stem by a membrane which breaks free as they grow and remains as a ring around the stem. The gills are not attached to the stem, so that on mature fungi the cap rocks on the long stem. The top of the cap is rough with rings of frilly membrane.

The stems of parasols are too tough and stringy to cook, even when young, so only the caps are eaten. They are of a more delicate flavour than field or horse mushrooms, even when old and should be cooked only lightly. The skin on older mushrooms may be tough, so they should be peeled. A large, open mushroom can simply be steamed or cut into strips and cooked in an omelette. Smaller, cup-shaped parasols can be stuffed with sage and onion stuffing, covered with bacon strips and baked. They can then be served with apple sauce like pork.

CHANTERELLES

These much sought after fungi are surprisingly common on Exmoor in the autumn. They are usually found in woods, often under beech trees and can also be found on beech hedge banks. They are a mid yellow colour on top and underneath, with glossy skins and matt gills. They smell of apricots.

They look dainty but need to be stewed for longer than mushrooms. They are best sliced and stewed in milk and butter. The milk can then be used to make a white sauce to serve them in. They need little seasoning because of their delicate flavour but a little sugar and mace may be added.

GOOSEBERRIES

A common local variety between the wars was May Duke, which had a dark red fruit and a very good flavour after cooking.

Traditional method of bottling gooseberries:

The gooseberries were topped and tailed and used to fill wide-mouthed bottles. These were heated in an oven with the door open. The bottles were then topped up with boiling water nearly to the brim. A piece of clean sheep's bladder was then tied over the mouth. If tied successfully the bladder would be drawn into the neck of the bottle as it cooled.

LEEKS

Leeks seem to be a regular ingredient in Westcountry food, although they have no particular association with the region. They often seem to be used as a tasty alternative to meat or to eke out a meagre supply of meat. As such they were traditional fare at Lent, when no meat was allowed. They are usually added to potatoes and bacon in soups and pies or served with fish. They braise better than they boil and are best cooked in the oven. On their own they are best cooked in a buttered oven dish with a little milk or stock. If the dish has a tight fitting lid, the leeks will cook in their own juice. They should then be served in the liquor from the dish.

MARROWS

There are no traditional recipes for vegetable marrows as they were only introduced to England in the late nineteenth century. There are many different kinds, with the younger ones being used as vegetables and the older ones for preserving. They are commonly grown on Exmoor, with courgettes being the most fashionable at present.

The most usual way to cook a marrow is to stuff it. The end of the marrow is cut off and the seeds scooped out and stuffed with a variety of fillings. Marrow is very moist, so the fillings are made dry to absorb the moisture. The most usual filling is a mixture of breadcrumbs and tomato. Other fillings are pork and beans, ham and spinach or spring beans. The end of the marrow is held on with a skewer and the stuffed marrow baked. The marrow is served tilted on a wedge-shaped piece of bread to aid scooping out the filling.

NETTLES

Eating nettles is by no means confined to Exmoor but has been common in poor country areas. They have a high nutritional value, providing many minerals, and are a source of fresh greens at a time of year when there are few other vegetables around. The young leaves are picked, before the nettles start to flower, and are stripped from the stalks. They are cooked like spinach and will substitute for spinach in many recipes. Like spinach, they reduce down considerably when cooked. The simplest way of cooking them is to sweat them over a gentle heat for about 20 minutes in a covered pan with a couple of tablespoons of water and a knob of butter.

NUTS

HAZEL OR COB NUTS

Many old Exmoor woods have an understorey of hazel bushes. It was quite common to pick the nuts for sale and a way for children to make pocket money. In *Within Living Memory* by Margaret Bate it is recalled how children at North Molton used to hang precariously over old mineshafts to collect the best nuts from overhanging trees.

A famous North Molton man, the poet Dicky Slader, who died in 1926, was renowned for selling nuts. He

Dicky Slader, pedlar poet, Simonsbath c1900
Exmoor Photographic Archive

was an eccentric pedlar who walked great distances with his donkey to sell eggs, blackberries, whortleberries and nuts at local markets. He would carry some nuts in a sack over his shoulder and some in a wicker basket. He would sort them out by putting them in a bucket of water. The good ones would sink and what he called the 'dreeve' ones – those which were empty or bad – would float. He would carefully dry them over the winter and sell them from door to door. The dreeve ones were kept to be sold to unsuspecting customers at fairs. He sold them at 8d instead of the usual 10d per pound.

Nuts were both sold and given as prizes at fairs. At the Lynton Revel in the nineteenth century a well-known character was a Mr Smith with his shooting range: 'Penny a shot and forty nuts every time you win'. A Mr Thornby of Barnstaple and Jennie Morris of Combe Martin sold nuts, gingerbreads and comfits.

WALNUTS

Walnuts are introduced trees and were much prized in Norman and medieval times. They were planted around the edges of Exmoor, particularly to the north east. The Aclands planted many on their Holnicote

Estate for wood for gunstocks rather than nuts but many produce edible nuts. Bossington was famed for its large walnut trees and one was reputed to have the largest girth in the country. Villagers used to gather the nuts in autumn and use them in pies, puddings, sauces, cakes, soups and stuffings. A walnut and honey tart was often part of harvest festivities.

ONIONS

Onions were used considerably in local cooking. Large onions were often baked in their skins on a bed of coarse salt. This was done slowly until they were tender. The skins were then peeled and they were opened up, seasoned and covered with a knob of butter. This made a tea or supper savoury dish, served with bread and cheese.

PLUMS

There are several species of Prunus, or the plum family, growing wild on Exmoor. Blackthorns and cherries are dealt with separately. The wild plum or damson and the cherry plum were introduced from SW Asia and thrive in the milder parts of the West Country. The bullace, a subspecies of wild plum, is widely regarded as native as it grows far from cultivation, although this is unlikely. It is usually called a cristling on Exmoor. All such plums grow in hedgerows and woodlands around the edges of the moor and are not particularly common here in the wild. The Heddon Valley has both wild damsons and bullaces, which are also common around Monksilver. Bullaces are small and best treated as sloes, for making jam and drinks.

There are few really old recipes using plums. This is mainly because sugar is a relatively recent addition to poor people's larders and because sweet varieties of plums are also relatively recent. There is an old variety of sweet plum known as the Dunster plum as it is common in gardens in that area. Its fruit are purple and juicy with a wonderful flavour. Its origin is obscure but presumably it was a hybrid developed in a Dunster garden and is similar to a Victoria. Over in North Devon is a yellow variety called the Landkey Yellow. This is propagated by suckers, so probably originates from one tree. It is reputed that it is only possible to grow it in hedgerows. A common variety in Devon was the Dittisham plum. Legend has it that in the nineteenth century a German cargo ship arrived at Dittisham in South Devon with a cargo of plum trees. Unable to sell them, the skipper just dumped them on the docks and they all rapidly found new owners. There is also a sweet variety of christling cultivated in North Devon.

Most old recipes containing plums usually refer to dried fruit which was imported. In this case plums could refer to raisins, currants, figs, dates or prunes (dried plums). Such fruit was expensive and used by common people mainly on festive occasions. The fruit was equally used in sweet and savoury dishes.

POTATOES

Until the eighteenth century potatoes seem to have locally been a garden crop for the wealthy. They were left in the ground over winter and dug as required. By the next century, however, they were extensively grown and became a mainstay of the poor. This change of diet was common in the west of Britain when the Napoleonic Wars forced up the price of corn. Luckily for Exmoor people sheep farming remained important and they did not become so totally dependent upon potatoes as some people in Ireland.

There is an old local variety of potato known as Exmoor Blue. It was developed from a North Devon strain of the Scottish Edgehill Blue. It is very hardy and adaptable, being suitable for both early or maincrop according to the time of planting. When fresh from the ground it is a deep bluish purple colour, turning more red as it dries. Exmoor writer Hope Bourne has tried to keep the strain going for many years by distributing a proportion of her seed crop amongst local friends.

RASPBERRIES

Some locals associate Exmoor with wild raspberries but, although they are common, I do not know that they have any particular association with the area. Wild raspberries taken and cultivated soon produce larger fruit and most cultivated varieties are comparatively modern. Many local varieties, such as Devon and Mayfair were raised at the Pyne nurseries at Topsham early in the twentieth century and Exeter Yellow at the Veitch nurseries at Exeter in the nineteenth century.

SAMPHIRE

There are two, unrelated types of samphire: rock samphire and marsh samphire, more commonly known as glasswort. As their names suggest, the former grows on rocky cliffs and shingle; the latter, on salt marshes. The former is quite common on exposed cliffs, the latter only found at Porlock Marsh and Weir on Exmoor and on the Taw\Torridge estuaries. I bought some fresh glasswort in a local supermarket recently but it was imported from France. It is so rare to find in the shops, fresh or pickled, that you usually need to pick your own.

Rock samphire smells of sulphur and has a taste of acid drops. It is well described as an acquired taste. It was

Rock Samphire at Ilfracombe

Brian Pearce

preserved in vinegar or brine and served as a pickle with mutton. A traditional pickle was made with pickled samphire, cucumber and capers chopped together and boiled with vinegar, spices and lemon juice. It was served on top of the mutton, which it helped to tenderise.

I prefer marsh samphire, as it lacks the sulphury taste. It is extremely salty and contains so much soda that it was used as a source of that chemical for the glassmaking industry – hence its other name. It contains many trace minerals and is no doubt good for you in small quantities. It is difficult to imagine eating large quantities but it is good to add to many dishes for its saltiness and bright green colour. I like it plain boiled or steamed, with melted butter, served with fish dishes.

SEAWEEDS

On the Exmoor coast seaweeds have had a variety of uses. Their main use was as a fertiliser and large amounts were taken by packhorses to fertilise market

gardens, along with the lime-rich, shelly sand from Barnstaple Bay. It is also likely that it was burned for the production of potash for fertiliser or chemical industries.

Some was fed to livestock as a tonic. Geese and ducks flock to the shore for it. Seaweeds are an important source of trace minerals and one of the few natural sources of iodine in the diet. Most seaweeds are edible, although some more edible than others. Although they can be eaten raw, their surprising toughness means that much boiling is required to soften them. Some, like carragheen, were just boiled for a long period after which the seaweed was discarded and the liquid used for thickening soups and broths.

Porphyra umbilicalis, commonly known as laver, is the seaweed traditionally associated with Exmoor cookery. It was mentioned in the Anglo-Saxon chronicles and in those days was eaten to cure bladder stones. Its ancient name was sion. Sometimes the name was applied to Ulva, the sea lettuce, which looks similar but is always green. Another species of Porphyra – Porphyra palmata – is known as sloke in Wales. Porphyra is a transparent red seaweed found growing on stones and boulders in the mid range of the tide, particularly where there is also sand. The tidal range is so great in the Bristol Channel that it is only here that the laver beds are extensive enough for the seaweed to be gathered in commercial quantities. One delicatessen on Butchers Row, Barnstaple currently sells about 400 lbs per week. Most of that, however, is gathered from the Torridge estuary, not the Exmoor coast. It is supposed to be picked only when there is an r in the month. This is possibly to give it chance to grow in the summer months, when it takes on a greenish colour.

Collecting and preparing it was usually women's work, and hard work it could be. Combe Martin women were renowned for scaling the cliffs at the Rawns between Little and Great Hangman to collect laver. Here there were sheep tracks over dangerous and constantly slipping cliffs used by iron miners. After an initial wash in sea water the wet and heavy weed was carried up the cliffs in baskets and later washed several times (traditionally eight times) in the River Umber to remove the sand. It was sold loose in markets, where it was weighed into customers' own jars, or in fishmongers or butchers shops. It is found all along the Exmoor coast as far as Watchet and Porlock was particularly renowned for its potted laver. Pickled laver was sealed in earthenware pots with butter and sent inland to Bridgwater, Taunton and even Bath and London.

Laver is boiled for 2-3 hours in sea water or in a bain marie, using an earthenware pot. During this process it reduces greatly. The resulting pulp is packed into small pots and covered with a layer of clarified butter or suet.

Laver at Bloody Beach, Martinhoe

In this state it keeps for several days, although vinegar is often added to preserve it further. On Exmoor pickled laver is simply reheated in a double saucepan (to prevent it sticking) and used as a condiment with fish, especially herrings, hogs puddings or other fried foods. Cooper, writing about Lynton in 1853, stated that laver: 'is found on this coast and brought to the door, prepared for the table. It is considered a luxury, and generally eaten with cold meat; others prefer it with hot.'

Traditionally, fresh laver was made into a sauce for marshland mutton. It could be added to a white sauce, simply heated with butter and lemon or sharp orange juice or added to thicken the mutton gravy. It was beaten together with a silver fork and brought to table on a hot water dish. Mrs Rundell, in her *System of Domestic Cookery* of 1806 recommended adding Seville orange juice to it to dress Welsh lamb and for a while it became popular for this throughout the country. Until then it was little known away from the Bristol Channel. A little earlier, a Bridgwater physician had send a pot of laver as a gift to his sons famous tutor, Dr John Hunter. Dr Hunter thought that it was some kind of a student joke, suggesting that he had been sent a pot of cow dung. The son had to demonstrate its use as mutton sauce to the incredulous doctor before he became a convert and was pleased to receive a regular barrel of Exmoor laver. Another well-known devotee was poet Robert Southey, who acquired a taste for it whilst staying at the Ship Inn, Porlock. Coleridge's friend and benefactor, Tom Poole of Nether Stowey, used to send him jars of Porlock pickled laver to his home at Bristol or the Lake District. Coleridge also sent him jars as souvenirs of his occasional return visits to Nether Stowey. By the middle of the nineteenth century the fame of laver had spread and the Rev. William Thornton reported of a lady from Carhampton who was regularly supplying it to Fortnum and Masons. There was for some years a very brisk trade in potted laver with Porlock and Watchet sending supplies to grocers in Bridgwater, Taunton, Minehead, Nether Stowey and Bath. Earthenware pots of it were sold as souvenirs.

The Welsh mix laver with oatmeal to a cake-like consistency to produce laverbread, which is fried. They pronounce it like 'lava' and Exmoor people like 'layver'. Exmoor laverbread is a stew of different kinds of seaweeds. Do not confuse this with laver bread, which is a wholemeal bread made with laver and coated with crushed, toasted laver. This modern invention can be purchased in local delicatessens and is absolutely delicious: I could live on that alone. Exmoor people may also fry laver in bacon fat to eat with bacon and locally pork and laver sausages have become fashionable. The Irish mix it with mashed potato. Bubble and squeak made with laver is a more widespread variation on this and laver soup is traditional throughout the west of the British Isles. The Japanese dry it into paper-like sheets and toast it as a wrapping for sushi or shredding and using in soups. The popularity of eastern cooking and the fact that laver has few calories but many important trace minerals has meant that laver, once a poor man's dish, has now acquired a certain trendiness. Some pregnant women, for whom it is an important source of iron, have cravings to eat it. Many, however, regard it with revulsion and laver eating contests are a popular

Three kinds of laverbread

spectator sport in North Devon pubs. The record seems to be about 8 lbs in one session.

Chefs are now beginning to introduce laver to top restaurants, where variations on laver soup are becoming popular. It is certainly popular toasted as eaten by the Japanese and one chef even crystallises it for toppings for puddings. Bob Deville of Martinhoe, says:

'Laver is one of the least understood natural products of the Exmoor area. Warmed up and served as it is with bacon, sausages etc, it is rather an acquired taste and off-putting to a newcomer. However, it has many more subtle uses, if it is thought of as a condiment or seasoning rather than a food. Here are some suggestions:

A tablespoonful added to any casserole will add an indefinable depth to it.

Some added to mayonnaise and whipped up in a processor will make a delicious dip for prawns etc.

Cook some triangles of fried bread and put ½ teaspoon of laver and a cooked mussel on top for an unusual warm canapé.

Take an oyster in its half shell, add a little laver, sprinkle some cheese on top and put under the grill until the cheese bubbles. This makes a delicious starter.

Mix some laver with fine oatmeal until you can roll it into croquettes and fry in butter – a good accompaniment to chicken.

Mix some laver with orange juice and some meat stock for a good sauce to go with fried liver.

The sky is the limit: do experiment with this lovely vegetable of the sea. My favourite way is to mix a little lemon juice with laver as a perfect partner for simply cooked white fish.'

SLOES

Sloes are the fruit of the blackthorn, a member of the plum family. Blackthorns grow in hedgebanks throughout Exmoor, but seem to be more prolific near the North Devon coast, where true 'blackthorn winters' can be seen when the shrubs are in full white bloom in April. The sloes are traditionally picked after the first frost, if any can still be found by then. The frost loosens the texture and helps the juice to flow. It is usually easier to pick them as soon as they are ripe and put them in a freezer overnight, which has the same effect as the frost. They acquire a blueish bloom as on a grape as they ripen and they should be picked well ripened, when the bloom completely covers them. A taste of a raw fruit is never forgotten. They are extremely,

Laver canapés and dip

Steve Guscott

tongue-curling sour but it is amazing what a little sugar will do and they are good in jam and the famous sloe gin.

STRAWBERRIES

One may not associate Exmoor with strawberry growing but for a time it was one of the main centres of the strawberry growing industry, at least around the fringes of the moor. Large cultivated strawberries were certainly around in Tudor times, but the earliest variety grown locally was small like a wild strawberry and known as 'pinkies'. Later came larger varieties such as Royal Sovereign, Laxton, Glorious and Madame Cowee. Between the wars a popular variety was Madame Lefebre, known locally as Phoebes. Since the Second World War, Talisman and Redgauntlet were popular.

Strawberries and cream

The main strawberry growing area was Combe Martin, which was a centre for market gardening and early vegetables in particular. The south western facing side of the Umber valley is known as sunnyside and, as well as having plenty of sunshine, has well drained and fertile soils, sheltered in small medieval strip fields. The valley produced lime, which was useful for early potatoes, which were often grown in rotation with the strawberries. The industry seems to have begun on a commercial scale in 1865 and grown with the tourist industry. It had its heyday between the wars. The valley has little frost and the strawberries were early by the standards of the day, flowering in March and cropping in June.

Everyone helped with the picking and there was much 'mitching' or truanting from school, as there was in other parts for whortleberry picking. The picked fruit was packed in wicker maunds holding from 12 to 25 lbs of fruit. The early fruit was mainly sold locally but main crops tended to be taken by steamers around the Bristol Channel. From the Second World War until the 1950s there were special fruit trains running from Barnstaple. Between 1913 and 1925 a jam factory operated in Combe Martin, using the surplus main crop strawberries. They advertised as 'Combe Martin Jams, the Best in the West'. They made marmalade and other jams to keep them busy through the year. Their downfall was the high cost of sugar and rationing following the war combined with the depression and rumours that they eked the fruit out with mangolds.

Strawberry picking at Combe Martin

Combe Martin Museum

Combe Martin strawberries ready for transport

There was a special strawberry show each year until the 1950s with over 50 different classes alone. The industry declined with competition from other parts of Europe and transport charges. Combe Martin strawberries are, however, still grown and well known locally and there is an annual Strawberry Fayre street fair.

WHORTLEBERRIES

'Quaint, lovely Lynmouth, that land of cream and whortleberries, of cream and blackberries' wrote a nineteenth century journalist. Whortleberries or myrtleberries are local names for plants with a huge variety of local names but more commonly known elsewhere as bilberries. When raw they are a great source of vitamins and minerals and were bottled to be used in the classic Exmoor dish, whortleberry pie. They cannot now be purchased fresh locally and you have to pick your own or use bottled eastern European or American blueberries.

The berries ripen in late July and are nowadays most bountiful where they have not been overgrazed by sheep, such as on hedgebanks, cliffs and verges. They are easier to pick from hedgebanks, as there is less stooping, and the famous pedlar poet, Dicky Slader, reckoned that the best were found on the hedgebanks by the road from Moles Chamber to Sandyway: 'The best whorts in Devon. Pick 'em in me own 'at so 'ems mus' be clean' he would say. If you had seen him and his hat you would not have thought that was a good selling point!

They were once picked commercially but the process was very labour intensive and it became unprofitable to pick the tiny wild whortleberries against larger cultivated varieties. Pickers stooped or sat on mats and combed the bushes with their fingers or by raking into baskets with wooden or homemade wire combs. The combs cut down picking time on the moors but increased time later spent picking out the leaves and stalks which they also raked up. Leaves were usually removed by spreading the whortleberries out on a sheet and fanning them. Whatever method was employed, pickers' hands and clothes became stained blue and old clothes were always worn. It was a dry weather job as the berries could not be sold wet, although the wet berries could be bottled and used for home consumption. Crops varied from year to year. If there had been a late frost when the shrubs were in flower the crop would be poor and good pickings would be jealously guarded. Each parish would have what was regarded as their own territory and within that everyone had their own secret patch.

The whortleberries were measured in quart pots. Between the wars 4d to 6d per quart was the usual wage when the berries were scarce, dropping to 3d or 2½d at the height of a good season. The price rose to 2s per quart during the last war and 2s 6d later. Each area had its own local dealer. Between the wars in the Wootton Courtenay area it was Tom Webber and his sister, who had a horse and cart which carried small barrels for the fruit. In the Porlock area the whortleberries were bought by Cecil Westcott, the local fruiterer. He packed them in punnets and took them to

Minehead station to be sent to London and the Midlands. His largest consignment was of one ton.

Whortleberries on North Hill, Minehead

It was never well paid work and was largely undertaken by women and children. There are many accounts from school records of children 'mitching' or truanting in the summer term to pick worts or urts, although this was only when the season was early and picking usually carried on in the summer holidays. In villages in the Vale of Porlock the headmaster and vicar would negotiate the timing of summer holidays each year according to when the children started truanting. At North Molton during the Second World War the headmaster took his children wort picking for the war effort. The berries made the blue dye for RAF uniforms.

Mothers and children would set off early in the morning, usually on foot and walking several miles to the moors. Sometimes wagons would be laid on for groups. They would pick until tea time, when they would have to leave to prepare the evening meal. They would take lunch with them – usually sandwiches wrapped in a knotted handkerchief and bottle of cold tea tied to the waist. The children would have to earn their lunch by filling their mother's basket to a preset mark from the mugs and pint pots they collected their berries in. Usually there was a short play time before going home. Children who stayed at home because they were too young were often taken a sprig of whortleberry by their older brothers and sisters. The children were usually allowed to keep the money earned on the last day. The rest of the money was often used to pay for the children's clothes for the coming school year and the end of the season was marked by a trip to town to buy winter clothes and as a treat for the children.

Setting off from Dulverton for whortleberry picking c1916

Exmoor Photographic Archive

Wort picking still remains vivid in many local memories. In *Within Living Memory* an old lady called Edna gives an account of 'wert' picking at North Molton between the wars:

> Every fine day except Sundays, after doing the morning chores and preparing a picnic and suitable baskets, one each, mothers and their children would set off about 9 am to walk three miles to the moors. This would take about one hour, then leaving for home again about 5 pm. Often about sixty plus people were on the moors picking. They came from Heasley Mill, North Molton, Twitchen, Brayford and other places. Those from Brayford arrived on their bicycles. About 4 pm, if the children had been good and filled their baskets, we could have a little time of play, before setting off one the long walk home, as long as we kept well away from the people who were picking the fruit.

Details of whortleberry picking at Luccombe were given by W. J. Turner in his *Exmoor Village* book of 1947:

> Apart from their household use of it the fruit has a ready sale in other districts, and for many generations the Exmoor people have looked upon the errts as one of their annual harvests. Nowadays lorries come each day to the picking grounds and buy up the fruit at about 2s 6d per quart, but prices vary slightly with the season, and some dealers buy by weight. During war-time the fruit is valuable as a dye as well as for food. In the old days when agricultural wages were very low the Exmoor cottagers used to rely on the money they received from their whortleberry harvest to provide the whole family with clothing for the coming year.

Frank Summers of Oldways End remembers walking up on to Rhyll, Anstey and Molland Commons in his summer holidays. He remembers being chased off Venford Moor by the farmer. Permission was required from the landowner for commercial picking, even on common land.

The commons in North Molton parish belonged to the Poltimore Estate and about the twentieth July Lord Poltimore used to put up notices declaring the commons open for three or four weeks for whortleberry picking, usually to coincide with the school summer holidays. Sometimes gypsies would come with their horse-drawn caravans for the picking. As they could stay up on the commons all day, this gave them an advantage over the locals. They would also start picking before permission was given and in an early season the villagers would press the lord to allow them to start picking when the gypsies arrived.

A dealer from South Molton used to drive his trap out to Molland Moor Gate to take provisions to the gypsies

and bring back their whortleberries. He would box them and send them off by train the next morning, half a ton at a time. Apparently they were very popular with the miners of Yorkshire and South Wales because whortleberry pies kept moist down in the pits.

SAUCES AND CONDIMENTS

APPLE PICKLE

Old recipe from Mrs A M Cole of Chittlehampton:

Boil 2 lbs brown sugar, ¼ lb salt, 1/4 lb ginger, ½ lb raisins, ¼ oz chillies, ¼ oz mustard seed, together in 3 pts vinegar for ½ hour, add 30 large apples sliced and boil till apples are cooked.

SWEET PRESERVED APPLES

This is an old method of storing eating apples. The apples are peeled but cooked whole in cider with their stalks on. Sugar to roughly half the weight of the apples is added to the cider, along with lemon juice and cloves. Once tender, the apples are bottled in the liquid.

RAW APPLE CHUTNEY

Old recipe:

1 lb apples
1 lb onions
1 lb dates
1 lb sultanas
1 lb brown sugar
1 pt vinegar
Seasoning
Pickling spices

Brian Pearce

Peel, core and chop the apples. Peel and chop the onion. Stone the dates and put all through a mincer.

Add the other ingredients, with the pickling spices in a bag. Stir occasionally and bottle after a day.

MUSHROOM KETCHUP

Traditional method:

When they have become black and soggy, mushrooms are best for making ketchup, the local answer to Worcestershire sauce. This was made by salting layers of whole mushrooms in an earthenware jar and heating in a slow bread oven or range. The resulting mush was pressed through muslin to remove the liquid, which was then spiced with pepper and nutmeg, brought to the boil and corked in sterilised bottles whilst still hot. Made this way it will keep indefinitely and is used to flavour soups, stews and squab pie.

It can also be preserved by adding one part of home-made red wine, such as elderberry, to four parts of mushroom juice.

PICKLED RED CABBAGE

Recipe from Rosemary Tucker of West Luccombe:

1 small red cabbage
1 medium onion
4 cooking apples
1 oz\25 gms sugar
2 teaspoons vinegar
2 ozs\50 gms butter
Salt and pepper

Thinly slice the cabbage, onion and apples and place in layers in an ovenproof dish. Sprinkle on the sugar and vinegar, dot with butter and season well. Cover and cook in a moderate oven for 1½ hours. Serve with roast pork.

PICKLED SAMPHIRE

Old recipe:

3 lbs young samphire leaves
6 ozs salt
3 pts water
2 pts vinegar
1 oz mixed spice
6 peppercorns

Mix the samphire in a large bowl with the salt and water until the salt is dissolved. Cover with a plate to keep the samphire immersed and leave for 24 hours. Meanwhile boil the vinegar with the spices, cool, leave for two hours and strain. Rinse the brine from the samphire, which is then stored in jars with the vinegar. Store for at least 3 months.

PICKLED WHORTLEBERRIES

Old recipe:

3 lbs whortleberries
¾ pt vinegar
12 ozs sugar
Cloves

Boil vinegar, sugar and cloves together until the sugar is dissolved. Cool and leave for two hours before straining. Cover the whortleberries with the vinegar and store in well sealed jars for at least three months, preferably a year.

SOUPS

A SOUPÇON OF EVERYTHING

Recipe from Joanna Hearth of Dulverton. Joanna lives at the former Dulverton Weavers premises overlooking the churchyard and writes poems on a variety of subjects, including the view from her windows.

I've washed and peeled the veg and made the stew
and while it cooks I know what I should do.
I ought to write the recipe
and leave it to posterity.
Maybe I'll reach the hall of fame for veggie stew – a household name!

So find a pan – with lid that's large enough and
suitable to stir fry all the stuff.
Begin with olive oil – of course.
Add mushrooms, chopped – improves the sauce.
In fact, chop everything youve got
and now the main things for the pot:
the mushrooms, carrot, parsnip, swede – to start
(its bound to warm the cockles of your heart)
and celry or some beans will do –
its fun to variate this stew.
Then, when alls fried and stirred around,
pour boiling water on the mound.

And, after that, potatoes go in too.
Tis now you add more flavour to the brew: some
liquid seasoning – not too much –
and powdered bayleaf, just a touch.
Tomato puree – that goes swell
with peanut butter mixed as well.

And last, small bits of broccoli and peas. Then let it
simmer, stirring as you please.
Oh! I forgot – black pepper, ground: its best to put it
in, Ive found,
and when its cooked – about an hour –
just thicken with a little flour.

Now, eat your fill and,
if youve left some, to your sorrow,
Id say its even better on the morrow.

Enjoy

DUNKERY NETTLE SOUP

Recipe from Katie Garnsworthy of South Molton:

Ingredients for 4 persons:
1 lb\450 gms young nettles
1 oz\25 gms butter
1 small onion
1 oz\25 gms cornflour
1½ pts\750 mls milk
2 egg yolks
3 tablespoons cream
Nutmeg, salt and pepper

Steve Guscott

Wash the nettles well, then cook in the minimum of water and sieve like spinach. Cook the onion in the butter until translucent, add cornflour, mix well and cook for 1 minute. Add milk, stirring well and simmer for 3 minutes. Pour over sieved nettles, return to the heat. Mix a little of the soup with egg yolks and cream, return all to the pan with seasonings and re-heat gently before serving.

CREAM OF NETTLE SOUP WITH EXMOOR JERSEY BLUE CHEESE

Recipe from Jackie Payne of West Buckland. Jackie says: 'Pick (with gloved hands) the top few young leaves of nettles before the nettles flower.'

2 ozs washed nettles
2 potatoes
1 leek
1 onion
1 clove of garlic
1½ pts vegetable stock
1 pt milk
3 ozs Exmoor Jersey Blue cheese
Seasoning

Steve Guscott

Peel and chop all the vegetables. Lightly fry the garlic and onion and place in a saucepan with all the other ingredients except for the milk and the cheese. Bring to the boil and simmer for 20 minutes, until the potato is soft. Blend in a processor and put back into the saucepan. Stir in the milk and heat until almost boiling. Ladle into bowls, crumble the cheese on top and serve with warm crusty bread.

MIXED HERB SOUP

Recipe from Jackie Payne of West Buckland:

2 ozs\50 gms mixed herbs e.g. 8 large sorrel leaves, a
handful of mint and lemon balm leaves
1 medium potato, peeled and diced
1 medium carrot, peeled and diced
1 medium onion, peeled and diced
1½ pts\900 mls water
¾ pt\450 mls fresh milk
1 oz\25 gms plain flour
½ teaspoon soy sauce
Salt and pepper
Small fresh mint leaves to garnish

Put the herbs, chopped vegetables and soy sauce into a medium saucepan with the water and boil for half an hour to reduce the liquid to about a pint. Purée the soup with the flour in a blender or food processor. Reheat, gently adding the milk, allow to thicken and season to taste. Garnish with mint and serve hot with homemade croutons and granary bread rolls.

HUXTABLE FARM CREAM OF WILD MUSHROOM SOUP WITH HERB CROUTONS

Recipe from Jackie Payne of West Buckland: Jackie says: 'Wild field mushrooms grow from July to November, usually after a long dry spell of weather followed by a shower of rain. They occur singly or in scattered groups or rings. The fields around Heasley Mill produce some wonderful mushrooms!'

Steve Guscott

1 lb field mushrooms
2 onions
1 pt vegetable stock
2 ozs plain flour
1 large potato
1 pt milk
Seasoning

For herb croutons:
Chop bread into cubes and leave to dry on a warm cooker for two or three hours. Lightly fry until golden in a shallow pan of olive oil, salt, finely chopped parsley and thyme. Serve warm with soup.

Peel and stalk the mushrooms. Cook the mushrooms, potato, onions and stock in a pan for 30 minutes. Purée the mixture with the flour in a processor. Bring to the boil gradually, stirring in the milk as the soup thickens. Simmer for 20 minutes, season and serve.

KETTLE BROTH

This soup was common throughout the West Country, particularly in Cornwall, and its ingredients varied locally and with the seasons. It was called kettle broth because it was cooked in a kettle, which was an iron cauldron held over an open fire. Sometimes the broth was served with a scattering of marigold petals, said to give good health. This is a modern variation:

1 lb leeks
2 onions
2 ozs bacon fat
3 ozs white bread, cubed
2 pints chicken stock
Punnet mustard and cress
3 ozs clotted cream
Salt and pepper for seasoning

Chop the onions and washed leeks and, in a large pan, fry them slowly in the bacon fat until soft but not brown. Add the bread and chicken stock and bring to the boil. Cool, add the mustard and cress and blend or liquidise. Return to the heat, adjust the seasoning and stir in the cream just before serving.

LAVER SOUP

Old recipe:

6 ozs potted laver
6 ozs butter
½ lb chopped onions
½ lb chopped potatoes
4 ozs chopped carrots
4 pts lamb or fish stock
Seasoning: salt, pepper, sugar

Cook the vegetables in the butter in a covered saucepan for 5-10 minutes until browned. Add the stock and laver and simmer for about 20 minutes until the vegetables are soft. Liquidise or rub through a sieve, season and reheat for serving.

LIKKY SOUP

This is a variation of Kettle Broth.

Old recipe:

1 lb potatoes
2 large leeks
2 rashers fat bacon
1 pt stock
2 ozs clotted cream
½ oz butter
Seasoning and parsley

Chop the bacon and fry in the butter. Peel and dice the potatoes, wash and slice the leeks, and add to the pan. Add the stock and parsley and simmer until the vegetables are soft. Add the clotted cream just before serving.

WATERCRESS SOUP

Old recipe:

Ingredients for four persons:
8 ozs watercress
8 ozs potatoes
2 onions
1 oz butter
1 pt water
1½ pts milk
1 oz grated cheese
¼ pt double cream
½ teaspoon nutmeg
Seasoning

Peel and slice the potatoes and onions and boil in the water until soft. Save the water and mash (or process) the potatoes and onions. Prepare the watercress by picking out the large stalks and withered leaves and cook the remainder gently in the butter. Add the potato and onion mixture to the pan with the watercress, then add the water and milk. Simmer for 15 minutes, liquidise or process (sieve originally). Reheat with the nutmeg and seasoning and serve with grated cheese.

Steve Guscott

SAVOURY DISHES

APPLE AND ONION PIE

This is the basic version of squab pie – without the squab.

Traditional method:

Line a pie dish with short crust pastry. Cover the bottom with a layer of peeled, cored and sliced apple. Cover with a layer of peeled and sliced onion. Keep adding alternate layers of apple and onion, seasoning with, salt, pepper, sage and mace as you go and adding sugar to the apple if necessary. Dot with clotted cream and cover with a pastry lid. Bake in a hot oven.

ASPARAGUS TART

Recipe from Derek and Val Pritchard of Wootton Courtenay: Derek says: 'There is no finer flavoured asparagus than that which we grow here; the season lasts from Easter until 21st June. We have developed this recipe as the ideal way of utilising the thinner spears.'

For the pastry:
2 cups plain flour
1 egg
½ level teaspoon salt
3 tablespoons double cream
2\3 cup butter

Sieve the flour into a bowl. Make a well in the centre of the flour, break the egg into the well, then add the salt, cream and butter. Blend together and then knead until smooth. Chill in a refrigerator for two hours before rolling out. Roll out and line a 9 inch tart dish.

For the filling:
½ lb fresh, thin asparagus spears
1 cup crème fraîche
1 cup milk
4 eggs
1 level teaspoon salt

Part cook the asparagus in a steamer for about 10 minutes. Lay the spears evenly over the pastry base. Beat the crème fraîche, salt, eggs and milk together. Pour the mixture over the asparagus. Cook in a pre-heated oven at 350°F\180°C\ Gas Mark 4 for about 30 minutes, until the filling is just set. Serve warm or cold, accompanied by one of Dunkery Vineyards dry white wines.

CARROT ROULADE

Recipe from Lesley Orr of West Buckland, Wellington:

4 ozs butter
1½ lbs carrots
6 eggs
Parmesan cheese
seasoning

For the filling:
½ lb cream cheese
1 large clove garlic
2 tablespoons chives

Steve Guscott

Preheat the oven to 400°F\200°C\Gas Mark 6. Line a large Swiss roll tin with Bakewell paper. Finely grate the carrots and cook them gently with the butter in a large frying pan until soft. Separate the eggs and mix the yolks with the carrots in a large bowl. Season well. Whisk the egg whites to soft peaks and carefully fold into the carrot mixture. Pour into the prepared tin and bake for 10-12 minutes, until golden brown and springy to the touch. Cover with a damp cloth and leave to cool. Chop the chives and mix with the other filling ingredients, beating well and seasoning. Turn out the carrot roulade onto a sheet of paper, or a cloth sprinkled with Parmesan cheese. Peel off the paper, spread with the filling, roll up carefully and serve.

HERBY PIE

Poor Exmoor families would often go without meat. There are many stories of, even in quite recent times such as the depression between the wars, subsisting on whatever green vegetables and wild plants could be found cooked in a suet crust.

Traditional method:

Mix and chop together green vegetables and herbs in season: spinach, watercress, scallions, parsley, leeks etc Line a pie dish with bacon and cover with the vegetable mixture. Add more bacon if wished. Beat two eggs with a little water or stock and add to the dish. Cover with a short pastry crust and bake in a moderate oven for about 1½ hours.

LANKCOMBE COURGETTES

Recipe from Sylvia Harrop of Lynton:

Ingredients for 3 people:
3 medium courgettes
2 ozs\50 gms chopped hazelnuts
1 Coxs apple
1 tomato
2 ozs\50 gms mushrooms
2 lemon slices
Basic white sauce
Lemon juice and rind
Parsley, seasoning

Steve Guscott

Boil the courgettes until tender and allow to cool. Slice lengthways and scoop out flesh, mix it with diced apple, lemon juice, salt and freshly ground black pepper. Re-stuff shells and top with finely chopped tomato and nuts. Grate lemon rind over, cover with foil and heat for half an hour in a medium oven. Serve covered in white sauce flavoured with lemon juice, with lightly fried mushrooms and garnished with parsley and lemon slices.

LIKKY PIE

This was eaten whenever leeks were in season but particularly at Lent. Strict observers of Lent would omit both the bacon and the egg.

Traditional method:

The leeks are washed and sliced and stewed gently with a little butter and milk or water. A pie dish is lined with short crust pastry and the leeks packed in tightly with a little chopped streaky bacon and some pepper. The pie is given a pastry top and baked in a moderate oven until the pastry is slightly browned. An egg is beaten in enough milk to fill the pie to just below the crust and the mixture is poured through a hole in the crust. The pie is put back in the oven and cooked just enough to set the custard. As with many local pies, a little clotted cream may be placed under the crust before serving.

FRIED POTATOES

Fried vegetables were traditionally diced whilst cooking with a special chopper. This was a long knife with a cranked blade. Crediton seemed to have been a centre for the manufacture of such knives.

Traditional method:

Cook the potatoes in their jackets. Remove from their skins and cook in bacon fat in a pan over a medium heat. Season and, whilst cooking, chop into a fine dice. Shape into a neat round and press down with a plate. When the underside is brown, serve by turning upside down on a plate.

PARMESAN POTATOES

Recipe from Ian Hamilton of Allerford:

To serve 4 persons:
1½ lbs potatoes, peeled, washed and diced into ¾" cubes
1 oz melted butter
1½ ozs Parmesan or grano cheese, grated

Blanch and refresh potatoes. Butter an oven proof dish and add layers of potatoes, cheese, butter and seasoning. Bake uncovered for 35 mins in a hot oven. Garnish with parsley and serve. Substitute Cheddar cheese for the Parmesan and you have Cheddar Gorge potatoes!

MEDLEY

This was a kind of bubble and squeak made to use up cooked vegetables and used to accompany meat pies, hogs puddings, faggots and other meat dishes.

Old recipe:

1 lb cooked mashed potatoes
8 ozs boiled cabbage
8 ozs chopped boiled onions
2 ozs butter
Seasoning

Mix together the vegetables and seasoning and fry in the butter. Keep turning the mixture, adding more butter if needed to prevent sticking, until browned on the outside and thoroughly heated in the middle.

SWEDE, PARSNIP AND CARROT PURÉE

Recipe from Jackie Payne of West Buckland:

1 large swede
3 parsnips
4 carrots
2 ozs butter
¼ pt milk
Seasoning

Peel and dice the vegetables. Place in a pan and cover with boiling water. Bring to the boil and simmer for about 20 minutes until tender. Drain and purée, a little at a time, in a processor with the butter, milk and seasoning. Serve hot.

EXMOOR WILD MUSHROOMS IN CIDER

Recipe from Mark and Sarah-Jane Ravenscroft of Challacombe: 'They say: This is our most popular vegetarian breakfast choice. We are only a small B&B, so dont have dinner recipes, but this one could be used for dinner as an accompaniment for pork, as a starter or, in larger quantities, as a vegetarian main course served with rice and seasonal vegetables.'

To serve two people:
6 ozs local wild mushrooms
Large knob of West Country butter
3 tablespoons cider (local scrumpy is best)
2 tablespoons double Devon cream
1 tablespoon flour and butter paste
Dash of lemon juice
Black pepper
Parsley

Fry the mushrooms in the butter. Add the cider and boil to reduce. Lower the heat and add the cream. Cook for a further 5 minutes. If required, add the flour and butter paste to thicken. Add lemon juice and pepper to taste. Serve on hot toast and garnish with chopped parsley.

MUSHROOM POTS

Recipe from Brian Pearce of Martinhoe:

Ingredients for 4 persons:
1 lb field mushrooms
8 ozs bacon
1 oz butter
2 ozs farmhouse Cheddar cheese
2 ozs clotted cream
Parsley
Salt and pepper to season

Trim the rind, then chop the bacon. Fry the bacon pieces until crisp. Chop the mushrooms into large pieces. Add the butter to the pan and cook the mushrooms gently until tender. Stir in the cream until well mixed. Spoon the mixture into individual ramekin dishes and top with grated cheese. Place under a grill to melt the cheese and serve garnished with chopped parsley.

SCALLOPED POTATOES

This traditional method of cooking potatoes is supposed to have replaced shellfish at times when few were around. Potatoes are cooked and mashed with butter, milk, chopped parsley and a little cayenne pepper and mustard. The mash is put in scallop shells, cheese grated over and browned in a hot oven.

JAMS AND PRESERVES

APPLE JAM

Old recipe from Edith Nott of South Molton:

To 6 lbs apples add 4½ lbs lump sugar; put few cassia buds, cloves and stick cinnamon in muslin bag and place with apples and sugar; add ½ teacupful water and boil gently 3 hours. The rind and juice of 1 lemon, or a little lemon peel cut into small pieces may be added.

APPLE BUTTER

Fruit butters and cheeses are thicker than ordinary jam, being just the fruit pulp and sugar. As such they tend to be made when there is a glut of fruit because it takes more fruit to make the same amount of jam. They are not normally eaten straight away but left for the flavours to blend and mature. Apple butter is normally kept until Christmas, when it is served as a dessert with clotted cream and sprinkled with chopped hazelnuts. It is also served as a jam.

Old recipe:

3 lbs windfall apples
5 fluid ozs cider
1 teaspoon mixed spice
¼ lb preserving sugar to each pound of pulp

Wash and chop the apples. Simmer them with the cider in a large pan until reduced to a pulp. Sieve the pulp and weigh. Return the pulp with the appropriate amount of sugar and the spice to the preserving pan and boil gently until thickened. Pot, seal and cover in the usual way.

CIDER MINCEMEAT

Old recipe:

12 ozs chopped cooking apples, peeled and cored
12 ozs raisins
8 ozs currants
3 ozs butter
6 ozs soft brown sugar
¼ pint cider
Grated rind and juice of one lemon
4 teaspoons mixed spice

Mix all the ingredients and bring to the boil in a large saucepan. Simmer for about 1½ hours. Cool and seal in jars. This will not keep for as long as ordinary mincemeat. Keep cool and eat within a month.

EXMOOR WILD FRUIT JELLY

Recipe from Brian Pearce of Martinhoe:

A variety of wild fruits can be mixed to produce a dark, sharply flavoured jam. Whortleberries can be mixed with other fruit but are in season before most hedgerow fruits and have a subtle taste which can be drowned by mixing with other flavours, so they are best used on their own. Sloes and crab apples work well together and a good mix is sloes, elderberries and blackberries, with a few hips and haws thrown in. Because of pips and stones, most wild fruit jam must be sieved.

4 lbs\2 kgs mixed wild fruit of your choice
About 3 lbs\1½ kgs preserving sugar
Water

Remove all leaves and stalks from the fruit. Chop crab apples if used. Place in a large pan and add enough water to reach the top of the fruit without it floating. Simmer gently for about 30 minutes. Sieve well to retain juice and pulp but discard seeds and stones. Weigh the juice and pulp and add an equal amount of sugar. Return to the jam pan, bringing to the boil whilst stirring and continue boiling until setting point is reached. Pot, cover and seal in the usual manner.

MAZZARD JAM

The mazzards have a strong flavour and are usually mixed with other red fruits in season.

Old recipe:

3 lbs mazzards
3 lbs preserving sugar
½ pt raspberry juice
¾ pt redcurrant juice

Stone the mazzards and simmer gently in a preserving pan with the juices and the mazzard stones tied in a muslin bag. Remove from the heat and remove the bag of stones. Stir in the sugar until dissolved. Boil briskly whilst stirring. Skim and test for setting when necessary. Pot, cover and seal in the usual manner.

NETTLE SYRUP

Recipe from Stuart Wheaton of South Molton:

Young nettle tops
Water
Sugar

Gather the tops of young nettles, wash well and to every pound add a quart of water. Boil for an hour and strain. Add a pound of sugar to every pint of juice, boil for a further 30 minutes and allow to cool before bottling.

HUXTABLE FARM SLOE JELLY

Recipe from Jackie Payne of West Buckland: Jackie says: The best time to harvest the sloe is after the first frost in October or November, which makes their skins softer and more permeable. Sloe gin is very popular with the guns and beaters during the shooting season.

6 lbs washed and dried sloes
4 pts \ 2.5 litres water
1½ lbs sugar
Juice of two lemons
Juice of two oranges

Steve Guscott

Simmer the sloes in the water in a preserving pan for two hours. Strain through a jelly bag overnight. Reheat the liquid, adding the sugar and fruit juices, stirring continuously until the sugar has dissolved, then boil rapidly until the jelly sets when tested (approximately 15 minutes). Allow to cool slightly and pour into jars. Serve with poultry and game dishes.

RHUBARB AND FIG JAM

Recipe from Jackie Kingdon of Umberleigh:

4 lbs \ 2 kgs rhubarb
1 lb \ 500 gms dried figs
4 lbs \ 2 kgs sugar
1 oz \ 25 gms butter

Wash the fruit well and chop into small pieces. Place in a bowl with the sugar, mix well together, cover with a cloth and leave overnight. The next day, tip into a preserving pan or heavy-based saucepan, stir well and heat until the sugar is dissolved. Heat to boiling point

and continue cooking, stirring frequently to avoid burning, until setting point is reached (approximately 30-40 minutes). Add the butter towards the end of cooking to prevent scum forming. Pour into sterilised jars and seal when almost cool.

ROWAN JELLY

This has an unusual, slightly smoky flavour and is used as a condiment like redcurrant jelly. It is a traditional accompaniment to roast venison. Recipes vary as the fruits are quite light and dry and apples are often added for bulk. I add a few cloves and the juice and rind of a lemon to the mixture before cooking.

Old recipe:

6 lbs \ 3 kgs rowan berries
3 lbs \ 1½ kgs cooking apples
About 3 lbs \ 1½ kgs preserving sugar
Water

Remove all stalks from the berries and chop the apples. Put in a pan with enough water to reach the top of the fruit without it floating. Simmer gently for about an hour until the fruit is soft. Put the fruit into a fine muslin bag and hang over a pan to drip overnight. For each pint of juice add 1 lb (450 gms) sugar and return to the pan. Bring to the boil, stirring to dissolve the sugar, and continue boiling until setting point is reached. Pot, cover and seal in the usual manner.

COMBE MARTIN STRAWBERRY JAM

There is nothing local about this recipe except that it is the simple way in which Combe Martin housewives used up the main crop strawberries. Nothing but sugar is added to the fruit. The proportions are 3 lbs strawberries to 3½ lbs preserving sugar. The fruit is boiled with half of the sugar for 20 minutes. The rest of the sugar is warmed and added and the mixture boiled to setting point.

WHORTLEBERRY JAM

Bob Deville of Martinhoe, says: 'I vividly remember, just after the last war visiting Yenworthy Farm, high above the Exmoor coast, with my parents and having a superb cream tea of cut rounds smothered in home made, deep yellow clotted cream and topped with whortleberry jam. The taste of this feast stays with me now.'

The whortleberries need sharpening with something acidic. Bob uses a few tablespoons of cider vinegar and blackcurrant juice. In this old recipe the lemon can be replaced with ½ lb of rhubarb. As the season for rhubarb and whortleberries does not coincide, bottled rhubarb is used.

Old recipe:

3 lbs whortleberries
3 lbs preserving sugar
Juice of 1 lemon or ½ lb rhubarb
1 tablespoon water

Add the water to the whortleberries in a preserving pan and simmer for a few minutes until the juice runs. Remove the pan from the heat and stir in the lemon juice or rhubarb and the sugar until it is dissolved. Return to the heat and boil rapidly, stirring frequently. Skim when necessary and test for setting. Pour into sterilised pots, seal and store.

HONEY

Honey was used to sweeten food throughout most of the history of Exmoor cookery. It is thought that its use to make drinks goes well back into prehistoric times and the drinks metheglin and mead were certainly made on Exmoor for centuries. Wild honey was protected in the Royal Forest but the domestication of bees must have been introduced by the Romans. Exmoor bee skips or skeps varied in design. In the Vale of Porlock they were made of wheat straw but on the high ground where wheat did not grow well they were made from ropes of oat straw, called thumb-beans because they were made by coiling straw around the thumb, rather like the ties for corn stooks. The thumb-beans were coiled into a dome and held together by long brambles stripped of their thorns.

The larger houses had bee-boles cut into garden walls to hold the skeps – usually skep-shaped niches in south facing walls. These are common in sixteenth century gardens in the area but the most accessible example is in the eighteenth century garden of the Pack o Cards inn at Combe Martin. Normally the skeps would be put out in an orchard in the summer, or a sunny corner of a south-facing field might be enclosed for the purpose. Barbara Reed recalls the reminiscences of her father-in-law from Knighton Farm, Withypool:

> They made straw skips or hives themselves and at the end of the summer killed all the bees in the older hives and took the honey from them, leaving the new swarms. They would follow one of their swarms miles to claim it and bring it home. I expect you have heard of the old adage,
> > A swarm of bees in May is worth a load of hay,
> > A swarm of bees in June is worth a silver spoon,
> > A swarm of bees in July isnt worth a fly.
> The May swarm would make enough honey to keep themselves during the winter. The June swarm might need a little help. But the July

swarm would be useless unless you were prepared to feed them completely.

The honey was used to sweeten puddings such as apple dumplings and cakes, rhubarb and wild fruits such as whortleberries. A honey and vinegar dressing made a common salad dressing.

Today many locals produce honey on a small scale and there are larger businesses at Exmoor Honey near Timberscombe and Quince Honey Farm at South Molton. The latter, run by Paddy Wallace and his wife Jean, uses 1500 hives and ranks among the largest honey producers in the country. Paddy has built the business up since 1949. It has twenty bee colonies in its exhibition at South Molton. The hives are placed out all over the Exmoor area. They are transported by lorry to fields on the edge of heather moorland for the heather flowering season in August and September. They are taken at night, when the bees are resting in the hives. Bee keepers from all over the West Country bring their hives to Exmoor for the heather, which itself smells of honey. Production is erratic as the heather only produces nectar if the weather is warm and moist. Heather honey forms a jelly in the cells of the comb and needs a special piece of machinery called a loosener to extract it.

The number of local beekeepers has reduced by over half in the last twenty years. This is mostly due to the difficulties of controlling an introduced pest – the varroa mite. Like many such pests, it is thriving as a result of the changing climate with milder winters. There are new methods of biological control but both domestic and wild bee colonies are still suffering.

BAKED PUDDINGS

APPLE DUMPLINGS

This is a classic Devonshire dish, not particularly confined to Exmoor. People from the Somerset side of the moor used to call the folk on the Devon side of the moor 'Devon dumplings' in a similar way to which one might refer to the French as 'frogs', referring to what they ate.

One dumpling should be a satisfying pudding, but there are stories of Exmoor farmers consuming prodigious amounts. A story from the 1940s surrounds two young farm workers, Tom Marley and Anthony Huxtable, who became huntsman with the Devon and Somerset Staghounds. One evening after a hard days work at a farm belonging to two sisters they consumed a huge main course and were left to help themselves to apple dumplings boiling in a cauldron over the kitchen fire. When one of the sisters returned she found one left out of 33 dumplings. Before she could take it for herself the two lads divided it and consumed it. Another story concerns Withypool farm worker Dick Turpin. He was inordinately fond of apple dumplings and always helped himself to the largest. One day the maid decided to cure him of this by wrapping a turnip in dough and baking it with the apples. Dick duly took the baked turnip and was the butt of much laughter.

There are many variations on the dumpling recipe, with much depending on the type of pastry covering. Suet pastries or pudding mixes were usually boiled and other coverings such as puff or short crust pastry, baked. Mrs Beeton and Elizabeth Acton recommended filling the cored apples with marmalade and presenting the dumplings in specially knitted cotton squares.

Old recipe for boiled apple dumplings:

6 apples
3 ozs moist brown sugar
6 cloves
Suet crust pastry made using:
12 ozs flour
5-6 ozs suet
½ teaspoon salt
1½ teaspoons baking powder
Cold water to mix

Peel and core the apples. Mix the pastry and divide into six. Roll out each portion into a circle. Put an apple in the centre of each pastry and fill the hole left by the core with sugar and a clove. Pull the pastry up over the apple, damp the edges and crimp firmly together. Tie each apple in a floured pudding cloth and simmer for about 40-50 minutes.

Old recipe for baked apple dumplings:

4 cooking apples
Demerara sugar, to taste
½ teaspoon cinnamon
Water

Scone dough made with:
½ lb plain flour
1 oz butter
1 oz sugar
½ teaspoon bicarbonate of soda
1 teaspoon cream of tartar
¼ pt milk
Pinch of salt

First make the scone dough by rubbing the butter into the flour and mixing with the sugar, cream of tartar, bicarbonate of soda and salt. Mix with the milk to make a moderately soft dough. Divide into four and roll each piece out into a round on a floured board. Prepare the apples by peeling and coring. Put one apple on each round of dough and filled the hole where the core was with demerara sugar and a little cinnamon. Sprinkle a little water over the apple and edges of the dough. Close up the dough around the apples, pressing firmly to seal the join. Turn the dumplings over and place them on a greased baking tray. Bake at 425°F\220°C\ Gas Mark 7 for 10 minutes, then cover with greased paper and cook for about another 15 minutes until the apples are tender. This can be ascertained by testing them with a skewer.

APPLE DAPPY

Old recipe from Bob Deville of Martinhoe:

10 ozs self raising flour
4 ozs lard or margarine
5 crisp eating apples
2 tablespoons golden syrup
2 ozs butter
¼ pt water
About 1 cupful milk
Sugar

Brian Pearce

Rub the lard or margarine into the flour. Add the milk and mix until the mixture leaves the sides of the bowl. Roll out into a square about ¼ inch thick. Peel, core and dice the apples and spread over the pastry. Sprinkle a few teaspoons of sugar over the apple to taste and roll up into a sausage shape. Cut up like a Swiss roll into inch thick slices and lay them flat side by side on a greased dish which will just take them all. Press down lightly so that the spaces are filled. In a saucepan warm the syrup, water and butter and stir until combined. Pour over the Swiss rolls. It will look rather watery at this stage. Bake at 350°F\180°C\Gas Mark 4 for about 40 minutes until the top is brown and the liquid has all disappeared. Serve hot with a sprinkle of sugar and clotted cream.

APPLE OMELET

Old recipe:

3 cooking apples
½ oz butter
2 tablespoons caster sugar
2 tablespoons crushed macaroons
2 eggs
Cinnamon

Peel, core and cook the apples in a pan with sugar and a little water until a pulp. Add the butter and mix well with cinnamon, macaroons and egg yolks. Whisk the egg whites until stiff and fold into the mixture. Pour the mixture into a buttered ovenproof dish. Dredge with caster sugar and bake in a moderate oven for 20 minutes until brown.

AVILLE APPLE IN AND OUT

This is an adaptation of an old recipe, so named because the pudding mixture works its way between the apples whilst cooking. Some people used to add elderflowers or elderflower cordial to the apples.

Recipe from Beryl Priddle of Minehead:

1 lb cooking apples, peeled, cored and roughly chopped
8 ozs self raising flour
6 ozs sugar
6 ozs suet (beef or vegetarian)
Milk to mix
Pinch salt

Steve Guscott

Put chopped apple into a mixing bowl. Add other dry ingredients, mix well, then add enough milk for a stiff consistency. Stir well again. Put into well greased shallow dish. Bake at 400°F\200°C\Gas Mark 6 for approximately 45 minutes. Cut into squares and serve with cream or custard.

APPLE PUDDING

Old recipe from Kathryn Brown of Wootton Courtenay:

Put 1 tablespoon of butter in an ovenproof dish and put the dish in an oven at for the butter to melt. In a bowl beat 2 eggs with 4 ozs caster sugar. Add 2 ozs of white breadcrumbs. Peel and core ¾ lb of cooking apples and grate into the egg and breadcrumb mixture. Add 3 teaspoons of lemon juice and grated rind of a lemon. Take the dish from the oven, swill around the butter and pour it into the apple mixture. Stir well and return mixture to dish. Dust with nutmeg. Bake at 350°F\180°C\Gas Mark 4 for 40-45 mins. Serve at once.

EXMOOR SURPRISE PUDDING

This is a modern version of the former apple pudding recipe from Suzanne Powell of Lynton:

Ingredients for 6 persons:
4 ozs\100 gms plain flour
1½ teaspoons baking powder
4 ozs\100 gms white breadcrumbs
3 ozs\75 gms caster sugar
3 ozs\75 gms shredded suet
1 large cooking apple
1 egg
6-8 tablespoons milk
2 tablespoons Exmoor honey
Large pinch of salt

Thoroughly butter a 2 pint pudding basin and pour in the honey. Mix together the flour, salt and baking powder and add the breadcrumbs, sugar and suet. Add the grated apple, the beaten egg and enough milk to achieve a soft consistency. Cover with greaseproof paper, then a pudding cloth and tie tightly. Stand basin in a saucepan with enough water to come half way up the side, cover and steam for 2 hours.

APPLE AND ALMOND PUFF

Recipe from Penny Webber of Minehead:

1 pkt frozen puff pastry

For the filling:
8 ozs cooked sliced apple
4 ozs ground almonds
2 egg yolks
3 ozs sugar
2 tablespoons cider or brandy - optional
2 tablespoons cream or full milk
A little beaten egg

Mix together all filling ingredients except apple. Roll out half the pastry to line a 7" flan tin or flat plate. Spread on filling mix and top with cooked apple. Cover with the remaining pastry and pinch edges to make a sealed flower shape. Use beaten egg to seal and glaze. Bake at 450°F\230°C\ Gas Mark 8 until brown and golden. Sprinkle with icing sugar and serve with clotted cream.

BISHNYM FARMHOUSE PUDDING

Recipe from Simon Robinson of South Molton:

17 fluid ozs\750 mls vanilla ice cream
14 ozs\400 gms blackberries
6 ozs\150 gms caster sugar
3 egg whites
Sponge flan case

Place the flan case on a heatproof serving dish. Place the ice cream on top and spoon the blackberries over it. Whisk the eggs whites and gradually add the sugar until stiff peaks are formed. Cover the ice cream and sponge base with the mixture and bake in a hot oven, 425°F\220°C\Gas Mark 7 for 5 minutes and serve immediately.

FRUIT DESSERTS

PEARS IN WINE

This was a dish sold from market stalls at Barnstaple Fair, which is held in September. Cider can be substituted for the wine.
Old recipe:

2 lbs pears
½ lb sugar
½ pt red wine
Blanched almond slivers
cloves or cinnamon stick

Steve Guscott

Peel the pears carefully and insert the almond slivers around them. Poach them gently in a syrup made from

the wine, sugar and spice. When the pears are cooked but still firm, arrange them upright in a dish and serve warm or cold with clotted cream.

PLUM JELLY

Old recipe from Mrs Ball of Ilfracombe:

Stew 2 lbs red plums with sugar to taste and see that there is nearly 1 quart pulp etc; stir in 1 oz gelatine powder, taking care that there is sufficient to dissolve it; crack stones and add kernels to jelly; pour into wet mould, turn out when cold and serve.

FRUMENTY OR PLUM PORRIDGE

This dish developed as a simple porridge in early medieval times, made into a broth with meat bones. It was later sweetened with honey and then fruit and wine were added for special occasions. A medieval verse said that it was coloured with saffron and sweetened with sugar candy for the wealthy and poorer people sweetened it with black sugar. The fruit included prunes, which gave rise to the term plum pudding. Locally it was used as an accompaniment for venison. Eventually meat disappeared, the fruit became the dominant ingredient and the frumenty turned into Christmas pudding, made popular by Prince Albert in the nineteenth century. It was also associated with Lent and Mothering Sunday in particular. The older form of frumenty, which was once widespread, remained in Somerset. It was a traditional harvest home dish in most parts of the country but locally it was a cereal dish rather like a custard pudding.

Traditional method:

Add to a simmering beef broth dried fruit, spices and a fruit liqueur with a thickener of breadcrumbs or semolina.

Old recipe:

10 ozs wheat
1½ pts water
2 pts milk
4 ozs dried fruit: currants, raisins, sultanas or prunes
2 egg yolks
Grated rind of 1 lemon
Sugar and mixed spice to taste

The wheat used for this recipe is pearled wheat or fresh wheat with the husks removed. In some parts of Somerset housewives would take wheat gleaned fom the field to the local blacksmith to burn the husks off. Barley can be used as a substitute. The wheat is washed and covered with the water in an earthenware jar. It is stood in a warm place for at least a day to cree:

the top of a Rayburn is ideal. The wheat will absorb the water and make a gelatinous gruel called creed wheat. Boil the creed wheat in the milk and when it begins to thicken add the sugar, spice, fruit and lemon rind. Finally stir in the egg yolks to thicken the mixture further. A little flour mixed with the milk can also be used as a thickener. Without the fruit it can be used as a breakfast porridge and with the fruit as a muesli or dessert.

WHORTLEBERRY MERINGUE

Recipe from Rosemary Pile of Countisbury:

Ingredients for 6 persons:
12 ozs\350 gms frozen whortleberries
2 ozs\50 gms butter
2 ozs\50 gms cornflour
4 ozs\100 gms caster sugar
2 large eggs
¾ pt\450 mls milk
Pinch of salt

Defrost whortleberries. Melt butter in saucepan large enough to hold all ingredients, add cornflour and heat until bubbling. Add milk, stir well until boiling then simmer for 3 minutes. Remove from heat, add salt, fruit and half the sugar and stir well. Beat in the egg yolks and pour the mixture into a buttered, ovenproof dish. Whisk the whites with the remaining sugar until stiff, pile in the centre and dust with sugar. Cook for 30 minutes at 300°F\150°C\Gas Mark 2 until meringue is lightly brown. Serve hot with Devonshire cream.

WHORTLEBERRY WONDER

Recipe from Jackie Kingdon of Umberleigh:

Ingredients for 6 persons:
5 ozs\125 gms plain flour
2 teaspoons baking powder
5 ozs\125 gms sugar
2 ozs\50 gms butter
2 fluid ozs\50 mls milk
1 lb\450 gms whortleberries
1 tablespoon lemon juice
½ pt\300 mls water
Pinch of salt

Place the whortleberries, 4 ozs of the sugar, lemon juice and water in a saucepan and boil, stirring constantly for 3 minutes. Sift together the flour, baking powder and salt, add the rest of the sugar and the butter cut into small pieces. Tilt the bowl and chop the butter again with a sharp knife, without handling it. Add the milk and mix to a soft dough, roll gently into half inch thick rounds and drop onto the boiling fruit. Cover and simmer for 10 minutes. Do not remove lid, or the

dough will not rise. Serve, as hot as possible, with clotted cream, custard or both.

RICE FLUMMERY

Old recipe from Mrs King of Ilfracombe:

Boil 3 or 4 cherry laurel leaves, a bit of cinnamon, and a little lemon juice in 1 pint milk, and sugar to your taste; take out leaves and cinnamon, and pour in 6 ozs rice flour mixed with milk smooth, but not thin, and keep constantly stirred until very thick, pour into well scalded mould and serve with wine sauce (½ pint milk, well sweetened, cream and wine to taste), and cream round.

RASPBERRY TRIFLE

This is more like a summer pudding than a trifle.

Old recipe from Mrs Houlford of Ilfracombe:

Put into a saucepan 1 quart raspberries, ½ lb sugar, and ½ pint water, and allow to stew for 5 minutes; have ready a buttered basin lined with slices of bread or sponge cake; pour in some raspberries while hot, then a layer of thin bread or sponge cake, then another layer of raspberries, and so on till basin is full, finishing with bread or sponge cake; let it remain till next day and turn out on dish.

SUMMER PUDDING

This originated in the eighteenth century, when it was known as 'hydropathic' pudding. It was designed for the sick and convalescing as a lighter alternative to the rich pastry desserts fashionable at the time.

Steve Guscott

This is not a recipe confined to Exmoor but I like to give it an Exmoor flavour with a preponderance of whortleberries and clotted cream. I use frozen whortleberries to add to summer fruit in season. Keep the proportion of strong-flavoured fruits such as blackcurrants quite small.

2 lbs mixed soft fruit as available
e.g. whortleberries, raspberries,
redcurrants, blackcurrants,
mazzards (stoned), blackberries,
a few strawberries
4-6 ozs caster sugar
juice and finely grated rind of 1 lemon
small white bread loaf

Wash the fruit and remove all stalks and stones. Heat gently with the sugar, lemon juice and rind and stir occasionally until the fruit is tender and the juices run. This can be done in a heavy saucepan but I use a microwave on medium power for a few minutes, taking the fruit out for a stir and returning it to the oven. I like to stir in a little port to the fruit after cooking. White bread is essential for this pudding. Slice the bread thinly to about ¼ inch and cut off the crusts. Use the slices to line a 1 pint plus pudding basin. I cut around the top and bottom of the basin to make the corresponding pieces of bread and cut wedge-shaped pieces for the sides. Make sure that there are no gaps: cut pieces to shape to fill any spaces. Half fill the lined basin with the fruit, add a layer of bread and fill just short of the top, reserving any surplus juice. Put a lid of bread on the top. Cover with a saucer which just fits the size of the basin and weight it down. Then chill in the fridge for a few hours.

The pudding should be carefully turned onto a dish which will hold the juice when it is cut. Use the remaining juice to colour any patches of bread which remain white. Serve with clotted cream.

TARTS

Tarts were usually eaten cold as the bake in a bread oven would be weekly. It was usual to make tarts with a top crust only, but serve them with the crust underneath the filling and with cream on top. Again, it was usual to serve them cold as the cream would melt on hot tarts.

DULVERTON FRUIT TART

Old recipe from Mrs P. Thrift:

For the pastry:
6 ozs\150 gms plain flour
2 ozs\50 gms cooking margarine

1 oz\25 gms lard
1 oz\25 gms caster sugar
1 egg yolk
Pinch salt
Cold water to mix

For the filling:
2 dessert apples
2 ozs\50 gms raisins
2 ozs\50 gms sultanas
1 oz\25 gms glacé cherries, chopped
1 oz\25 gms mixed peel
1 teaspoon grated lemon rind
1 tablespoon soft brown sugar
3-4 drops rum essence
2 ozs\50 gms cooking margarine
2 ozs\50 gms caster sugar
2 eggs
2 ozs\50 gms ground almonds
A few flaked almonds

Grease an 8 inch\ 20 cm flan ring and stand on a greased baking tray. Make up the pastry in the usual way and use it to line the tin. Peel, core and slice one of the apples and spread the slices over the pastry. Peel, core and grate the other apple and mix with the dried fruit, peel, rind, essence and brown sugar. Stir well together and spread on top of the apple slices. Cream the margarine and caster sugar together until light and fluffy. Gradually add the eggs, beating well after each addition. Stir in the the ground almonds and spread the mixture on top of the fruit. Bake in a moderately hot oven at 375°F\190°C\Gas Mark 5 for 15 minutes, then reduce to 350°F\180°C\Gas Mark 4 for a further 20 minutes.

SPICED APPLE FLAN

Recipe from Julia Brown of Winsford:

Ingredients for 6 persons:
1 lb\450 gms peeled cooking apples
4 ozs\100 gms moist brown sugar
3 tablespoons cider
1 teaspoon mixed spice
4 ozs\100 gms sultanas

For the pastry:
8 ozs\225 gms flour
2 ozs\50 gms lard
2 ozs\50 gms butter

Make up the shortcrust pastry, adding enough water to make a paste, and line a 9 inch flan tin with half of it. Cook the apples, brown sugar, cider, sultanas and spice together until the apples are slightly softened. Leave to cool slightly, then place in pastry case. Cover with rest of pastry, sprinkle with caster sugar and bake in a moderate oven for 15-20 minutes.

HUXTABLE FARM ELDERFLOWER, GOOSEBERRY AND HAZELNUT TART

Recipe from Jackie Payne of West Buckland: Jackie says: 'A harvest from the farm. The hazelnuts have been stored since Autumn waiting for the end of May and beginning of June, when the gooseberries in the large fruit garden mature and the elderflowers blossom.'

4 ozs\100 gms sugar
4 heads elderflowers
2 ozs\50 gms soft butter or margarine
2 tablespoons plain flour
2 ozs\50 gms ground hazelnuts
1 large egg
8 ozs\225 gms gooseberries
*Shortcrust pastry lined and partly cooked
in an 8 inch dish*

Steve Guscott

Process the sugar and elderflowers in a processor. Remove about a third of the mixture and save for the topping. Add the butter, flour, hazelnuts and egg to the remaining mixture and process until creamy. Line the partly cooked pastry case with the gooseberries and spread the elderflower creamy mixture over the top. Sprinkle the top with the sugar and elderflower mix reserved earlier (this will give the tart a crunchy texture when cooked). Bake for approximately 20 minutes at 350°F\180°C\Gas Mark 4.

SPICED PEAR PIE

Pears were one of the first fruits to be cultivated in England and commonly grown in the West Country, where some have become naturalised. Pear pie was mentioned from Elizabethan times onwards

Old recipe:

For the pastry:
6 ozs plain flour
2 ozs butter
1 oz lard
Cold water to mix

For the filling:
2 lbs cooking pears
2 ozs sultanas
1½ ozs granulated sugar
1½ ozs soft brown sugar
1½ ozs butter
1 tablespoon plain flour
1 teaspoon ground mixed spice
Grated rind of ½ lemon and 1 tablespoon of juice
Grated rind and juice of an orange

Mix and roll the pastry, using half to line an 8 shallow pie dish. Mix together the sugars, flour and spices and scatter a little over the pastry lining. Mix the grated rinds with the rest. Peel, core and slice the pears and arrange the slices over the pastry. Sprinkle with the sugar and spice mixture, fruit juices and melted butter. Use the remaining pastry to make a lid for the pie, crimping the edges together with the base layer. Sprinkle the lid with sugar. Bake at 400°F\200°C\Gas Mark 6 for 20 minutes, then lower heat to 375°F\190°C\ Gas Mark 5 for 25 minutes. Serve hot or cold with clotted cream.

RHUBARB AND STRAWBERRY TART

Recipe from Jackie Payne of West Buckland:

For the pastry:
6 ozs plain flour
4 ozs butter
1 oz sugar
1 egg
½ pt custard

Process together, roll and use to line a pastry cake dish. Bake blind (with clay beans on top to stop the pastry rising) for 20 minutes at 375°F\190°C\Gas Mark 5. Line the bottom of the tart with the custard.

8 ozs rhubarb
2 tablespoons chopped stem ginger
10 ozs sugar
Strawberries

Heat together gently the rhubarb, ginger and sugar in a pan for about 15 minutes until a puree. Pour the puree over the custard in the tart. Arranged sliced strawberries on top and sprinkle with sugar. Continue cooking the tart in the same oven for 15 minutes

WHORTLEBERRY TART

Recipe from Heather Burnett-Wells of Withypool:

For a sweet short-crust pastry:
1 lb plain flour
4 ozs butter
4 ozs lard
4 ozs caster sugar
3 fluid ozs milk

For the filling:
14 ozs whortleberries
4 ozs sugar
4 ozs melted jam or jelly

Steve Guscott

Work the fats in with the flour until the mixture resembles fine breadcrumbs. Mix in the sugar and sprinkle the milk over the mixture. Work the mixture until smooth but do not over work. Allow the dough to rest at least 30 minutes before rolling out to fit a flan dish. Bake blind for 20 minutes at 375°F\190°C\ Gas Mark 5. Fill with the fruit, sprinkle over the sugar and pour the melted jam or jelly over the mixture. Return to the oven for 10-20 minutes until firm and set. Serve warm or cold with clotted cream.

WHORTLEBERRY AND RASPBERRY TART

Recipe from Mrs M Trelford of Dulverton:

1 pint\450 gms whortleberries
½ pt\225 gms raspberries
5 ozs \125 gms caster sugar
6 ozs\150 gms self raising flour
3 ozs\75 gms lard or margarine
Pinch of salt, water

Place the fruit and sugar in a pie dish (not too shallow). Make the pastry with the fat, flour, salt and water and cover the dish, sealing the edges well. Brush with a little beaten egg and bake in a moderate oven for at least half an hour. Sprinkle with sugar and serve with clotted cream.

WHORTLEBERRY AND REDCURRANT PIE

Recipe from Doreen Orton of Milverton:

Ingredients for 6 persons:
For the pastry:
8 ozs\225 gms flour
2 ozs\50 gms sugar
5 ozs\125 gms butter or margarine
1 egg
Pinch of salt

For the filling:
12 ozs\350 gms whortleberries
4 ozs\100 gms redcurrants
8 ozs\225 gms sugar
2½ tablespoons minute tapioca
1 tablespoon currant or apple juice
Pinch of salt

Line a 7 or 8 inch flan ring with pastry and chill in refrigerator. Mix fruit together. Combine sugar, salt and tapioca, place a quarter on the pastry base, mix the rest with the fruit and pour on top. Add fruit juice, cover top with lattice pastry strips and bake in an oven pre-heated to 425°F\220°C\Gas Mark 7 for 10 minutes. Lower heat to 350°F\180°C\Gas Mark 4 and cook for a further 35-40 minutes. Serve warm or cold with double or clotted cream.

WEST COUNTRY TARTS

'My landlady brought me one of the West Country tarts, and this was the first I met with, though I asked for them in many places in Somerset and Devonshire; it is an apple pie with the custard all on top, its the most acceptable entertainment that could be made me; they scald the cream and milk in most parts of those counties and so its a sort of clouted cream as we call it with a little sugar and so put on the top of the apple pie' wrote Celia Fiennes in her journal of her tour of Devon and Cornwall in 1698.

Apple pie has been popular since medieval times and has been part of both everyday and festive fare. They were particularly popular at apple harvest time. For feasts, dried fruits and spices were added to the apples. In Tudor times they added candied orange peel, cloves, cinnamon, rose water, dates and other dried fruit. In Georgian times, fresh lemon peel and lemon juice and often sliced quince were added. Later, the dried fruit was often soaked in rum. They were usually baked as pies but the more elaborate versions were sometimes baked as open tarts.

A traditional Westcountry apple tart was made with sweet or rich shortcrust pastry. Sliced apples and currants were arranged in layers on the pastry and sprinkled with brown sugar and cinnamon or mixed spice. It was then dotted with butter and baked in a moderate oven for about 45 minutes. It can be baked with a custard on top. An old recipe for such is as follows:

1 pt milk
2 ozs sugar
2 eggs
1 tablespoonful arrowroot, cornflour or potato flour

Beat together the eggs, sugar and starch. Pour on hot milk, stirring all the time. Put the mixture in a pan and heat gently, stirring all the time until it thickens. Pour on top of the apples in the pastry case and bake in a moderate oven.

SWEETS

FUDGE

Old recipe:

1 lb granulated sugar
3 ozs clotted cream
4 fluid ozs milk
Few drops vanilla essence

Gently heat the sugar in the milk in a heavy pan, stirring to dissolve the sugar completely. Stir in the cream and bring to the boil, with only an occasional stir to prevent sticking. Boil to the stage when a drop of the mixture cooled in cold water will roll into a soft ball. Remove from the heat immediately and beat the mixture with the vanilla essence until it becomes thick and creamy and sugar grains begin to form. Add any flavourings whilst beating. Pour the mixture into a buttered tin and mark into squares before completely set.

TOFFEE

In *Within Living Memory* by Margaret Bate an old lady called Doris recalls her childhood in North Molton:

'My grandmother used to make daffy (toffee), Granny Goviers daffy. I used to have it in a basket, all wrapped in greaseproof paper, and go around selling it so much a stick while the sheep fairs were here. I can see that oblong basket now with a bow of ribbon on each side.'

Old recipe from Mrs Philpot of Ilfracombe:

1lb sugar, 2 ozs butter, 1 tablespoonful vinegar and a small cupful water. Put all into a saucepan, boil until brittle (to test put a spoonful into cold water), but do not stir, and turn out into buttered tins.

HAZELNUT TOFFEE

Old recipe:

1 lb granulated sugar
1 oz butter
5 fluid ozs water
4 ozs chopped hazelnuts
1\8 oz cream of tartar

Put the sugar and water in a heavy pan and heat gently, stirring all the time until the sugar is completely dissolved. Stir in the other ingredients and bring to the boil but do not stir any more. Keep boiling the mixture, testing every so often by dropping a little into cold water. When the drop will roll into a firm, but not brittle, ball, pour the mixture into a greased tin. Mark into squares with a knife before the toffee sets hard.

EXMOOR HONEY TRUFFLES

Recipe from Elizabeth Jessup of Brendon Hill:

9 ozs\225 gms icing sugar
5 ozs\125 gms cooking chocolate
3 ozs\75 gms butter or margarine
1 oz\25 gms Somerset honey
Drinking chocolate powder

Melt the chocolate and butter in a bowl placed over a pan of hot water, add honey and stir until dissolved. Sieve the icing sugar into a bowl and stir in the chocolate mixture and mix well. Leave to cool slightly, then roll into 1 inch diameter balls and toss in chocolate powder.

SLOE LIQUEUR CHOCOLATE

After making sloe gin the sloes are usually discarded. They are somewhat shrivelled but contain gin and sugar and are delicious. They are a little fiddly to stone. You can try an olive stoner but some of the pulp can be removed simply, if messily, by squeezing the sloes between your fingers.

Recipe from Bob Deville of Martinhoe:

Pulp from making one bottle of sloe gin, including split almonds if used in making the gin
8 ozs good plain chocolate

Melt the chocolate in a double boiler very gently. You can use a saucepan if you apply heat slowly. When the chocolate is just melted, add the pulp and stir gently until mixed. You can add a couple of tablespoons of double cream if you like milk chocolate. Pour into a small tray and refrigerate until set. Cut into chunks and it is ready for a Christmas Eve adult treat!

⚜ The Dairy ⚜

The dairy was a cool room, usually with windows kept open for draught and netted against flies and well fitting good doors to keep out domestic animals, rats and mice. It was usually at the back of the house and away from the kitchen for coolness but not far from the scullery with the copper boiler. The large wooden pails and earthenware utensils had to be kept scrupulously clean and much hot water was needed. The eighteenth century inventory of Thomas Estcott of Withycombe shows that he had a boiler in his dairy, with fire complete with firedogs, brandises, 20 brass pans, kettles, earthen pans and earthen dishes. Some dairies had racks for cheeses but larger houses usually had their separate cheese chambers.

Cattle produce more milk than is needed by the calves, unless they have twins, and hand milking stimulates the cows to produce more milk. The surplus milk was usually turned to butter, cream and cheese. Something had to be made daily with the milk if it was not to go off. There was too much milk for it all to be sold locally and no refrigerated transport to take it further afield.

Traditionally calves would be born in April and milking would continue until November. The milking, which takes place twice daily, was usually women's work and the farmers wife generally had the assistance of a dairymaid. The women also made the cream, butter and cheese, which were an important source of cash income.

CATTLE

The standard Exmoor cattle for many years were the Red Devons, originally bred by the Quartly family of Great Champson, Molland in the late eighteenth century. They became popular in the following century. Elihu Burritt, an American walking from London to Lands End in 1864, stopped to visit one of the Quartlys:

> He showed me a herd of cows, all of the purest Devon blood. He winters from seventy to eighty head, including about twenty milking cows. He sells calves from six to eight months old at from thirty to seventy guineas, averaging £40 each. The cows produce on average five pounds of butter a week in the pasture season.

At the time butter was fetching 8d to 10d per pound according to quality. C.S. Orwin mentioned the Devon

cattle in his account of the Exmoor part of the Fortescue Estate at the time of the publication of his book *The Reclamation of Exmoor Forest* in 1929:

> There are sundry sales of butter, cream and eggs in the summer, and of rabbits in the winter – in fact, these items are said to produce enough to pay for the housekeeping – but the main dependence of the farmer is on the autumn sales of store stock, both sheep and cattle. As regards cattle, few but the Devons are seen. The cows are all spring-calvers. Calves are hand-reared, on skimmed milk and meal, the cream being scalded or made into butter.

Previous types were much smaller black cattle descended from ancient Celtic breeds. These black cattle were half wild and survived on the moors better than many breeds succeeding them but were extremely small and had much bone compared to meat. The Red Devons of North Devon were smaller than their South Devon counterparts and produced less milk. Their use for milk production died out in the 1950s. They were used mainly for breeding and calves were sold for fattening by lowland farmers, particularly on the Somerset Levels. Some were crossed with hardier breeds to make them more suitable for the moors. Generally only the wealthier farmers were concerned with improving breeds. The coming of the railways enabled small cattle markets such as at Blackmoor Gate to be set up for stock to be sold up country. A few cattle were kept indoors as, when cash was needed, there was always a ready market for a fattened calf.

MILK

There have never been many dairy farmers on Exmoor but there is much dairying in surrounding, lower lying areas and most Exmoor farmers kept a house cow for their own needs. On the Exmoor part of the Fortescue Estate it was a customary entitlement for shepherds to keep two cows and other workers to keep one. They were allowed grazing on Duredon and it was said that the cows found their own way home for milking each evening. The custom died out around the Second World War. With a tendency towards smaller families, less milk was needed and house cows later were often shared between several families.

It is only comparatively recently, with refrigeration and pasteurisation, that farmers have been able to sell large quantities of milk. They often had enough milk to sell surplus to neighbours, as with cream and butter, which was sold by the farmers wife, often at the local pannier market.

In the book *Within Living Memory* Lady Stucley recalls her childhood days at Court House, North Molton:

> Our herdsman was assisted by his two daughters and his wife who made the butter and scalded the cream in the old fashioned scalder in the dairy. I spent most of my spare time with them learning to milk the Guernsey cows, feed the calves and poultry and churn the butter. The farm was one of my favourite places and I used to sneak up there at 7 am, when I knew that the milking would be in full swing and I could milk a cow or two before breakfast.

It is a long time since Devon cows were used for milking in the Exmoor area. In recent times it has been the Channel Islands cattle which have supplied the rich milk for cream and butter production. This does not happen now on a small scale and it is no longer possible to buy Exmoor cream. Bert Verney gives one explanation in his *Reflections*. Speaking of the late 1970s, he says:

Farming was changing once again. The milk, which had for years been collected in churns, would now be collected by bulk tankers. This meant that the milk on the farm had to be stored in a tank, cooled and sucked into tankers. Very nice and easy, with no more heaving and lifting of ten gallon churns. But to John, the death knell of his Guernsey herd as the milk was mixed with Friesian milk and could not be kept separate. He would only get the Friesian price and lose his 14p per gallon premium. Although he struggled on for about three years the profit margin, without premium, was not high enough to make it worthwhile. The herd would have to be sold and many years of my work and all John's, to date, would now have to be cast aside.

Milk quotas do not seem to have made a great difference to overall milk production in the area but may have had an effect on the number of businesses. Again, however, small scale production for cream has been affected by legislation. Jackie Payne, of Huxtable Farm, West Buckland, was trying to provide traditional dairy produce for her guests in the 1980s:

> Three Jersey cows produced rich creamy milk, served fresh on the breakfast table, whilst the

Rhoda Blackmore, local milk supplier, with churns at Oldway's End, c1930

Exmoor Photographic Archive

remainder was made into clotted cream so that there was always a large bowl of clotted cream on the sweet table in the evening. Pigs were kept and fattened on the skimmed milk, the by-product of the clotted cream production. Unfortunately, due to the Milk Licensing Law of 1987, we had to cease putting our jug of milk and clotted cream on the dining table unless we obtained a licence, which was financially not feasible, so the Jersey cows were sold and subsequently the pigs, a sad end to an era!

WHITE FOAM SOUP

This is a common dish throughout the dairying parts of the West Country, with local variations.

Old recipe:

1½ pts milk
1½ ozs butter
1½ ozs flour
2½ ozs grated cheese
2 eggs
1 small onion
1 tablespoonful chopped parsley
Seasoning

Melt the butter in a pan; add the flour and heat until the mixture leaves the sides of the pan. Gradually add the milk, add the onion and bring to the boil. Separate the yolks and whites of the eggs. Add the yolks and cheese to the soup when it has cooled and the onion has been removed. Return to the fire, but do not allow to boil. Beat the egg whites very stiffly. Put the soup in a tureen and scatter with chopped parsley and lumps of the egg white.

BEASTINGS

Now usually know as colostrum, beastings are the milk from the first milkings of a cow after calving. The milk is yellow and thick as cream and any surplus not needed by the calf was used for puddings. The beastings were usually thinned down with about four times the amount of ordinary milk and a little water and either sweetened and flavoured or just left in a warm place to set. The unflavoured beastings formed curds and whey and the curds were strained from the whey to make cheesecakes.

BISKEY PIE

This is a form of junket which does not require rennet for setting. The beastings were usually taken from the third milking of a cow after the birth or her calf (about 36 hours). To these were added sugar and a few raisins and left in a low oven to set.

JUNKET

The West Country is renowned for junket making. The word was originally applied to the rush mat on which cream cheeses were served but in medieval times it became synonymous with a dish of sweetened curds and scalded cream. Although a simple, everyday dish, it was also used on special occasions and the name became associated with feasts. At such times it was made with the top of the milk. Junket is best made with fresh, creamy milk from Devon or Channel Island cows. Traditionally it was made by taking milk still warm from the cow and setting it in bowls on the slate shelves of the dairy. It is set with rennet, an enzyme taken from the lining of calves stomachs. Double the quantity of rennet is needed for pasteurised milk. In more recent times it has been sweetened with sugar and flavoured with rosewater, rum or brandy. Modern recipes suggest flavouring with fruit syrup, coffee or cocoa. Other variations include adding a beaten egg with the rennet or putting crushed biscuits in the base of the serving dish before the junket mix is poured in.

Walter Isaac in *The Way 'Twas* remembers his parents entertaining the local preacher to Sunday lunch:

> This meant a fire in the front room, best behaviour and, in summer time, always a large bowl of junket with nutmeg and lashings of cream for afters.

JUNKET

Old recipe:

1 pt fresh milk
1 tablespoon sugar
1 teaspoon rennet

Warm the milk to blood heat, remove from heat and stir in sugar until dissolved. Stir in rennet and pour into the dishes from which it will be eaten. Leave in a cool place to set – a pantry or similar. When set (in a few hours), dust with nutmeg and serve with single cream.

Steve Guscott

DEVON JUNKET

Cornish junket was similar but was flavoured with lemon and omitted the dusting of spice. To make an Exmoor junket, this can be decorated with whortleberries or slices of local strawberries.

Old recipe:

2 pts milk
5 fl ozs brandy
2 ozs caster sugar
1 tablespoonful rennet
Clotted cream, grated nutmeg or cinnamon,
caster sugar or jam for decoration

Warm the milk with the brandy and sugar to blood heat. Add the rennet, doubling the quantity if pasteurised milk is used. Pour into serving dishes and leave to set at room temperature. Chill when set and before serving top with clotted cream, a dusting of spice and a dusting of sugar or dollop of jam.

BUTTER

Butter is made from cream. The cream can be separated from the milk by churning but on Exmoor it was usually separated by the scalding process used in the making of clotted cream. This did not give it a very smooth consistency and, combined with the smoky taste from the fire, this meant that it was not generally marketable, although prized by locals who had acquired the taste. Some local market towns had their butter crosses where such commodities were sold before the days of indoor markets. Most locals preferred their clotted cream and rough butter to any small profit made from selling churned butter further afield. Churns were a comparatively recent introduction to the area, coming largely in the nineteenth century, when transport improvements allowed for the sale of butter in other parts of the country. Even so, much butter was spoiled by not working it enough to remove the air and remaining

Butter churn at Allerford Rural Life Museum

buttermilk which caused it to go off. Butter making classes for women became common in local villages.

Small quantities of butter for home consumption were simply made by beating clotted cream in a large bowl. On the moor farmers did not usually produce enough milk to make butter each day and probably the production of clotted cream originated as a way of storing cream to produce enough butter for sale. The scalding process was equivalent to todays pasteurisation. The butter was usually heavily salted, more so in previous centuries when travel took longer. Diaries of the Huxtable family at Challacombe show how the daughters had to carry the butter by pony and trap to Barnstaple pannier market in the 1920s. They had to make at least 30 shillings from the butter to pay the farmworkers' wages. Many potential customers would taste the butter first and would not buy if it was too salty.

Off the moor there was more dairying. Bert Verney remembers the inter-war days near Landkey:

> Every two days in the summer the remainder of the cream was put in a churn and churned to butter. The hotter the weather, the longer it took. An average time of a quarter of an hour of steady churning would do the trick. The churn was turned by hand but later by petrol engine. The churn, with wooden beaters on the inside, was turned over and over on a wooden frame, mixing and banging the cream until it was a fairly solid mass, and now butter. Any surplus milk left by the separator was poured away, by removing a bung in the end of the churn and perhaps as much as a pint would be removed from the cream. This was known as butter milk and fed to the pigs.
>
> The butter was then removed from the churn into a wooden frame with a notched roller. Some salt was added and then rolled and worked into the butter, then weighed into half pound or pound slabs. It was then taken between two

wooden butter bats and patted into the cube shape required. It was now ready for the market and many customers from the village.

BUTTERMILK

This is the milk which remains after churning milk for butter. As such it was not commonly produced on Exmoor, where it was replaced by scalded, skimmed milk, which kept better. Buttermilk would rapidly sour and there was little use for large quantities. Much ended up as pig food but small quantities could be used for making cutrounds for cream teas.

CLOTTED CREAM

The production of clotted cream is traditional in the West Country and is suited to the rich milk produced by Devon and Channel Island breeds of cow. There are few dairy herds on Exmoor and clotted cream has not generally been produced commercially on the moor but often in the past small quantities were made for home consumption where farmers kept a house cow. Excess cream was usually made into butter. In Exmoor recipes cream and butter are often interchangeable as the two are so similar. The extra effort required to make butter meant that cream was often used as a substitute, although the butter was more easily churned when made from scald cream.

Today very few farmers keep a house cow and most cream is produced by large commercial dairies. The cream is separated from the milk mechanically. Between the wars it was done by a Lister separator in which the milk was made to flow over fast spinning cups. The differences in density of the cream and milk meant that the cream stayed near the cups whilst the milk was thrown out and drained off. On hand operated machines a bell sounded the correct speed of operation; others were engine powered. The separated milk was mixed with a food supplement and used to feed calves or pigs. In *The Lychford File* Richmond Harding of Winsford remembered how until the early 1960s his parents would make much of their spare cash – about 15% of their income – by selling clotted cream to a restaurant:

> …when I was a child I used to take it to the main road here, such as it is, and there was four service busses a day and there was one went down past here at eight o'clock mornings – between quarter to eight and eight o'clock – and it was my duty from about 7 or 8 year old to carry cream down and put it on this bus in about 5-6 lb containers.

Clotted cream was made at home by allowing fresh milk to settle, scalding it and drawing off the top. The house cow was milked morning and evening and the day's milk was taken to the dairy and strained and left to cool and settle in brass or earthenware pans on the slate shelves. The next morning the milk was moved carefully to a slow cooker to be scalded. This process usually took from about nine in the morning to about three in the afternoon, long enough to set the cream. It was important to get the temperature just right to pasteurise the milk but not to let the milk boil. It is said that the temperature was right when the outline of the bottom of the pan was picked out in bubbles on the surface. The pans would be taken back to the dairy to cool and the cream was skimmed off the next morning. The process was described in detail by R. D. Blackmore in *Lorna Doone* during a conversation between Annie and the Counsellor:

> …they are brought in here to cool, after being set in the basin-holes, with the wood ash under them, which I showed you in the back-kitchen. And they must have very little heat, not enough to simmer even; only just to make the bubbles rise, and the scum upon the top set thick; and after that, it clots as firm, oh, as firm as my two hands be.
>
> Have you heard, asked the Counsellor, who enjoyed this talk with Annie, that if you pass across the top, without breaking the surface, a string of beads, or polished glass, or anything of that kind, the cream will set three times as solid, and in thrice the quantity?

The basin holes referred to are usually called creamers. They are shallow hollows in the recesses of stone walls, usually in farmhouse kitchens. Hot embers from the fire were put in the hollows and the cream basins stood on top. Sometimes there was a flue but generally the smoke from the embers would escape into the kitchen, eventually to be drawn up the main chimney. Originally the basins would be stood on a cauldron of hot water over a peat fire. In this case it was much more difficult to get the temperature right. Whichever method was employed, the cream always took on a characteristically smoky flavour now sadly lost. The smoky flavour was not appreciated further afield, however, when the cream was turned to butter. In more recent times, when it became possible to transport butter further, some farms had special portable charcoal cookers or cream ovens which looked like chimney pots on which the basins sat. They were made of cloam (earthenware), usually by the manufacturers of cloam bread ovens. They burned charcoal and the heat was controlled by bellows. This was a much less smoky process and more suited to commercial cream production.

Today the top of a Rayburn is ideal. The heat sets the cream, which can then be skimmed off the surface, traditionally with a scummer, a large broad spoon with holes to drain off the scalded milk. As it is skimmed, the cream ripples like cloth and dollops of cream were called 'clouts', or 'rags', hence its original spelling as clouted cream. The poet Coleridge referred to 'clouted cream' as his favourite food whilst in the West Country. The cream is amongst the richest, with over 55% fat, and keeps better than untreated creams. It is possible to freeze it but this is not good practice.

Modern method from Bob Deville of Martinhoe:

You will need a large earthenware mixing bowl. Fill it to about 2/3 with the freshest full cream Channel Island milk you can get. Cover and keep in the fridge for 24 hours. Then, without shaking it, put the bowl into the warming plate of an Aga or Rayburn cooker or put a thick asbestos mat between the bowl and an electric or gas ring on low and leave until the cream forms into a big yellow blob in the centre: it will take several hours. Cover and refrigerate or leave in a cool place for another 12 hours. Remove the creamy crust with a fish slice or slotted spoon and it is ready to enjoy. The remaining scald milk is good to use in scones, coffee or just to drink when cold. It will also freeze well, as does all skimmed milk.

CREAM TEAS

These seem to be largely a nineteenth century invention, as there was little jam around before then. In fact they were often served with honeycomb instead of jam. Hall, writing in 1849, mentioned a visit to an inn at Porlock:

On entering our little parlour, we found the tea things laid out on a clean white tablecloth, some excellent home-made bread, fresh butter and honey in the comb, with the addition of a large glass of clotted cream, which luxury we had hitherto erroneously believed to be only had in its true excellence in the south of Devon; a neat little handmaid soon followed with the chops, hot and delicious, and then the kettle boiling from the fire, and we set to in good earnest.

The cream is used as a substitute for butter and is spread on the bun or scone first. Scones are not an old tradition and seem to be an outside influence. Tuffcakes or splits – plain or sweet yeast buns, of which there were several variations – were the normal accompaniment. The local cream was rarely plentiful enough to be given to tourists and cream tended to be bought in from surrounding areas for the purpose. Not long ago it could be purchased loose at markets: you took your own container. With modern regulations it comes packaged and from pasteurised milk and is usually Westcountry but not local to Exmoor.

The well known Horner Tea Gardens were set up just after the First World War by a Mrs Floyde and her niece, Alice. In season a Mrs Partridge would carry at

Horner tea gardens c1950

Alfred Vowles Collection

least three pounds of clotted cream daily from Luccombe to Chapel Cross, where Alice would meet her and exchange empty pots for full. The three pounds of cream at 2s 6d per pound seven days a week provided a good income for Mrs Partridge when farm workers were receiving about 28s-32s per week in wages.

CREAM AND FOOLS

There is no clear distinction between custards, creams and fools. They are all based on cream. It is merely the manner of serving them which differs. Custards usually had a pastry base whereas creams and fools were served on their own or with a fruit base and elaborately garnished. It is only recently that egg white or gelatine have been added to stiffen the mixture.

Old recipe and traditional method from Mrs Reed of Ilfracombe:

Take ¼ lb cream, white of 1 egg, flavouring to taste, and sufficient sugar to make moderately sweet. Beat all together until nice and thick and put into custard glasses. It is enough for six glasses.

BLACKBERRY CREAM

Recipe from Heather Burnett-Wells of Withypool:
Apples can be mixed with the blackberries.

8 ozs blackberries
2 ozs caster sugar
3 teaspoons powdered gelatine
½ pt double cream

Steve Guscott

Place the blackberries and sugar in a pan and simmer gently, leaving a few blackberries for decoration. Dissolve the gelatine in a little of the juice. Put the

blackberries through a sieve and add the dissolved gelatine to the puree. When the mixture is cool, whip the cream and fold it in. Set in a mould and when turned out decorate with the remaining blackberries and sprigs of mint.

BAKED DAMSON CREAM

Old recipe:

1 lb damsons
3 ozs white breadcrumbs
½ pt double cream
3 ozs caster sugar
Grated rind of ½ lemon
1 egg, separated
Nutmeg to taste

Stone the damsons and cook gently in a pan with the sugar until soft. Allow to cool. Whip the cream lightly and mix in the breadcrumbs, lemon rind, egg yolk and nutmeg. Fold in the damsons. Whisk the egg whites until stiff and fold into the fruit mixture. Spoon into a buttered dish and bake in a pan of water in the oven for 30-40 minutes at 325°F\170°C\Gas Mark 3.

APPLE AND CIDER FOOL

Recipe from Suzanne Powell of Lynton:

Ingredients for 6 persons:
1 lb\450 gms cooking apples
2 tablespoons sweet cider
2-4 ozs\50-100 gms Demerara sugar
½ pt\300 mls whipping cream
2 pinches cinnamon
2 or 3 cloves

Wash and quarter the apples and poach with the cinnamon, cloves and sugar in the cider. After 10 minutes purée by rubbing them through a sieve. Leave to cool. Whip the cream until stiff and fold into the purée, adding a little green food colouring if preferred. Pipe into individual glasses and chill. Serve, decorated with cream and chopped nuts, with boudoir sponge finger biscuits.

BERRY BOMBE

Recipe from Penny Webber of Minehead:

¾ pt double cream
3 ozs icing sugar or Exmoor heather honey
½ teaspoon vanilla essence
2 egg whites
4 ozs crushed macaroons
2 tablespoons sherry, marsala or liqueur
1 lb berries: whortleberries, raspberries, blackcurrants,
strawberries or a mixture of these.

Whip cream until thick. Stir in the icing sugar and essence. Whisk the egg whites until stiff then fold into the cream. Stir in crushed macaroons and liqueur. Add the chosen berries to the mixture, pour into a basin and freeze. To serve dip the basin in very hot water up to the rim, put a plate over the top and turn over. The bombe should drop out with a little help. Leave in the fridge for half an hour before serving and decorate with berries and cream.

CHESTNUT SOUFFLÉ

Recipe from Heather Burnett-Wells of Withypool:

4 eggs
6 ozs caster sugar
4 tablespoons cold water
10 ozs pureed cooked chestnuts
4 teaspoons gelatine powder
8 ozs double cream
Brandy to taste

To decorate:
Whipped cream
Whole chestnuts or marrons glacé
2 ozs grated plain chocolate

Steve Guscott

Whisk the egg yolks, sugar and 3 tablespoons of water in a bowl over simmering water until pale and creamy. Fold into the chestnut purée. Dissolve the gelatine into the remaining water and brandy (placed over simmering water) and when cool stir into the mixture. Whip the cream and fold into the mixture. Whisk the egg whites until stiff and carefully fold in. Pour into a prepared soufflé dish tied round with a collar of greaseproof paper so that the mixture is well above the top of the dish. Leave in a refrigerator to set and decorate with the chocolate, cream and chestnuts.

WHORTLEBERRY MERINGUE CREAM NEST

Recipe from Mrs G Payne of Brompton Regis:

Ingredients for 6 persons:
12 ozs\350 gms whortleberries

or:

6 ozs\150 gms whortleberries
6 ozs\150 gms blackcurrants

½ pt\100 mls water
1 teaspoon rum
8 ozs\300 mls whipping cream
4 tablespoons sugar
1 dessertspoon gelatine
2 ozs\25 gms caster sugar
2 ozs\25 gms sieved icing sugar
2 egg whites

Cook the berries, water and sugar over a low heat for a little while to soften the fruit. Strain, and sprinkle the gelatine into the warm juice and dissolve by stirring over a low heat. Allow to cool. Pulp the fruit in a blender, whip the cream and fold in the fruit, juice and rum. Leave in a cold place to set. Whisk the egg whites until stiff, gradually adding the caster sugar and fold in the icing sugar. Pipe or spoon into a nest shape on baking paper and cook in a very low oven until dried. To serve, spoon the fruit mixture into the centre of the nest and decorate with whole berries and a little cream.

WOODY BAY DESSERT

Recipe from Peter Fuller of Barnstaple:

Ingredients for 6 persons:
1 pt\600 mls double cream
7 tablespoons Exmoor honey
1 tablespoon lemon juice
1 oz\25 gms pine kernels

For the sauce:
4 ozs\100 gms whortleberries
1½ tablespoons icing sugar
1 egg white

Heat one tablespoon of the honey in a small saucepan and roast the pine kernels in it. Leave to cool. Whip the cream until stiff and fold in the honey, pine kernels and lemon juice. Freeze for 12 hours. Simmer the whortleberries with the sugar for 5 minutes, then liquidise them with the egg white until doubled in volume. Lay slices of the ice on cool plates and pour the warmed sauce over them.

HUXTABLE FARM WHORTLEBERRY AND ELDERBERRY CREAM FUDGE

Recipe from Jackie Payne of West Buckland. Jackie says: 'This dessert can also be made in individual glass dishes and with other soft fruit as desired.'

2 ozs\50 gms whortleberries
2 ozs\50 gms elderberries
Sugar to taste
½ pt whipping cream
¼ pt clotted cream
½ pt natural yogurt
2 tablespoons soft brown sugar

Line the bottom of a glass bowl with the whortleberries and elderberries and sprinkle with sugar to taste. Whip the cream, mix with the clotted cream and yogurt and spread over the fruit. Sprinkle the brown sugar on top of the creamy mixture and leave to stand in a cold place for an hour, to let the sugar soak into the cream.

WHORTLEBERRY CRÈME BRULÉE

Recipe from Kay Smith of Williton:

Ingredients for 4 persons:
½ lb\225 gms whortleberries
¼ pt\150 mls Somerset cider
1 tablespoon lemon juice
2 ozs\50 gms caster sugar
½ pt\300 mls double cream
4 small egg yolks
2 ozs\50 gms unrefined sugar
1 teaspoon cornflour
Pinch of nutmeg and cinnamon

Simmer whortleberries in a heavy saucepan with the cider, spices, lemon juice and half of the sugar. Thicken with cornflour and continue heating for 5 minutes. Divide between four ramekins and leave to cool. Scald the cream in a heavy pan, beat the remaining sugar and egg yolks in a bowl and gradually whisk in the cream. Return to the pan over a low heat, stirring constantly, but do not boil. Allow to cool slightly and pour over the fruit mixture. Refrigerate for at least 2 hours but preferably overnight. Top each dish with unrefined sugar and caramelise under a hot grill. Chill before serving.

DUNSTER PLUM AND APPLE MOUSSE

Recipe from Heather Burnett-Wells of Withypool:

1 lb Dunster plums
1 lb cooking apples
2 tablespoons lemon juice
3 teaspoons powdered gelatine
3 tablespoons Exmoor heather honey
½ pt double cream
Whites of 3 eggs

Peel, core and slice the apples. Halve the plums to stone them. Put the fruit in a saucepan with the lemon juice and a tablespoon of water, cover and heat gently until soft. Leave to cool slightly, then puree in a blender. Dissolve the gelatine in 3 tablespoons water and stir into the plum and apple mixture with the honey. When cool, fold in the whipped cream and whipped egg whites. Spoon the mixture into individual serving dishes and chill in the refrigerator. Decorate with mint sprigs and slices of freshly cut dessert apple just before serving.

POSSETS

Possets were supposed to be complete meals taken by invalids. They were always served hot in a covered china dish and usually contained sweetened milk or cream and some type of sweet wine used as a tonic. However, they varied greatly and could have been like a porridge or a drink.

OATMEAL POSSET

Old recipe:

2 ozs oatmeal
1 pt milk
6 ozs grated dessert apple
2 tablespoons sherry
1 oz sugar
1 oz clotted cream
Cinnamon and nutmeg

Simmer the oatmeal with the milk and a little cinnamon until cooked. Heat the sherry and sugar in a separate pan and stir into the porridge with the grated apple. Leave over the heat for a minute or two and serve in a bowl with grated nutmeg and clotted cream on top.

SYLLABUBS

Somerset claims to be the birthplace of syllabubs. Originally they were made with creamy milk – often literally straight from the cow so that it frothed – in a bowl of sweet home made wine, cider or beer. The word is supposed to have derived from the French 'Sille', a light sparkling wine, and 'bub', Tudor slang for a fizzy drink. They first became popular in the seventeenth century and became traditional for May Day and Midsummer Day. They then developed into something more solid with the use of cream and lemon juice. Later they became whipped and flavoured. Traditional recipes have roughly equal quantities by volume of cream, honey or sugar and wine, sherry or cider, with various flavourings. The whipped mixture was then left for at least eight hours for the cream and liquor to separate. The liquor was then spooned up or drunk through the cream like Irish coffee. Modern recipes tend to have a greater volume of cream, making a stiffer mixture which is consumed earlier to avoid separation. This is usually served with sponge fingers or shortcake.

Steve Guscott

SYLLABUB

Old recipe and basic method:

One teacupful each cream, sherry, and white sugar, juice of two lemons. Beat all well together, pour into glasses and let stand for 24 hours before using.

Old recipe dating from Tudor times:

½ pt double cream
4 tablespoons brandy
4 tablespoons Exmoor heather honey
1 lemon

Finely grate the rind from the lemon and extract the juice. Add the juice and rind to the cream and honey and whisk until thick. Gradually fold the brandy into the mixture. Spoon into serving glasses and chill before serving.

RHUBARB SYLLABUB

Recipe from Heather Burnett-Wells of Withypool:

1 lb young rhubarb
4 ozs honey
1 teaspoon ground ginger
7 fl ozs white wine
1 pt double cream
4 tablespoons caster sugar
lemon juice to taste
stem ginger for decoration

Cut the rhubarb into large chunks and simmer gently in a pan with the ginger and honey until tender. A couple of minutes in a microwave with a stir in between will do just as well. While the rhubarb is cooling, mix the wine, caster sugar and lemon juice and

leave until the sugar is dissolved. To make the syllabub, stir the cream into the wine mixture then whisk vigorously until thick and forming peaks. Divide the rhubarb between serving glasses and spoon the syllabub on top. Decorate with chopped stem ginger and decorate before serving.

ELDERFLOWER SYLLABUB

Recipe from Brian Pearce of Martinhoe:

½ pt double cream
2 tablespoons elderflower cordial
2 tablespoons homemade white wine such as
gooseberry or rhubarb
1 tablespoon caster sugar

Whip the cream and fold in the wine, cordial and sugar. Spoon into serving glasses and chill before serving. Serve within a couple of hours if you wish to retain the lightly whipped texture.

SOMERSET SYLLABUB

Locally, in the seventeenth century, syllabubs were most commonly made from cider and were a common treat given to harvesters and farm workers in the late summer. It was more of a frothy drink than this set dessert:

Old recipe:

¼ pint cider
Rind and juice of 1 lemon
2 ozs caster sugar
½ pint double cream
Grated nutmeg

Stir together the cider, lemon rind, nutmeg and sugar. Stir in the cream and whisk until thick. Fold in the lemon juice. Spoon into individual glasses and chill before serving.

CHEESE

Most cheeses produced on Exmoor were skimmed milk cheeses, produced from the scalded milk left from cream making. As such, rather bland cheeses were produced which did not reach the fame of the full milk and cream cheeses produced elsewhere. There is a story passed on by author Tim Burton that an old Exmoor farmer who was very fond of cheese was once given a really ripe Limburger as a treat. Limburger is possibly the smelliest of European cheeses. Some days later the donor asked the farmer if he had tasted anything like it before. 'No,' came the reply, 'Us reckons us never as eaten un afore, but us as often trodden in un.'

However, cheese presses or cheesewrings were common in Exmoor farms. Every Knight farm had at least a dairy cow and some had dairy herds. Full use was made of the local Devon cattle. These cattle could be summered on the moor and wintered on the recently reclaimed land and were good for both beef and dairy farming. Normally the calves were fed on skimmed milk, the cream being saved for clotted cream and butter. Some of Frederic Knight's tenant farmers who came from other areas made full cream cheeses. There are several references to the excellent Stilton produced by Mr Meadows of Leicestershire, who farmed Larkbarrow. There were also dairies at Honeymead, Emmetts Grange and Warren. A dairyman and dairymaid were listed for Winstitchen in the 1851 census and cheese was later made at Driver. William Hannam from Wincanton, who kept the dairy at Honeymead and then Cornham, had a herd of Devon\Hereford cross yearlings and made a Cheddar type cheese. His dairy makes fascinating reading and is a good record of the hardships of the Knight tenants:

> In the year 1850 we had to contend with Bad times and for a year or two previous our Cheese we could not gett more than 5d; or 6d to retail ther was such a Quantitey of Americen Cheese Brought over – I advertised a Sale by Auction in Barnstable and tryed it on serveall wicks in the

Cheese presses at Driver Farm 1929

Alfred Vowles Collection

Month of April and in aney could not make more than I name and I no doubt at the present time the same Qualitey would make 10d per lb we had ovr one Hundred Cheese in number that averaged over 56lbs Each altho we did not make a Sattisfactorey price then I believe the Publick Auction did good as I think it established the thing it gott into many Peepls Heads and that reccommended others and since or in the last three Seasons we have sold none less than 8d per lb at any time of the Year and if it had been kept to the age of what I sold by Auction no doubt it would have made 10d. The following spring I took neir 30 hundred weight into a Room at the Golden Fleece and Tryed it wickly I sold about 10cwt weight by retail I sold the reminder to Mr May about a Ton weight In the year of 1856 and for maney years before and after it would make 8d and 10d per lb I supplyed over 400 diferent Peeple with Cheese ay 8d pr lb all the respectable Inhabbetents of the North and South of Deaven.

Cheese provided valuable winter income for farmers' wives. The cheeses were stored on racks in the dairy or in a cool upstairs room. Such cheeses did not keep long and were usually sealed with butter. As they aged they naturally became 'vinid' or veined with mould. Later, cheese mites would enter the veins. Some people actually enjoyed eating the mites. The infamous Parson Froude of Knowstone once served an unwelcome guest with Devon Blue Mould – a hard, flavourless, scald milk cheese.

Full cream cheese is now being made by Alan Duffield of Exmoor Blue Cheese at Willet near Crowcombe. Mr Duffield makes both Exmoor Jersey Blue and Somerset Blue cheeses. They are made from unpasteurised milk and their production is threatened by government plans to outlaw the sale of such milk. Although farmers could still sell it to cheese producers, the demand was still not high enough to continue its production.

Ewes' milk was used for cheese until medieval times and that and goats milk cheese has only recently been produced again in the district. Ewes' milk cheese is being produced at Middle Campscott Farm near Ilfracombe. The owners, Lawrence and Karen Wright, have 70 milking ewes and produce a variety of organic cheeses on a small scale for local consumption. The hard cheeses are matured for two or three months and the rind forms naturally as the cheese has been brined in sea salt. Most cheeses are made from the curd, which separates from the whey after renneting. However, the Wrights also make a whey cheese, unknown outside Scandinavia. It is a sweet and salty, soft, dark brown cheese used as a savoury spread. The cheeses can be bought at

Barnstaple, Bideford, South Molton and Hatherleigh markets. After only two years in the business they won a British Cheese Award for a hard pressed cheese with a Cheddar like texture.

EXMOOR GOATS' CHEESE ON GARLIC CROUTS

Recipe from Ian Hamilton of Allerford:
To serve four persons:

Crumb mix:
1oz fresh grano cheese, grated
1oz fresh breadcrumbs
Exmoor goats' cheese balls in oil
4 rounds of bread sliced ½ inch thick
Garlic butter

Brian Pearce

Lightly toast bread and cool. Spread with garlic butter. Cut the cheese balls in halves and place three halves on each crout. Sprinkle with crumb mix. Grill or bake in a hot oven for 3-5 minutes. Serve with salad garnish of raddichio, endive and iceberg lettuce with ceasar or vinaigrette dressing and toasted pine kernels.

CURD AND CHEESE CAKES

There are many variations on this and curd cakes are found throughout England. They were traditionally served on Mothering Sunday, along with a stuffed bacon joint. The addition of cream and eggs makes the local variation more like a custard tart. The custard can be placed on top of cooked apple to make West Country apple tarts.

Old recipe:

¾ lb curds
6 ozs butter
4 ozs caster sugar
4 ozs currants
2 ozs ground almonds
2 teaspoons ground cinnamon
4 eggs
5 fluid ozs sweet sherry or Madeira
2 tablespoons clotted cream
About ¾ lb rich or sweet shortcrust pastry

Use the pastry to line patty tins. It should make about two dozen patties. Cream the curds with the butter and cream and gradually mix in the sugar, spice, almonds and currants. Beat together the eggs and sherry and blend with the rest of the ingredients. Spoon into the patty cases – not too full, as the mixture rises – and bake for 20-25 minutes at 350°F\180°C\Gas Mark 4, until slightly brown on top. The top can be sprinkled with grated nutmeg before or after baking.

WHORTLEBERRY CREAM

This recipe from Barbara Payne of West Buckland was overall winner of the Taste of Exmoor competition:

1 lb\450 gms stewed whortleberries
8 ozs\225 gms cottage cheese
4 ozs\100 gms caster sugar
½ oz\10 gms gelatine
Toasted nuts
Clotted cream

Beat together the cottage cheese and the sugar, add the stewed fruit and continue beating until smooth. Add the gelatine softened in a little water (and, for special occasions, add 2 tablespoons kirsch or other liqueur). Pour into individual bowls and leave to set. Decorate with flaked, toasted nuts and serve with clotted cream.

BERRY TORTE

Recipe from Suzanne Powell of Lynton:

Ingredients for 6 persons:
2½ ozs\60 gms unsalted butter
7 ozs\180 gms crushed digestive biscuits
8 ozs\180 gms caster sugar
5 large eggs
1½ lbs\750 gms full fat soft cheese
2 teaspoons vanilla essence

For the topping:
1 teaspoon grated lemon rind
2 teaspoons cornflour
12 ozs\300 gms whortleberries, or other soft fruit
2 tablespoons water

Steve Guscott

Pre-heat the oven to 350°F\180°C\Gas Mark 4. Butter a loose-based 8 inch round cake tin. Melt the butter in a medium-sized pan and add the biscuits to combine. Press the mixture into the tin with a wooden spoon. Beat the cheese until smooth using a hand-held mixer, then add the sugar and beat again to combine. Add the eggs one at a time and beat well, finally adding the vanilla essence. Pour into the cake tin. Bake for 35 minutes, leave to cool, then chill overnight before turning out, biscuit side down. Combine the berries, lemon rind, water and cornflour in a saucepan over a moderate heat and cook for 3-5 minutes stirring once or twice. Allow to cool before spreading over the torte. Serve with clotted cream.

PLUM CHEESECAKE WITH
ELDERBERRY SAUCE

Recipe from Jackie Payne of West Buckland:

10 ozs\300 gms plums
¼ pt\150 mls water
4 ozs\100 gms sugar
2 teaspoons gelatine
2 teaspoons water
7 ozs\200 mls whipping cream
6 ozs\175 gms soft cream cheese
5 ozs\150 gms crushed digestive biscuits
3 ozs\75 gms butter

For the sauce:
5 ozs\150 gms elderberries
2 ozs\50 gms sugar
¼ pt\150 mls water
1 teaspoon arrowroot

To make the base, melt the butter in a pan and stir in the crushed biscuits. Press into a 7 inch loose bottom flan tin. Stew the plums with the water and sugar until the stones can be easily removed. Mix the gelatine with the 2 teaspoons of water and stand for a minute, then microwave on high for 50 seconds, stir into the stewed plums and leave to cool but not to set. Whip the cream until stiff. Add the cream cheese and whip in quickly. Fold the plum mixture into the cream and cheese and pour over the biscuit base. Place in the fridge to set for an hour. Garnish with sprigs of elderberries. To make the sauce, boil together the elderberries, water and sugar until the sugar is dissolved. Mix the arrowroot with a little water until it forms a smooth, runny paste. Add to the elderberry mixture, stirring all the time over a gentle heat. Allow to cool and serve with the cheesecake.

Cheesemaking class at Brushford, c1920

❧ The Bakehouse ❧

Farmers often used to grow some form of corn on Exmoor, usually oats or barley for animal rather than human consumption. In days when fresh meat was not available in the winter bread was often the staple diet and, combined with poor communications, some subsistence farming of corn was necessary. Rye was the main crop for the poorer soils of the moors and would grow well where other cereals would fail. Often rye straw can be found in the lower layers of the thatch on local buildings. It seems to have been commonly grown, although in small quantities, until the early eighteenth century and continued to be grown for a while for thatching straw.

Barley bread eventually replaced rye but was coarse and considered second best and usually eaten only by the poor. Wheat bread for ordinary people did not really become affordable until cheap North American grain began to flood into the country in the late nineteenth century. Flour was then produced for large bakeries and the local corn mills were largely kept working for cattle feed. Until the nineteenth century a kind of porridge or gruel made of coarsely ground grain simmered in water was a common meal for poor Exmoor folk. It was locally known as girts or groats and may have been the origin of the grits of the southern states of the USA. Some groats were even exported and they were commonly used to eke out sweet or savoury dishes, such as frumenty or potten pudding.

Before the First World War, when many local watermills were still running, farmers would usually take their own corn to the mill for grinding. Sometimes

Oat stooks above Farley Water

Brian Pearce

they just wanted a mash of unseparated grain for the animals. If they wanted flour they could often have it milled free, as the miller kept the separated bran to sell as horse feed. Some farmers grew a little wheat for flour for baking but Exmoor was not a good place for growing wheat and after the First World War locals started using better quality imported flour, bought from bakers shops. The coming of railways had meant that bulky goods such as flour and animal feed could be economically brought from further afield.

Town Mills at Dulverton continued working until 1973. The Warren family had worked it since the early nineteenth century. In the twentieth century Canadian and Russian wheat arrived at Avonmouth docks and was sent by train to Dulverton Station. From there it was fetched by horse and cart, later by lorry, in 1½ ton loads, up to five loads per day. The grain was ground, bagged and weighed into 2 cwt bags and delivered, mostly to farmers for cattle feed. The current interest in healthy eating has resulted in the restoration of some local mills. The best known is Dunster Water Mill. Two mills were recorded at Dunster in the Domesday Book. The present mill dates from 1680 and continued to grind flour and feed for the home farm of the Luttrell

estate until 1962. It was restored in 1979 and now grinds flour for local bakeries as well as for sale in shops.

At the same time as bulk wheat imports were growing, deliveries from shops to outlying areas became frequent and the practice of baking ones own bread started to decline. The open fire tended to be used mainly for boiling water and ranges had mainly replaced bread ovens. Fred Rawle, however, remembers his childhood at Ashott, near Exford, where there were no bakers deliveries and bread continued to be cooked in a hearth oven baker under the open fire until the 1930s.

From ancient times until the twentieth century many Exmoor villages had their communal bakehouses where people would take their own meals to be cooked. A bakehouse was built for Frederic Knight at Simonsbath in 1856. He had been concerned at the cost of delivery of bread and flour, which was brought from South Molton. In that town a pound of flour cost 2d and a 6 lb loaf 1s whereas in Simonsbath the flour cost 3d and 1s only bought a 5 lb loaf. He was adamant that South Molton and Barnstaple tradesmen would not

Dunster Water Mill

Brian Pearce

make money out of his venture. In the 1920s in Dulverton there were two such bakeries: Broomfield's and Darch's. The day would begin at 6.00am with the lighting of the faggot to fire the oven. Two batches of white bread in 2 lb and 4 lb loaves were baked daily. Delivery in town was by two-wheeled trolley, or further afield by horseback with the bread basket strapped to the rider's back. On Sundays between 11.00am and 1.00pm family dinners were baked for 2d a time. Fred Rawle remembers his mother baking bread until the 1930s at Ashott near Exford because there were no deliveries there. The last village bakehouse he can remember working was at Brendon, where the baker delivered with his horse and trap. He remembers people taking meals to be baked there. It was usual to take the heavy earthenware lid from a crock used to keep water hot by the fire or pot boiling, put it on a warmed milk pan and take them to the bakehouse to keep the food warm on the way home. At one place the tradition remains. This is at Sewards bakers at Bampton, which has been in the same family since 1908. Each Christmas Day they offer the service of roasting their customers' lunches free of charge. This involves cooking about forty turkeys at once.

BREAD

·Until the late nineteenth century most Exmoor farmers' wives would make their own bread. Often this involved flour from their own grain and yeast from their own brewery. Then commercial bakeries took over and most Exmoor villages had their bakers shop. The yeast would come in 7 lb hessian bags and was creamier than todays fresh yeast. Fresh yeast is now difficult to obtain as few local bakers bake their own bread.

At Combe Sydenham near Monksilver is the national museum of bakery and the home of Monksbread, where an attempt is being made to revive the taste for real bread. There the flour is ground by an ancient watermill. It is argued that the old slow method of grinding preserves more of the goodness and texture of the flour than today's high speed mills, which bruise the grain at higher temperatures. No flour improvers or chemicals are added to the bread and water from the Monks Spring is used to make the dough. The other ingredients are vegetable fat and rocksalt. Monksmill Foods have developed a double wrapping method for the bread, which gives it a very long shelf life without the need for freezing.

LUCKWELL BRIDGE WHOLEMEAL BREAD

From Gay Brown, Luckwell Bridge: Gay produced this recipe by experiment to suit her own Aga cooker and food mixer. It should, however, work well in any kitchen.

Steve Guscott

2½ lbs\1250 gms wholemeal flour
½ lb\250 gms strong white flour
3 ozs\90 gms butter
2 ozs\60 gms granulated sugar
1½ teaspoons\7.5 mls salt
2 packets fast action dried yeast (the sort that requires only one rising of the dough)
1½ pints\900 mls or a fraction over, lukewarm water

If making by hand, rub the fat into the flour, then mix well with the sugar, salt and yeast. If using a mixer, mix all the dry ingredients thoroughly first, then cut the butter into small cubes and add to the mixer, mixing well until it is incorporated into the flour – like pastry mix. Add the lukewarm water and mix just until the mixture holds together. For most mixers the mixture will have to be divided to mix smaller quantities at a time. Turn the dough onto a floured surface and let it rest whilst you grease your bread tins. You will need 4 6½x3 inch bread tins. Knead the dough, dusting with the strong white flour as necessary, until the mixture feels pliable – about 5 minutes. Divide the dough equally between the tins. Cover each tin with a clean damp tea towel and leave over the Aga or in any warm place until the dough has doubled in size. Cook at the bottom of the hot oven in the Aga for 15 minutes then turn around and bake for another 15-20 minutes. When cooked the base of the tin will make a hollow sound when tapped. Tap loaves out of tins, place on a wire rack and return to the oven for 5 minutes. For other ovens, preheat oven and cook at 375°F\190°C\Gas Mark 5 for 15 minutes, then turn the oven down and cook for another 20-25 minutes at 325°F\170°C\ Gas Mark 3. Turn out and leave to cool on wire racks.

YEAST CAKES

Yeast cakes are what we would now call fruit loaves. They were also known as brack or barm brack, barm being another word for yeast. There are many regional variations throughout the British Isles. Yeast was commonly available as a by-product from brewing. Today it is usual to use dried yeast but the packets usually give instructions on how to adapt old recipes for fresh yeast.

YEAST CAKE

Old recipe:

1½ lbs plain flour
4 ozs butter
2 ozs lard
6 ozs sugar
8 ozs dried mixed fruit
1½ ozs fresh yeast
½ pt milk
¼ pt water

Leave the yeast to rise in a cup of the warmed milk and water into which a teaspoon of sugar has been stirred. Rub the fats into the flour to make a crumb consistency. Mix in the fruit and sugar. Stir in the yeast mixture when it has started to froth and the rest of the warmed milk and water. Mix to a soft, spongy texture. Cover with a damp cloth and leave in a warm place to rise to double its size. Divide the mixture between two large, greased loaf tins and leave for another ten minutes in a warm place. Bake for about one hour at 325°F\170°C\Gas Mark 3 until browned. Serve sliced with butter.

PATSY'S EXMOOR TEACAKES

Recipe from Patsy Way of Minehead:

1 pt\600 mls milk and water
3 teaspoons raw sugar
1½ tablespoons dried yeast
2 lbs\1 kg 85% organic flour
2 teaspoons sea salt
3 teaspoons mixed spice
3 ozs\75 gms soft brown sugar
4 ozs\100 gms butter or margarine
2 ozs\50 gms dried fruit
2 ozs\50 gms cut mixed peel

Bring the milk, water and raw sugar to blood heat in a saucepan, sprinkle in the yeast and leave until frothy. Sift the flour, salt, spice and brown sugar into a bowl and rub in the butter or margarine. Pour in the bubbly yeast mixture and knead on a floured board. Leave to double in size in a warm place, then knead again and divide into approximately 16 pieces. Knead each one, incorporating a little of the fruit and peel and place on a greased baking tin in a plastic bag to prove in a warm place for 15 minutes. Bake at 425°F\220°C\ Gas Mark 7 for 20 minutes until golden. Serve cold or split and lightly toasted with butter and conserves.

REVEL BUNS

Revels were parish celebrations held to mark the anniversary of the saint to whom the church was dedicated. They usually commenced on the Sunday nearest to the Saint's day and could last several days. Most disappeared with the spread of Nonconformity and disapproval of festivities on a Sunday and the violent form of wrestling which traditionally accompanied the revels. Revels survive at Hawkridge and Parracombe but are more like village fêtes now.

Special food and drink accompanied the revels. The buns were forerunners of hot cross buns and similar to the larger saffron buns traditional in Cornwall. Saffron is also a traditional ingredient in Devon. It is said that in ancient times traders from the Mediterranean exchanged it for local minerals. As saffron is an extremely expensive spice, it tended to be used only as a treat for special occasions such as Christmas, birthdays and revels.

At Lynton revels were on a Sunday and a barrel of beer and revel cake were placed near the church gate to greet people coming out of church. The cake contained dark flour, currants and caraway seeds. Revel buns were common throughout the West Country and there were many local variations. Some were baked in sycamore leaves.

Old recipe:
A richer recipe substituted clotted cream for the cream and butter for the lard.

1 lb flour
6 ozs currants
2 ozs lard
1 egg
¼ pint cream
3 tablespoons milk
½ oz fresh yeast
1 teaspoon sugar
A pinch each of salt, cinnamon and saffron

Warm the milk, sugar and saffron in a pan. Remove from the heat and sprinkle in the yeast. Leave until the mixture is frothing. Sieve the flour with the salt and cinnamon and add to it the melted lard, cream and egg. Add the yeast mixture and knead to a smooth dough. Leave covered in a warm place for about an hour, and then knead again, working in the currants. Shape into 15-20 balls and place on greased baking trays. Cover and leave to prove in a warm place for about for about 20 minutes. Bake in a hot oven for about 25 minutes.

SAFFRON CAKE

This is a bread traditionally associated with Lent. Although now eaten all year round, it is still commonly eaten at Easter. It seems to have originated in the late fifteenth or early sixteenth as the pre-Reformation Lenten Bread. Then it was not a sweet bread and currants, sugar and rosewater seem to be refinements which crept in during Elizabethan times.

Old recipe:

1 lb strong white flour
6 ozs butter
1 oz fresh yeast (or ½ oz sachet dried yeast)
½ pt hot milk
6 ozs currants
2 ozs cut mixed peel
3 ozs sugar
1 teaspoon mixed spice
Good pinch saffron

name derives from the way of cutting them open diagonally from top to bottom without cutting right through. Sometimes they were made with dough folded in half and the halves were pulled apart after baking. They were filled with clotted cream and jam and are the traditional cream tea fare, rather than todays scones.

Old recipe:

1 lb strong white bread flour
½ pt warm water
3 ozs sugar
1 egg
2 ozs butter
½ teaspoon salt
1 oz fresh yeast

Infuse the saffron in the hot milk and leave for at least 30 minutes. Cream the yeast with a teaspoon of the sugar and stir into the saffron milk whilst still warm. Leave in a warm place until frothy. Sieve the flour with the spices and rub in the butter and sugar. Mix well with the liquid and knead in the currants and peel. Cover and leave in a warm place to double in size. Knead the dough on a floured surface and shape to fit a greased 8 inch round cake tin. Leave for about 40 minutes to rise and bake in a preheated oven at 350°F\180°C\ Gas Mark 4 for about an hour, or until golden and sounding hollow when tapped. Serve sliced with butter or clotted cream and jam.

SPLITS

There were many different names for these yeast buns, most of which come from south Devon, where different villages seem to have given names to them. Boveys and Chudleighs were common names and Tiverton had its own version known as Tiverton Chudleighs. In North Devon they were usually known as splits. The

Cream the yeast with a teaspoon of the sugar and stir into the water and beaten egg. Leave in a warm place until it froths. Sift together the flour and salt and rub in the butter and remaining sugar. Add the liquid and mix well. Knead to a smooth and elastic dough. Cover the dough in a bowl and leave in a warm place to double in size. Divide the dough into 12 parts and roll each into a ball on a floured board. Place on greased baking tins and leave in a warm place for another 40 minutes to rise. Bake in a preheated oven at 425°F\220°C\Gas Mark 7 for ten minutes.

Modern method from Bob Deville of Martinhoe:

Bob omits the egg, adds an ounce of lard and uses half milk and half water. The main difference is in using modern, quick acting dried yeast.

Combine the yeast, sugar and water and leave in a warm place until it looks frothy – about 15 minutes. Meanwhile, put the milk, lard and butter into a saucepan and stir over a low heat until the fats have melted (do not boil). Allow to cool. Sift the flour and salt into a food mixer and add all other ingredients, mixing until you have a soft doughy ball. Roll up into about 18 balls, put onto a buttered baking tray, cover with cling film and leave in a warm place (airing cupboard or warming oven) until doubled in size – about an hour. Bake in an oven preheated to 400°F\200°C\Gas Mark 6 for about 20 minutes – they should sound hollow when tapped lightly. They will freeze well.

SCONES

CUT ROUNDS

The term cut round seems to be equally applied to a bun of bread or scone mix. The way I understand it, however, is that a round is a yeast bun shaped by hand and a cut round is a scone cut with a pastry cutter.

Old recipe and traditional method from Mrs Garnish of Ilfracombe:

Steve Guscott

Take 2 lbs flour, 1½ ozs butter, pinch of salt, tablespoonful caster sugar, 2 teaspoonsful baking powder. Rub butter into flour, add rest of ingredients, and mix into firm paste with milk and water; roll to about ½ inch thick, cut into rounds and bake in fairly quick oven for ¼ hour.

WEST ILKERTON SCONES

A richer variation on the traditional cut rounds.

Recipe from Victoria Eveleigh of Barbrook:

2 lbs plain flour
8 teaspoons cream of tartar
4 teaspoons bicarbonate of soda
½ teaspoon salt
4 ozs butter
4 ozs sugar

Steve Guscott

Mix all ingredients with fingers or food mixer until fine and crumbly. Break 4 eggs into a measuring jug and make up to 1 pint with milk. Beat the eggs and milk together and then add (all at once) to the dry mixture and mix until it has a soft, dough-like texture.

For fruit scones add dried fruit (raisins, currants, sultanas and/or cherries) at this stage.
For cheese scones, forget the sugar and add grated cheese at this stage.

Turn out onto a floured board and knead until the dough is easy to handle. Roll out to about ½ inch thick. Cut into shapes with a knife or cutter and put these on a lightly floured baking tray. Sprinkle the tops of the scones with flour and bake at 450°F\230°C\Gas Mark 8 for between 8 and 15 mins, depending on the size of the scones. Serve hot with clotted cream and good quality jam.

EXMOOR APPLE SCONE

Recipe from Karen Williams of East Anstey:

Ingredients for 4 persons:
8 ozs\225 gms plain flour
4 tablespoons milk
½ teaspoon salt
2 teaspoons baking powder
2 ozs\50 gms butter
2 ozs\50 gms caster sugar
1 medium cooking apple, grated
2 medium cooking apples, sliced
1 tablespoon Demerara sugar

Sieve the flour, salt and baking powder together and rub in the butter. Add the sugar and grated apple and enough milk to form a soft dough. Turn onto a floured surface and knead lightly, then divide into two slightly unequal portions. Roll the smaller into an 8 inch circle, place on a greased and floured baking sheet and put the sliced apple on top, leaving a half inch gap round the outside. Roll the other portion out until it is large enough to cover, place on top and pinch the edges together. Brush all over with a little milk and sprinkle with sugar. Bake for 20-25 minutes at 400°F\200°C\ Gas Mark 6 and serve hot or cold with cream or custard.

TEA RUSKS

Old recipe from Miss Pickett of Ilfracombe:

Breakfastcupful flour
3 ozs butter
1 dessertspoonful baking powder
1 teaspoonful sugar
2 eggs

Rub flour and butter together, add baking powder and sugar, then eggs beaten with little milk; knead to a stiff dough, roll out, cut into small rounds, about ½ inch thick and bake; when well risen and baked through, cut in half and bake again until brown and crisp. Serve cold, buttered, or with clotted cream and jam.

BISCUITS

FLATS

Old recipe:

1 lb plain flour
½ lb caster sugar
8 ozs clotted cream
1 egg
Milk

Sift the flour, beat the egg and mix all ingredients together with enough milk to give a stiff dough like a

pastry mix. Roll the mixture out very thinly and cut into rounds. Place on greased baking trays and bake at 425°F\220°C\ Gas Mark 7 for ten minutes.

ROLLS

These are like flats, but the rounds are lightly folded in halves. This recipe substitutes honey for the sugar.

Old recipe:

8 ozs plain flour
2 ozs butter
3 ozs honey
1 egg
2 fluid ozs milk
1 egg
1 teaspoon baking powder
Pinch salt

Cream together the butter and honey and beat in the egg. Add the milk and gradually mix in the flour sieved with the baking powder and salt. Roll the mixture out until about half an inch thick. Cut into rounds and fold each round into half to make a semi-circle. Bake on a greased tray at 400°F\200°C\Gas Mark 6 for about 15 minutes until golden.

GINGERBREAD

Gingerbread was so called because it was originally made with breadcrumbs. It was a special occasion treat, used for festivities such as religious celebrations. Old recipes sweeten the crumbs with honey and make them to a paste with ale. Flavourings included ginger, liquorice, aniseed and peppers. It was rolled flat and cut into recognisable shapes, then dried gently until hard. It was thus a cross between bread, cake and biscuit. It developed into a biscuit through substitution of flour, fat and eggs for the bread. Sugar or treacle replaced the honey, but the biscuit was still baked hard until the eighteenth century. During the nineteenth century raising agents were added and the biscuit became a cake popular in the north of England. There were Westcountry variations but the gingerbread here tended to remain as a biscuit.

FAIRINGS

Originally a fairing was any gift bought at a fair, but the name came to be applied mainly to biscuits and sweets. Fairings are traditional biscuits throughout the West Country, with many local variations. They are generally large flat, crispy but slightly chewy, spicy biscuits with a predominant flavour of ginger. They are mostly a variation on gingerbread, but in the Exmoor area they were more like brandy snaps. They were sold from stalls at local fairs, and still can be bought at Bampton and Barnstaple fairs.

BARNSTAPLE GINGERBREAD FAIRING

Old recipe from Miss Bale of Barnstaple:

6 ozs treacle
3 ozs caster sugar
6 ozs flour
5 ozs butter
Powdered ginger

Rub butter, flour, sugar, and ginger together, warm treacle, and thoroughly mix. Drop small pieces on well greased tin, and bake in a very slow oven.

FLAPJACKS

Flapjacks are a variation of the basic gingerbread recipe. They seem to have appeared in most places where oats were grown, particularly in the north of England, and are by no means peculiar to Exmoor. There seems to be little written tradition of flapjack making, possibly because the basic recipe is so simple that there was no need to write it down. Some old recipes are, however, quite sophisticated and include a mixture of rolled oats and oatmeal, eggs and a variety of spices and fruits.

WESTERMILL FLAPJACKS

Recipe from Jackie Edwards of Exford:

12 ozs\350 gms margarine
12 ozs\350 gms sugar
1 lb\450 gms rolled oats

Whilst melting the margarine and sugar in a large saucepan, line an oblong baking tin (16"X12", 1 ½" straight sides) with Bakewell paper. Mix the rolled oats into the saucepan. Tip the contents into the baking tin and flatten evenly with a spatula. Bake in the top oven of an Aga for 20 minutes, turning the tin at half time. Remove when lightly browned. Mark into squares with a sharp knife when cool. Reverse onto a flat surface and break into sections.

SHORTCAKES

In former times these were sweetened with honey instead of sugar. Substituting honey for half of the sugar can vary this recipe. The basic recipe omitted the ground almonds and egg yolks.

Old recipe:

½ lb plain flour
4 ozs butter
4 ozs caster sugar
Yolks of two eggs
1 oz ground almonds
Milk

Sift the flour and rub with the butter to a crumb consistency. Mix in the almonds and sugar. Mix with the egg yolks, adding milk if necessary to make a stiff dough like pastry. Roll the dough out thinly and cut into rounds. Place on greased baking trays and prick the surface with a fork. Bake at 350°F\ 180°C\Gas Mark 4 for 15 minutes until golden but not brown.

EASTER CAKES

These are a richer variation on the basic shortcake recipe. According to legend, the Duke of Monmouth was fleeing from the Battle of Sedgemoor and fell into a ditch. A farmer's wife, thinking he was a bedraggled peasant, made these biscuits for him. They became popular at Easter.

Old recipe:

½ lb plain flour
4 ozs butter
4 ozs caster sugar
4 ozs currants
1 egg
1 teaspoon cinnamon
2 tablespoons brandy

Steve Guscott

Sift the flour and rub with the butter to a crumb consistency. Mix in the sugar, currants and spice. Beat the eggs together with the brandy and stir into the mixture to make a stiff consistency, adding milk if too dry. Knead the mixture and roll out slightly thicker than for ordinary shortcake. Cut into rounds and place on a greased baking tray. Bake at 350°F\180°C\Gas Mark 4 for about 20 minutes until golden but not brown.

EXMOOR TRIANGLES

Recipe from Miss P Tilsley-Green of Combe Martin:

Ingredients for 10 persons:
6 ozs\150 gms plain flour
2 ozs\50 gms caster sugar
4 ozs\100 gms butter

For the filling:
1½ ozs\35 gms butter
3 ozs\75 gms icing sugar
1 dessertspoon clear heather honey

Cream the butter and sugar until light and fluffy and mix in the flour to form a stiff dough. Roll out to ¼ inch thickness and cut into 20 X 3 inch triangles. Using the tip of a sharp knife, decorate half of them with the outline of a stag's head. Place on a greased baking sheet and cook for 15-20 minutes at 325°F\170°C\Gas Mark 3. Allow to cool before sandwiching with the well-beaten filling ingredients, placing the decorated triangles uppermost. Pipe on a little of the filling to outline the antlers.

CAKES

LARDY CAKE

This is also known as dripping cake and is a classic West Country tea time speciality. Its origins seem to be in the way that no part of a pig was wasted. The lard came from the flead, which is the inner membrane of a pig. It is a thin skin full of particles of lard. The lard is worked loose by beating the flead into flour, then

removing the membrane. Flead pastry was made by beating the flead into the flour with a rolling pin until the particles of lard were broken down, then adding a little salt and water to make a paste. Flead cakes were made in the same way, but omitting the salt and adding sugar and spice. The sweet pastry was then cut into squares and brushed with egg white and sugar before baking. Lardy cake evolved from this with the addition of fruit and rising agents to make a cake mix as opposed to a pastry. It may have had its origins in the traditional pig rearing areas of Gloucestershire but spread throughout the region with local variations. It is more commonly available now as a yeast cake basted with syrup. Although sold as West Country lardy cake, this recipe comes from Oxfordshire and is simply bread dough rolled and dotted with fruit and lard.

Old recipe:

1 lb plain flour
½ lb pork dripping
½ lb soft brown sugar
10 ozs dried mixed fruit
4 eggs
3 tablespoons milk
1 teaspoon baking soda
2 teaspoons mixed spice
White sugar

Sift the flour, soda and spice into a mixing bowl. Rub in the dripping, then mix in the sugar and fruit. Mix to a dropping consistency with beaten eggs and milk. Transfer to a greased and lined 9 or 10 inch cake tin and scatter the surface with white sugar. Bake at 350°F\180°C\Gas Mark 4 for about 1½ hours, until firm but not brown.

BOILED FRUIT CAKE

This cake seems to have a multitude of local variations. It keeps well and is best left for a week or two to mature.

Old recipe:

8 ozs plain flour
1 lb dried mixed fruit
4 ozs butter
8 ozs sugar
1 teaspoonful ground mixed spice
2 eggs
1 teaspoonful baking powder
¼ pt water

Simmer the fruit, sugar, butter, water and spice in the water for about 15 minutes. When cool, mix in the beaten eggs. Fold in the flour sieved with the baking powder. Turn into a greased 8 inch cake tin and bake for between 1½ and 2 hours at 300°F\150°C\Gas Mark 2 until cooked right through but not dried.

Steve Guscott

HEAVY CAKE

This is a West Country tradition with many variants. The name is thought to come from 'hevva', a local word for the hauling in of fish. The top of the cake was decorated with a criss-cross pattern to represent a fishing net. The basic old recipe is more of a flaky pastry than a cake. The current recipes are for sweeter, lighter cakes more like the one for Chittlehampton Cake, which follows.

Old recipe:

1 lb plain flour
1 lb butter
6 ozs currants
Milk

Sieve the flour and rub with a quarter of the butter until a breadcrumb texture is reached. Add the currants and mix with a little cold water to make an elastic dough. Roll out the dough on a floured board and dot with another quarter of the butter. Fold the pastry over, roll out again and repeat until the butter is used up. The pastry is usually rolled into a neat square or rectangle and scored with a knife to make a diamond pattern on the surface. It can then be brushed with milk and is baked in a hot oven for half and hour: usually 450°F\230°C\ Gas Mark 8 for 10 minutes and reducing the heat to 400°F\200°C\Gas Mark 6 for the remaining cooking time.

DEVON POT CAKE

This is a variation on the heavy cake recipe from Elizabeth Pring of Martinhoe:

12 ozs\300 gms self raising flour
4 ozs\100 gms butter
4 ozs\100 gms currants and sultanas
2 ozs\50 gms lard
1 egg
1 cup milk
Salt

Make a dough with the flour, lard, butter and pinch of salt, add the well-beaten egg and stir well before adding the fruit. Place the mixture on a floured surface and roll out to the size of the pan to be used. Place in the well-greased pan and cook in a moderate oven for an hour. Serve by spreading with butter, brown sugar and clotted cream while still hot.

NORTH DEVON BLACK CAKE

The term black cake seems to refer to any dark fruit cake. I use this as my Christmas cake recipe. It is a very rich fruit cake for special occasions and is not cheap to make. It matures well and the tradition is to make two

and keep one for the anniversary of the occasion for which the cake was baked. The Cornish variation of this cake omits the treacle, so it is not as moist and, therefore, not so much like a Christmas pudding after a year.

Steve Guscott

Old recipe:

½ lb plain flour
½ lb rice flour
12 eggs
¾ lb butter
½ lb caster sugar
6 ozs black treacle
4 lbs mixed fruit and peel
½ lb chopped almonds
2 tablespoons brandy or rum
2 teaspoons baking powder
4 teaspoons ground mixed spice

Whisk the eggs in a bain marie or a large bowl over a bowl of hot water until they are light and creamy. Cream together the butter and sugar and gradually add the eggs and warmed treacle. Gradually fold in the sieved flours, baking powder and spices. Mix in the fruit, nuts and spirits. Divide the mixture between two lined and greased 9 inch cake tins. Bake at 350°F\180°C\ Gas Mark 4 for 3 hours. Turn out the cakes when cool. It is best to leave them for at least a week before using, preferably longer. The one to be used soonest is covered with marzipan and decorated with icing a few days before the special occasion, the other is kept in a sealed tin for another year. Do not decorate until needed, as the treacle seems to permeate the marzipan and icing and all turns to a sticky mess.

MRS FROUDE'S POUND CAKE

Pound cake seems to be found throughout England with regional variations. There is also a pound pudding, which is like a Christmas pudding. The name refers to the fact that there is usually a pound of each of the butter, sugar, flour and fruit. There is also a half pound cake.

Recipe from Jan Ridler of Wootton Courtenay, compiled by his mother at East Lynch, Selworthy in the nineteenth century:

1 lb butter
1 lb sugar
1½ lb currants
1½ lb flour
16 eggs
4 ozs lemon peel
1 glass of brandy
½ teaspoonful mace and nutmeg
Saltspoonful of salt

Cream the butter and work in the sugar at twice, then the yolks of the eggs at twice, then the whites of the eggs at twice, then the spice and peel, then the flour and salt very gradually, then the currants and brandy, beaten well and lightly all together. Pour at once into a tin and cook immediately, not moving until done. (There is no mention of cooking instructions, but a rich cake like this would take long, slow cooking, probably in a warm oven at about 325°F\170°C\Gas Mark 3 for the first ½ hour and reducing the temperature to about 275°F\140°C\Gas Mark 1 for another 3½ hours: ideally suited to a bread oven.)

EXMOOR FARMER'S CAKE

Recipe from Audrey Vellacott of Brompton Regis:

8 ozs\225 gms chopped dates
8 ozs\225 gms caster sugar
3 ozs\75 gms butter
1 teaspoon bicarbonate of soda
1 beaten egg
1 teaspoon vanilla essence
10 ozs\250 gms plain flour
1 teaspoon baking powder
2 ozs\50 gms chopped walnuts
Water

For the topping;
5 tablespoons light brown sugar
2 tablespoons butter
2 tablespoons cream

Pour a breakfast cup of boiling water over the dates and add the bicarbonate of soda. Stir and allow to cool while mixing the rest of the ingredients. Combine the two mixtures, turn into a greased 10"X10" or 12"X9" baking tin and cook in a moderate oven for 35 minutes. Mix the topping ingredients together and boil for 3 minutes. Spread on the cooled cake and sprinkle with chopped nuts.

HONEY CAKE

Old recipe:

6 ozs Exmoor heather honey
5 ozs butter
3 ozs soft brown sugar
1 egg
7 ozs self raising flour
1 teaspoon baking powder
1 tablespoon water

To glaze:
1 tablespoon Exmoor heather honey
2 tablespoons water
2½ ozs icing sugar

Steve Guscott

Gently heat the honey, sugar, butter and water in a pan over a low heat until melted. Beat in the egg, followed by the flour, sieved in with the baking powder. Bake in a greased and lined 7 inch cake tin at 350°F\180°C\Gas Mark 4 for 45 minutes. Leave to cool in the tin before turning out. Warm together the honey, water and icing sugar and brush over the cake to glaze.

HEATHER HONEY CAKE

Recipe from Vicky Nash of Ralegh's Cross:

Ingredients for 6 persons:
8 ozs\225 gms caster sugar
4 ozs\100 gms margarine
¼ pt\150 mls single cream
6 ozs\150 gms plain flour
3 teaspoons baking powder
8 ozs\225 gms clear honey
8 ozs\225 gms whortleberries
2 large eggs

Whisk the eggs and sugar until thick. Bring the margarine and cream to boiling point and add, whisking all the time. Fold in plain flour and baking powder and pour into an 8\12 inch ovenproof dish. Bake at 400°F\200°C\ Gas Mark 6 for 20 minutes and serve hot or cold with the sauce made by mixing the whortleberries and honey.

POTATO CAKE

Usually known as 'teddy cakes', these seem to have been a Devonshire teatime treat but can be said to be a classic Exmoor recipe with numerous variations. The potato cakes can be sweet or savoury, baked or griddled and cooked as a single cake or in individual rounds. In rounds they are usually cut with a criss-cross design. Frequently 4 ozs of suet is added to this basic recipe.

Old recipe:

8 ozs self raising flour
8 ozs mashed potatoes
12 ozs currants
4 ozs brown sugar
3 ozs butter or margarine
2 eggs
½ teaspoon mixed spice

Add the spice to the flour and rub in the fat with the fingers until it makes a crumb texture. Mix in the mashed potato, then sugar, currants and beaten eggs. Put the mixture in a greased, fairly shallow baking tin and bake in a hot oven, 375°F\190°C\Gas Mark 5 for about 30 minutes. Cut into squares and serve hot. The cakes can be frozen and microwaved to reheat.

To fry potato cakes:
Omit butter and eggs. Mix other ingredients and roll out to ½ inch thickness, dusting well with flour. Cut into rounds with a pastry cutter. Heat a small amount of lard in a frying pan and cook on both sides until brown. Sprinkle with sugar and serve hot.

SOMERSET APPLE CAKE

There are many variations on this recipe and the cake is traditional throughout the West Country. Devon apple cake is almost identical.

Old recipe:

4 apples
3 ozs\75 gms butter
¼ pint\150 mls milk
2 eggs
2 ozs\50 gms plain flour
3 tablespoonfuls sugar
A few drops of almond essence

Peel and slice the apples and fry them in hot butter. Mix the milk, eggs and flour. Stir in the apples, melted butter and almond essence. Put in a greased 7" (18 cm) sponge sandwich tin and bake at 375°F\190°C\ Gas Mark 5 for 20 minutes. Turn out; sprinkle with sugar and brown in the oven or under a grill. Serve with cream or cold with ice cream.

APPLE SAUCE CAKE

This is a variation on the West Country apple cake theme which is similar to that traditional in Dorset. In Somerset it was usual to puree the apples instead of leaving them in pieces as in Dorset.

Old recipe:

½ lb plain flour
6 ozs apple sauce (unsweetened)
4 ozs raisins
4 ozs butter
½ lb brown sugar
2 teaspoons mixed spice
1 egg
1 teaspoon baking powder
Butter icing

Steve Guscott

Cream together the butter and sugar in a mixing bowl. Gradually beat in the egg. Mix in the apple sauce. Gradually stir in the flour sifted with the baking powder and spices, then mix in the raisins. Transfer the mixture to a greased, lined 8 inch cake tin and bake at 350°F\180°C\Gas Mark 4 for about one hour until brown but not too dry. When cool the cake can be iced with butter icing suitably flavoured: rum, cinnamon or vanilla work well.

APPLE GINGERBREAD

This is another variation on the apple cake recipe.

Old recipe:

> 4 ozs plain flour
> 2 ozs butter
> 1 lb cooking apples
> 2 ozs sugar
> 2 ozs golden syrup
> 1 teaspoon ground ginger
> ½ teaspoon mixed spice
> 1 teaspoon baking soda
> Milk
> Cinnamon icing

Melt gently together the sugar, butter and syrup in a pan. Add this to the sifted flour, soda and spices and mix well. Mix with enough milk to make a soft dropping consistency. Peel, core and chop the apples and add to the mixture. Turn into a lined and greased square cake tin and bake at 350°F\180°C\Gas Mark 4 for 1½ hours. When cool, ice with cinnamon icing.

SIMNEL CAKE

Steve Guscott

Simnel cake is clearly British but, although traditional on Exmoor, it has lost any regional origin in the mists of time. Different traditions associate it with mid-Lent, Mothering Sunday, Easter or Christmas. Mothering Sunday was even referred to as Simnel Sunday and

spiced ale was drunk with the cake. The word 'simnel' comes from the Latin 'simila', which is a fine flour. The original recipe was for a crisp bread made of fine wheat flour. No doubt it became richer as people were able to obtain other ingredients. However, it was clearly a cake for special occasions and contained the finest ingredients people could afford. During its evolution it was boiled like a pudding and the use of almond paste either in the cake, on it or both seems to be a recent invention, as is the now traditional decoration of eleven eggs or marzipan balls. As part of an Easter tradition, these are said to represent the eleven apostles who remained loyal to Christ.

Old recipe

> 5 eggs plus 1 yolk
> ½ lb butter
> ½ lb caster sugar
> ½ lb plain flour
> 2 lbs mixed fruit and peel
> 2 ozs black treacle
> 3 teaspoons mixed spice
> ½ teaspoon salt
> 1½ lbs almond paste
> apricot jam

Cream the butter and sugar and gradually beat in the five eggs. Fold in the sieved flour, spice and salt. Mix in the treacle and finally the mixed fruit. Grease and line an 8 inch round cake tin with greaseproof paper. Roll out the marzipan and use the tin to cut a circle to fit from about a third of the marzipan. Put half of the cake mixture in the tin, top with the marzipan circle and cover with the other half of the mixture. Bake at 325°F\170°C\Gas Mark 3 for 3½ hours. When the cake is cool, brush the top with jam and roll out the remaining marzipan to fit on top. Any trimmings can be used to make eggs for decoration. Brush the marzipan with the egg yolk and place the cake under a grill to brown it.

EXETER SANDWICH

This is a traditional Devonshire recipe which seems like it is going to be an ordinary jam sandwich cake but has a surprisingly firm texture.

Old recipe:

> 8 ozs plain flour
> 4 ozs butter
> 4 ozs caster sugar
> 1 egg
> 2 ozs split almonds
> Raspberry jam

Rub the butter into the flour, and then mix in the sugar, then the beaten egg. Roll out lightly and cut one half to fit a 7 inch sandwich tin. Press in to cover the base of the greased tin and spread with jam. Cover with the second half, pressing the edges lightly together to seal in the jam. Dot with split almonds and bake for 40 minutes at 375°F\190°C\Gas Mark 5.

SOMERSET CIDER SLICE

Recipe from Mrs C J Corbett of Minehead:

1½ ozs\35 gms margarine
8 ozs\225 gms soft brown sugar
4 ozs\100 gms raisins
4 ozs\100 gms sultanas
¼ pt\150 mls dry cider
8 ozs\225 gms malted wheatmeal flour
1 teaspoon mixed spice
1 teaspoon ground ginger
2 teaspoons baking powder
7 fluid ozs\175 mls water

Place the margarine into a pan with the fruit, cider, spices and water, stir well, bring to the boil and simmer for 2 minutes, then leave to cool. Mix flour and baking powder in a bowl, then stir in the cooked fruit mixture. Turn into a greased tin and bake at 350°F\180°C\ Gas Mark 4 for 30-40 minutes until firm and golden. Turn out and cool on a wire rack. Freezes well.

FROSTED WHORTLEBERRY SLICE

Recipe from Hannah Bradshaw of Dunster:

For the pastry:
2 ozs\50 gms margarine
2 ozs\50 gms lard
8 ozs\225 gms plain flour
Water

For the sauce:
1 lb\450 gms whortleberries
6-8 ozs\150-225 gms caster sugar
¼ pt\150 mls port

For the filling:
4 ozs\100gms soft margarine
4 ozs\100 gms self raising flour
4 ozs\100 gms caster sugar
2 eggs
½ teaspoon almond essence

For the topping:
8 ozs\225 gms sifted icing sugar
1 egg white

Heat the whortleberries and port until the skins begin to split, pour into a bowl, stir in sugar and leave to cool. Rub together fats and flour and make up to a soft dough with a little water. Roll out and line a greased 7"X 11"X 1" tin, trim the edges and prick with a fork.

Spread the cooled sauce over the base. Mix together caster sugar, flour, eggs margarine and almond essence, beat until light and fluffy and spread over the sauce. Bake in the centre of an oven for 30-35 minutes at 375°F\ 190°C\Gas Mark 5 until lightly browned and springy to the touch. Turn out when cold. Beat icing sugar and egg white together until light and fluffy. Spread over the top of the sponge and cut into 12 slices.

DUNSTER COBBLES

Recipe from Hannah Bradshaw of Dunster:

8 ozs\225 gms margarine
5 ozs\125 gms caster sugar
3 ozs\75 gms desiccated coconut
2½ ozs\60 gms corn flakes\bran flakes
5 ozs\125 gms Dunster wholemeal flour
1 tablespoon cocoa

Steve Guscott

Melt the margarine over a low heat and stir in the sugar, coconut, cocoa and corn or bran flakes. Gradually stir in the flour. Roll into ping-pong ball shapes; place on a greased and lined baking sheet, leaving space between each one to allow them to flatten. Bake for 20 minutes at 300°F\150°C\Gas Mark 2.

SAVOURY PUDDINGS

DUMPLINGS

These were used to eke out meagre supplies of meat, which was always expensive if you did not produce your own. Originally they were made using pieces of dough from bread making. When baking powder and soda were introduced in the nineteenth century it became usual to make dumplings with flour, baking powder, grated suet and salt and mixed with a little water to form a soft dough. They varied in size and were sometimes cooked separately like Yorkshire puddings but were generally added to stews and casseroles for the last twenty minutes of cooking time. Sometimes children were only given the dumplings with a little of the gravy and the meat was reserved for the hard-working men. They had various additional flavourings, mainly of herbs, and were sometimes lightened by adding bread crumbs to the mixture.

HERB DUMPLINGS

Old recipe:

2 ozs plain flour
2 ozs white breadcrumbs
2 tablespoons shredded suet
2 teaspoons chopped mixed herbs e.g. thyme, parsley,
marjoram, chives, sage
½ teaspoon baking powder
Grated rind of 1 lemon
1 egg
Seasoning

Mix together all ingredients except the egg in a bowl. Beat the egg and mix in well to form a soft dough. Add a little water if necessary, but do not make it too sticky. Roll into walnut-sized balls and add to a stew for the last 20 minutes of cooking time.

DEVON SUET PUDDING

Recipe from Hazel Milton of West Anstey; she has used this for many years to serve with roast lamb.

4 ozs suet
8 ozs self raising flour
1 egg
Pinch salt
Milk to mix

Put all the ingredients in a bowl and mix. Add enough milk to make the mixture of a dropping consistency. Put in a deep baking dish and bake for 30 minutes at 400°F\200°C\Gas Mark 6.

DONKEY PIE

Traditional method:

A pie dish was lined with thin short crust pastry. This was filled with a mixture of rolled oats, grated cheese and butter roughly in the proportions of two parts oats to one of oats and a quarter of butter. The mix was seasoned and devilled with a little cayenne or mustard and dampened with a little water. Another thin layer of pastry was placed on top and the whole baked in a moderate oven for about half an hour.

DODGERS

Traditional method:

These are cheese pancakes made with an oatmeal batter. Plain flour was mixed with fine oatmeal roughly in the proportion of eight parts flour to one of oatmeal. A little baking powder and seasoning was sieved in with the flour. Milk was mixed in to form a firm pancake batter. Diced cheese was added and the mixture fried in butter a few tablespoonfuls at a time, as small pancakes.

SWEET PUDDINGS

EXETER PUDDING

Old recipe:

7 eggs
10 ozs white breadcrumbs
6 ozs sugar
5 ozs grated suet
Ratafia biscuits
Butter
Raisins
Jam
Grated rind of 1 lemon
Rum

Beat together the eggs and sugar and rum to taste. Mix in the breadcrumbs, suet and lemon rind, beating all together. Line an ovenproof dish with ratafia biscuits stuck on with butter. Scatter with raisins and add a layer of the mixture. Dot with jam and cover with remainder of mixture. Bake in a moderate oven until firm and golden brown. Serve with a sauce of jam melted in sherry.

BATTER PUDDINGS

These were like Yorkshire puddings but were sweet, not savoury and used as desserts.

Traditional method:

Cream together the grated rind of a lemon with 2 ozs butter and 2 ozs caster sugar. Beat in two eggs and fold in 2 ozs plain flour. Make to a batter consistency with about half a pint of milk. Turn into a buttered and floured pudding dish and bake in a moderate oven for about 30-40 minutes. Serve immediately, with butter and sugar.

TIVERTON PUDDING

This is a local variation on the batter pudding recipe.

Old recipe:

3 dessertspoons flour
1 pt milk
4 eggs
1 dessertspoon sugar
Ginger and other ground spices
Grated lemon rind

Separate the eggs. Beat the yolks with the milk and stir in flour, sugar, spice and peel. Whisk the egg whites and fold in to the mixture. Put in a buttered pudding basin and steam until set. Serve immediately, as the pudding tends to sink as it cools.

EGGS

Eggs have been part of the Exmoor diet since time immemorial, although hens' eggs have never been as common as they are now. Asiatic jungle fowl have been domesticated for about four thousand years but, in Britain at least, it has only been since the mid nineteenth century that they have been selectively bred as meat or egg producing birds. Until then each hen would only produce about thirty eggs per year, which was hardly worth the input of feed. Battery hens now produce about eight times that amount.

Not surprisingly, wild birds' eggs were more commonly eaten in the past. Sea birds' eggs were probably the most common on Exmoor. These were largely taken from the colonies of auks and kittiwakes on the cliffs in spring. Herring gulls eggs taste fishy and were not greatly prized. Better are those of Black-headed gulls, but those birds are only winter visitors to Exmoor. Gulls' eggs are still collected in parts of the West Country and sold to hotels hard boiled. Some serve them nestling in a bed of moss. You crack the shells, dip the eggs in celery salt and eat them with slices of brown bread and butter.

From the Middle Ages onwards eggs were used as an ingredient in cookery: to thicken soups, custards and sauces; to bind stuffings; and to enrich pastry and cakes. As plain eggs – boiled, poached or fried – they rarely formed part of main courses. In the seventeenth century collops and eggs became the forerunner of the bacon and eggs which became popular as salt pork became a mainstay of the Exmoor diet. Eggs were also a common accompaniment of salt fish, the other mainstay for many poor people. However, it was only

Free range eggs from farmyard hens

Brian Pearce

when egg production rose in Victorian times that they became standard breakfast fare. Victorians introduced scrambled eggs on toast, boiled eggs coddled in hot water in a china hen, and plain omelets. Soufflés appeared about the same time, but they were a French invention and not for the common people of Exmoor. Today we worry about the cholesterol content of eggs but, until recently, on Exmoor it was common not only to fry eggs but to serve them with a dollop of clotted cream on each for breakfast, accompanied by bacon which was up to 90% fat! Bert Verney in his reminiscences remembers his mother's home help in the 1920s:

> She always lit the hearth fire and fried the breakfast for eight people: fat bacon from our own pigs, eggs and potatoes left over from the day before, and often batter pancakes. If anyone wanted toast, it had to be toasted on long-handled forks over the open fire. The taste was superb, and when covered with home-made butter, jam or marmalade, was really a meal on its own. She cooked or fried the breakfast in a huge frying pan, holding ten eggs at a time, balanced on a brandis over an open fire.

Surprisingly, I cannot find any Easter egg customs for Exmoor. However, there were Shrovetide customs. Shrove Tuesday was the day to use up any rich food before Lent – the forty days before Easter representing Christ's fasting in the wilderness. It was quite common for farmers and their labourers to feast on pancakes. Tradition had it that everyone had to toss a pancake over the open fire and eat it, wherever it had landed. Lent crocking or Lent sherding was a bit like trick or treating. Usually on the Monday before Lent, people would go around farms singing for crocks (cakes). If they were invited in, they were given a crock and a cup of cider. If not they would throw stones or broken crockery at the door. In some parts they would sing for eggs and, perhaps, other ingredients with which to make their pancakes next day. In the South Molton area they chanted:

> Once, twice, thrice
> I give thee warning.
> Please go make pancakes
> gin tomorrow morning.

On Shrove Tuesday itself the eggs for the pancakes were subject to the custom of 'shackle egg'. Everyone marked their own egg and all were placed in a padded sieve. The sieve was shaken and the winner was the last whose egg remained uncracked. This always then had to be cracked to prove that it had not been boiled.

It was considered unlucky to bring small bunches of primroses into the house of anyone who kept poultry, or the number of poultry reared that season would tally with the number of primroses in the bunch. Few

Exmoor farmers, however, kept many poultry. This was probably to do with the remoteness of the farms from markets. Another problem was that it was difficult to guarantee a regular supply. Output varies with day length; hens go broody from time to time and go off laying altogether at the winter moult, hence the cheer when they start laying again in spring. Modern commercial hybrid hens are kept laying with artificial lighting and do not go broody in their uncomfortable cages but are thrown out after the first moult as they never produce as frequently again. Traditional breeds allowed to continue their natural cycle produce fewer eggs but their rate of output does not diminish as rapidly with age. A problem, however, is how to store eggs for the winter. They are best kept cool but keep no better in todays refrigerators. They were sometimes preserved in buckets of waterglass (sodium silicate solution), which sealed the shells. Today eggs are cheap and waterglass is not worth the expense. In the past local farmers used lime as a cheaper alternative. An old recipe for preserving 800 eggs was: 1 bushel quicklime, 2lbs salt and ½lb cream of tartar mixed with enough water to float the eggs. Quicklime is extremely caustic and reacts violently with water, so the process must have been hazardous.

One Exmoor farmer was known for touting his eggs around local pubs, largely to pay for his drinking. However, it was the farmers' wives who were the main poultry keepers and sold eggs for housekeeping. In his reminiscences, Pat Pidler of Chittlehampton remembers his mother's duties:

> The houses were just beyond the garden in what we called the plat, where there were some apple trees. Each morning the fowls were fed, given water and eggs collected. I can see mother now going out with some corn in a bucket and scattering the grains on the ground, and all the fowls gathering around to eat it. In the afternoon she would often gather up her towser apron, which was made of light sacking tied around the waist with tape, and gather the eggs into it. When mother had any broken china she would break it up finely and give it to them to save buying grit. We had some eggs for use in the house for cooking and the rest were sold to Mr Venner from Filleigh whose lorry would come and collect them once a week.

Today, of course, hens are not generally fed broken china, although farmyard hens are still fed corn and they will eat almost anything. For commercial production, hens need a high protein diet to maintain a high output of eggs. This comes in the form of grain pellets which contain fishmeal. This is not so good for fish, as fish of any size are hoovered out of the sea in the process and potentially not so good for us either as they contain antibiotics and chemicals. Most contain chemicals to enrich the colour of the yolks. One, otherwise known as E161g, was banned as a colourant in human food because it caused eye problems. Dont be misled into thinking that free range eggs are different. The hens may be happier (although not necessarily) but they are usually fed the same pellets. Also, diet may affect the colour of the yolks but not the shells, and brown shelled eggs are no better than white. My hens are all truly free ranging and naturally fed, but each produces a different colour egg because each is a different breed or cross. That way I can tell which is laying and how much. So, ignore appearances and use your taste to judge eggs. Luckily most Exmoor poultry are genuinely free ranging and naturally fed and the eggs taste wonderful. The slight drawback is that you usually have to buy them straight from the farm.

EGGYOT

Heat two pints of beer in a pan. Beat two eggs with two tablespoons of sugar and beat into the beer until thick.

CHIPPLE TART

Steve Guscott

Chipples is a local word for spring onions. It obviously has the same root as the Italian for onions – cipolle – but I have not discovered the connection. This is an old and very simple recipe and instructions are not precise.

Old recipe

Grease a tart plate or shallow pie dish and line with short crust pastry. Cut chipples and streaky bacon into quarter inch lengths and cover the pastry. Break eggs over these carefully without breaking the yolks. Put a pastry lid on top, brushing it with milk and pricking it. Bake for about 30 minutes, according to size, at 350°F\180°C\Gas Mark 4 until the pastry is browned.

OYSTER OMELETS

Steve Guscott

You can use tinned smoked oysters for this dish, but there is nothing like fresh oysters if you can obtain them. Omelets are best cooked very lightly, stirring gently during cooking and removing from the heat as soon as the egg starts to set.

Old recipe

3 eggs
6 oysters
seasoning

Blanch and beard the oysters and cut the meat of each into four. Separate the eggs. Beat the yolks a little and mix with oysters and seasoning. Whisk the whites until stiff and stir lightly into the mixture. Cook with a knob of butter in an omelet pan for 2-3 minutes, stirring all the time.

DEVONSHIRE OMELET

An old recipe

To serve four persons:
3 large cooking apples
½ oz butter
2 tablespoons caster sugar
2 tablespoons crushed macaroons
2 eggs, separated
½ teaspoon powdered cinnamon

Peel, core and cook the apples in a pan with the sugar and 3 tablespoons water. Cook to a purée. Stir in the butter, cinnamon, macaroons and beaten egg yolks. Whisk the egg whites stiffly and lightly fold into the other ingredients. Butter a fireproof dish and pour in the mixture. Dredge the top with caster sugar and bake for about 20 minutes in a moderate oven until browned.

HONEYCOMB PUDDING

Old recipe from Miss M A Richards of Simonsbath

3 teacupsfull milk
3 eggs, separated
1 teacupfull caster sugar
½ oz gelatine
1 wineglassful cherry brandy (optional - if used, reduce milk by same quantity)

Soak the gelatine in the milk for half an hour then heat with the sugar in a saucepan, stirring until dissolved. Beat the yolks and stir into the mixture. Heat until simmering but not boiling. Stir in the cherry brandy, if used. Beat the egg whites until stiff and lightly stir into the mixture. Pour into wetted moulds and leave to cool.

RHUBARB AND CUSTARD PIE

If you prefer a meringue which is crisp through, bake at 100°F for three hours.

This is an old recipe, so instructions are not precise.

Roll out 6ozs shortcrust pastry. Grease an 8 inch flan tin and line with the pastry. Prick all over; cover the bottom with greaseproof paper and weight with baking beans or an ovenproof substitute. Bake blind in a moderate oven for about ten minutes until the pastry is cooked but not brown. Cut 1lb of rhubarb into 2 inch pieces place in a saucepan and stew gently till quite tender; sweeten well and use only enough water to prevent burning. Leave to cool. With the yolks of 4 eggs and ½ pint milk make a thick boiled custard and when nearly cold pour over flan base. Leave to set and pour the rhubarb over the custard. Whisk the egg

Steve Guscott

whites to a quite stiff froth and beat in one heaped tablespoonful dried sifted caster sugar for each egg used, till mixture is snow white and stiff enough to stand in points; cover fruit with this and bake in moderate oven about ½ hour, till top is light brown and quite crisp through.

❧ Drinks ❧

SPRING WATER

Most old Exmoor farmhouses were built along the spring lines of the hillsides, many tucked into a 'heal' or hollow at the top of a small combe. A good spring which did not dry up was essential to a farm. Many wells are marked on old maps but on Exmoor this usually meant where water welled up out of the ground and true wells were relatively uncommon on the high ground. Boreholes are, however, becoming more common. Some tap sources of water which has travelled considerable distances within the rocks. Some in the Combe Martin area are reputed to tap water which originated in Wales.

Borehole water usually contains more minerals and is more refreshing than the rather flat tasting, soft, surface water which is normal on Exmoor, although it can contain unhealthy proportions of some metallic salts. Surface water springs can also have problems – rarely through contamination from fertilisers but often through the action of acid moorland water on old lead or copper plumbing. Sources of really good tasting water are unusual on Exmoor but, where found, are exceptionally good. They are usually where the water has travelled some distance through the rocks and is naturally filtered by them. At the remains of the old Lynrock mineral water factory near Watersmeet the spring can be found gushing straight from the rock.

The Lynrock factory operated from about 1911 until the late 1930s. It used water throughout its working life: hydraulic power first worked the bottling machinery, then hydro-electric power and finally the remains of the buildings were washed away in the 1952 flood. Extravagant claims were made about the water: that it was the purest water in the world and that it was radio-active, giving it remarkable properties as a tonic. It was said to cure gout, rheumatism, liver complaints, kidney disease, dyspepsia, anaemia, constipation, blood and skin impurities. It was supposed to be naturally sparkling, but the company also aerated it and made sparkling soda, lemonade, ginger beer and ginger ale. There were other aerated water companies operating in Minehead from the 1870s until the Second World War. They grew with the interest in teetotalism around the 1880s. Temperance hotels were all the rage and non-alcoholic drinks were very popular. In the 1880s

Hayward's Aerated Water Company was selling 120,000 bottles of flavoured mineral water a year. They used the well known Codd's Patent bottles. These had a pinched neck which contained a loose marble. When full, the pressure of gas held the marble against a rubber ring in the neck, making it leakproof.

Many wells were ancient holy wells which were said to have magic or healing properties. They date back to Celtic times when the spirits of springs were worshipped. These tended to be female spirits and when locals were converted to Christianity in Saxon times they tended to dedicated the springs to female saints such as St Agnes' Fountain and St Catherine's Well at Allerford and Selworthy. Many wells were said to have curative properties attributed to their associated saints. Women would pray to St Catherine for a husband or child and a gift to her thrown in her well would help. Blindwell near Twitchen was said to have cleared eyesight. This was the origin of wishing wells.

St John's Spring at Combe Martin was long noted for the curative properties of its water. It was marketed as Coulsworthy Water from 1906 until 1934, when the Lynton to Barnstaple railway, which was its main source of distribution, closed. It was recommended for over-indulgence and dyspepsia and was said, like Lynrock water, to cure almost anything, including jaundice, appendicitis and dysentery. Tying it in with the Combe Martin tourist industry, it was recommended that one drank '8 ozs four times a day combined with a cure de repos, with a new and salutary regime, spent among the simpler scenes and more homely character of picturesque villages on the rugged coast of North Devon'.

There are several commercially used springs around Exmoor as spring water has now become popular again. The Exmoor Spring Water company at Huntscott was for a while very successful, winning a national blind tasting competition and even exported water to Saudi Arabia. Companies bottling water for sale are subject to stringent legislation. Most people swear by their own spring water, but testing often shows up contaminants and, luckily, there are still some good supplies in the area. A farm at Furzehill bottles its own water for sale. Combe Martin, where beds of limestone naturally filter some springwater, seems to be blessed and there are commercial wells at Hoyles Farm and Coulsworthy.

CORDIALS

SPARKLING ELDERFLOWER CORDIAL

Elderflowers vary greatly and it is important to pick them in full bloom and when dry. It is best to smell them first and use only those which smell sweet: reject any that smell musky.

Old recipe:

> 2 heads elderflowers
> 1 lemon
> 1 gallon water
> 2 tablespoons cider vinegar
> 1½ lbs sugar

Squeeze the juice from the lemon, chop the rind and mix with the other ingredients in a large jug. Leave to infuse for at least 24 hours. Strain and bottle tightly. Keep for at least two weeks before using.

ELDERFLOWER CORDIAL

Recipe from Mrs G Hill of Dunster:

> To make 4 pints:
> 20 elderflower heads, de-stalked
> 2 oranges, sliced
> 2 lemons, sliced
> 2 ozs citric acid
> 2½ lbs sugar
> 3 pts water
> 1 Campden tablet

Dissolve the sugar in boiling water for 5 minutes. Pour over the remaining ingredients and cover. Stir twice daily for 3 or 4 days. Strain – dont mash – and bottle.

RASPBERRY VINEGAR

This is an old country drink not confined to Exmoor, but is still made commercially by Brendon Hill Crafts. Vinegars can be made from a variety of soft fruits and are refreshing drunk diluted with water or soda.

Old recipe:

Take equal volumes of raspberries and white wine vinegar. Combine these and leave to stand for up to a week. Strain through a muslin bag, squeezing to remove remaining juice and add 1 lb of sugar to every 2 pints of juice. Heat in a saucepan and stir to dissolve the sugar, but do not boil. Cool the liquid, bottle and stopper firmly. It should be kept in a cool place.

TEA

Tea has been a popular drink with Exmoor people since it became affordable in the nineteenth century. Its popularity has started to dwindle slightly now, especially amongst younger people. There is, however, a revival of interest in herbal teas or infusions, which were the norm for country folk before the nineteenth century.

The well known Miles tea company of Porlock and Minehead started when Derek Miles moved to Porlock in 1961. He had come from a family tea blending business in Birmingham via a tea brokering company in London. He first ran a grocers shop in Minehead and undertook some part time tea inspecting at Avonmouth docks. There were always a few chests landed which did not easily sell and Derek bought them and blended them at his cottage at Porlock, selling to customers in Bristol.

The business soon took off and had to move to larger premises at the old coal yard in Porlock. He took over his old family firm in the Midlands and started manufacturing tea bags there, eventually moving that part of the business to Minehead in 1998. The firm now has 28 staff. Although the premises are ultra-modern, the tea is still tasted and blended in the old fashioned way. The tea for tasting is measured on an old pair of hand scales balanced by a sixpenny bit and the blending machine is pre-war and described as being a bit like a cement mixer. Up to twelve different teas are used to keep the Miles blend tasting the same and up to a hundred teas are tasted before each is selected for the blend. The firm used to claim that the tea was blended to suit the local water but it is now sold far and wide. Several different blends have now been added to their products, including organic tea, and single estate teas can be purchased from their shop in Porlock. Much of the business, however, is selling to catering outlets.

BEER

Home brewing was very common in the countryside until the end of the nineteenth century and beer was drunk more extensively than cider. It was generally weaker and even drunk by children, which was not the case with cider. Small quantities of beer were seen as a stimulant to encourage work and generally regarded as healthy, whereas cider was associated with drunkenness and a variety of disorders. Cider became associated with labourers and lower classes, whereas beer was an accepted drink for yeomen farmers and the middle classes. Accounts from the sixteenth to eighteenth centuries suggest that enough beer was produced in many households to supply about a pint per day to every man, woman and child.

The climate of Exmoor was not particularly suited for the growing of cider apples or grain, but grain could often be grown where apples could not. Barley did not become commonly grown in the area until the seventeenth century. Before that, oats and rye were the main grains, much more suited to the damp moorland climate. Oats can be and were malted for brewing. Even when barley became more common locally, it tended to be mixed with oats, rye or wheat for malting. The area was not known for quality oats and the beer was reckoned to be a taste acquired by the locals but unpalatable to most outsiders. Much of the best barley was grown in the Vale of Porlock. Today several farmers in that area concentrate on producing small quantities of the highest quality malting barley. They frequently win national and international prizes for this barley. Hops were introduced to Britain in the sixteenth

Hops at Bossington

Brian Pearce

century, but seem to have been a considerable luxury until the eighteenth century, when they seem to have been grown on some West Country farms. They were grown in the Vale of Porlock, where they still grow wild. An account of a storm at Porlock Weir in 1626 states that two acres of hops were washed out to sea.

Farms tended to have their own small malt houses, often at the back of the house next to the scullery, where the copper could heat the mash for brewing. To make malt, the grains were sprouted. These were spread out on a cloth made of felted hair. This was suspended over a small fire made of sticks or straw in a kiln-shaped building.

Pubs also commonly made their own beer. The earliest ones locally were the church houses. They doubled as the church hall and village pub. Such buildings often backed onto the churchyard and have now been converted to dwellings or other purposes as at Parracombe, Martinhoe and Luccombe. They often existed in large rural parishes where people would walk considerable distances to church and wished for some rest and refreshment before services. Church ales were a method of raising money and there were many festivities concerned with ale drinking on the local calendar. There were bride ales to assist a couple in setting up house or with a newborn child; bid ales for helping an individual in debt; and regular Whitsun ales to provide funds for the poor of the parish. There were also the annual revels where ale was served after church. Revel Sunday was nearest to the day of the saint to whom the church was dedicated. In Lynton a barrel of beer was set against the church gate in readiness for the congregation coming out of church. Naturally, any excuse for a festivity was invented by those wishing to sell or drink ale. In Skilgate at Easter, 1592 the church bells were rung to encourage people as far away as Taunton to come to church to drink. An Act of 1603 tried to put a stop to drinking in church or in the churchyard, but traditions died hard locally. Many local revels and festivities, including the Earl of Rone ceremony at Combe Martin were put an end to by nineteenth century clergy because they became too drunken and violent.

In the centre of Exmoor there were few inns until the mid nineteenth century because there were poor communications and few travellers. Simonsbath House had been licensed in the early part of the century but it ceased to be an inn when taken over by John Knight in 1818. He set up an inn at Gallon House in 1841. It was reputed to have gained this name because thirsty miners ordered their beer a gallon at a time. However, miners did not arrive in the area until five years later. Also on the Knight estate was the Acland Arms, at Mole's Chamber, which had a reputation for vice and smuggling. Both inns were closed in the 1880s. Another, the Sportsman's Inn, was built at Sandyway in 1851 and, due to its isolation, survived sporadically through the twentieth century. The only one which survived on the estate was an existing house and shop licensed as the Simonsbath Inn in 1855. Its landlord lost his licence a year later for keeping a rowdy house. It continued to sell beer until 1873 when Frederic Knight tried to reduce the proportion of wages spent on drink by allowing it to sell wine only. This had some effect, but encouraged home brewing. In the Edwardian era, as the Exmoor Forest Hotel, it became a temperance hotel and did not regain a full licence until 1933.

In the nineteenth century publicans often travelled around the houses selling beer in 4½ gallon firkins at 2d-4d per pint, according to quality. In the 1880s Dulverton had more than a dozen inns. The present Guildhall buildings partly occupy an old brewery and malthouse. In the 1890s a club was founded at Stogumber to promote the drinking of the local beer. The reason was that all pubs round about were tied to outside brewers and the local brewery had just reopened. It had been offered for sale a few years before together with the West Somerset and Tangier breweries in Taunton and eight inns in West Somerset and North Devon and appears to have closed before a sale was eventually agreed. In 1894 the brewers were described in Kelly's Directory as 'barley factors, wine and spirit importers, hop merchants and manufacturers of aerated waters', which included ginger beer, lemonade, orange champagne, kola champagne, potash water and a cordial known as Winter Cheer. The Stogumber Ale was promoted for its health giving properties and the brewers even offered dietary advice for convalescence:

Breakfast: a broiled mutton chop, a small quantity of home-made bread, one cup of coffee or tea made with soft water, with good sweet cream, and an egg boiled for two or three minutes – may finish with orange marmalade.

Lunch: hot mutton, a small piece of bread and one-third of a pint of the ale after the meal.

Dinner: venison, mutton or beef, and bread, no vegetables, no pastry, no wine or spirits, half to three-quarters of a pint of the ale.

Tea: one cup of tea or coffee with good cream, and home-made bread in moderation with butter or cream.

Another brewery which advertised the health giving properties of its ale was at Wiveliscombe. A postcard advertising Wiveliscombe Old Ale showed a picture of Betsy Bushen of Minehead taken in 1908, when she was a hundred years old. It reads: 'A great comfort to me has been Wiveliscombe Old Ale. I have had half a pint every night for 70 years; it gives me strength and

sleep'. Another well known twentieth century brewery was Crocombe and Son at Parracombe, which supplied inns in that area with beer and mineral waters. In recent years Exmoor has been known for the two breweries at Wiveliscombe: Cotleigh and Exmoor Ales. They share the same water and malt supplies and distribute in the same area but produce distinctly different beers.

Exmoor Ales was founded in 1980 by Tim Gilmour-White at the old brewery which was founded by William Hancock in 1807 and stands on Golden Hill. The original building was a cloth mill supplying the slave trade. Hancock's remained a family concern until 1955, when the last Hancock died and the business was taken over by Ushers of Trowbridge. The staff were bussed to work at the depot at Taunton. They were allowed two pints of cider at lunchtime as part of their wages but few kept their full ration and their job.

At first Exmoor Ales traded as Golden Hill Brewery, although its beers all had the Exmoor prefix. It was successful right from the start, winning the bitter award in the 1980 Great British Beer Festival and has since gone on to win many more prizes. In 1991 Adrian Newman took over as brewer and redesigned the brewery, increasing its capacity. A good relationship was built up with wholesalers and other small brewers (as guest beers) and Exmoor Ales became available in all parts of Britain. They went in with Marstons brewery to bottle Exmoor Gold, which claims to be the first regularly available single malt ale, using no colouring or additives.

It alone has won over thirty awards. Barrie Pepper of *What's Brewing* magazine describes Exmoor Gold as having: a sweet hoppy aroma and a delicate mix of malt and hops in the taste with a touch of toffee. As well as Exmoor Ale and Gold, the brewery also offers Exmoor Hart and Stag, the latter being originally brewed to celebrate the centenary of Somerset gaining first class status in cricket. It also brews two beers for winter consumption only: Exmoor Beast, a dark, very strong porter; and Exmoor Exmas, a ruby coloured and complex mix of three malts and whole hops. The brewery currently employs ten people and seems to be surviving in a competitive market by supplying high quality produce.

Cotleigh was started by Ted Bishop at Cotleigh just outside of Tiverton. It moved to Wiveliscombe about the same time as Exmoor Ales started and the two breweries operated literally side by side until 1985 when Cotleigh expanded into new premises down the hill. The brewery is long and thin and the beer progresses downhill through its processing and out onto a lorry at the end. Cotleigh delivers most of its beer within a forty mile radius and uses wholesalers to distribute further afield. Its original bitter was the regular Tawny and then came the darker, stronger winter ale, Old Buzzard. This was followed by a light summer ale called Harrier. The strong bitter Barn Owl was a promotion to sponsor the Hawk and Owl Trust but it became a permanent brew after it became Supreme Champion at the Maltings Beer Festival. Other occasional brews, following the birds of prey theme, have been Golden Eagle and Hobby. Cotleigh seems set to remain a small local brewery whereas Exmoor is continually expanding and now distributes bottled beer to the large supermarket chains.

CIDER

Cider (usually spelt cyder in Devonshire) is no longer made on Exmoor and probably never was in any great quantity, much of it being imported from surrounding areas. An eighteenth century survey of Devon reported that: 'Every estate has some orchards, every cottage some apples' and William Marshall, writing in 1796 said 'Their orchards might well be styled their temples and apple trees their idols of worship'. However, this was not necessarily so for the exposed moors. In Milles enquiry of Devonshire parishes of about 1750 the rector of North Molton remarked that the parish produced 'poor, meagre cider' and the rector of East Down, probably disapproving of cider drinking, replied that the cider was 'good for nothing, on the evidence of the parish'. Likewise at Mariansleigh there was 'little, bad cider' and at East Anstey the same was true and most cider had to be bought in. At Challacombe and Countisbury there was no cider at all.

Cider was very much a commercial crop in the West Country and farmers tended to sell their best cider and keep the worst to pay their labourers. Thus Exmoor people must have drunk a mixture of good quality bought cider and fairly appalling locally produced cider. Most of the cider orchards in the Exmoor area seem to have been in the more sheltered, lower lying areas of the Vale of Porlock and the northern edge of the Brendon Hills. Carhampton was singled out as being full of orchards, although this seems to have been mostly in the nineteenth century.

Records of cider drinking in the West Country date back to the thirteenth century. Cider had reached Normandy a century earlier and could well have been introduced by the Plantagenets. It seems to have been a drink of the gentry at first but, by the seventeenth century, was a common drink for all. Briefly in the eighteenth century it was taxed but the local reaction was akin to that to the poll tax. Before the tax cider was 2d to 3d per gallon when a man's weekly wage was about 7s. Even in 1965 it was possible to buy a pint of cider for 1s but, since then, duty has been imposed.

The practice of paying farm workers cider as part of their wages had died out by the Second World War and these factors have combined to greatly reduce the consumption of cider.

Even as this book was being written, two of the largest cider factories in the area: Inch's at Winkleigh and Taunton Cider at Norton Fitzwarren, were being closed down as their respective owners concentrated production elsewhere. Inch's was founded by Sam Inch in 1916 and produced up to a million gallons a year. It was bought out by its management in 1989 and later taken over by Bulmers. Hancock's Devon Cider at Trentworthy Mill, South Molton used hydraulic presses for over 50 years and won many awards. In the Tiverton area are Palmershayes Cider, which was started in 1905 and Clark's Farmhouse Cider, which is run more like a hobby by Lawrence Clark. Both use apples from local farms. In the Taunton area survives Sheppy's Cider, which has had many awards for its traditional style ciders. The Sheppy family has been producing cider for over 200 years and they have opened a cider museum at their works at Bradford on Tone.

Traditional cider is simply fermented apple juice. When apples drop to the ground they naturally start to ferment and no yeast needs to be added. The trees were shaken and the apples added to the windfalls, which were just shovelled up into heaps in the orchard and left until they all acquired a brown rot. The apples were not washed and, as all sorts of animals ventured into the orchard to pick at them, modern hygiene standards would definitely not have been met. The skill lies in blending the apples, although it is only since the nineteenth century that locals seem to have cared about the varieties – quantity was usually more prized than quality. Celia Feinnes, writing in the seventeenth century said:

> In most parts of Sommerset-shire it is very fruitful for orchards, plenty of apples and peares, but they are not curious in the planting the best sort of fruite, which is a great pity; being so soone produced and such quantetyes, they are likewise as careless when they make cider; they press all sorts of apples together, else they might have as good sider as in any other parts.

In some parts of the country cider is made from commonly found eating and cooking apples. Cider apples, however, are more akin to wild crab apples. They tend to be small, hard, blotchy and unattractive: so you would not find them in today's supermarkets. If you try eating them they tend to be very astringent – bitter and drying to the tongue – or, at best, bland. Their high tannin content makes them bitter but some are both bitter and sweet whilst others are bitter and sharp. Bittersharp varieties used nationally include Foxwhelp, Cowarne Red, Dymock Red, Joeby Crab, Kingston Black and Skyrmes Kernel. Common bittersweet varieties include Strawberry Norman, Knotted Kernel and Upright French. Some varieties are both culinary and cider apples and one local variety, called All Doer is triple purpose: culinary, dessert and cider. Local cider apple varieties include Bell Apple, Blue Sweet, Cider Lady's Finger, Coleman's Seedling, Crimson King, Dabinett, Dove, Fair Maid of Devon, Horners, Kingston Black, Kingston Bitter, Major, Morgan Sweet, Royal Somerset, Slack Ma Girdle, Stoke Red, Sweet Coppin, Taunton Fair Maid, Tremlett's Bitter and Wellington. Many of the varieties were named after the place where they were developed or the farmer who developed them. An Exmoor variety was named Coccagee as it came in the eighteenth century from Ireland, where its name means 'goose dropping'. Another local variety, Tom Putt, was reputedly named after Sir Thomas Putt, an eighteenth century Devon landowner. There were so many varieties because they do not grow true from seed. The seeds produce what were known as wilding trees onto which buds from the original trees were grafted. Often the wildings were allowed to grow on to see what sort of apples would develop from them.

Nowadays tastes are for less bitter ciders and cidermakers tend to concentrate on mixing bittersweets with regular apples such as Bramleys. Few of today's cider apple varieties are not of recent origin. If you wish to make your own cider you will need to experiment with different varieties but almost any can be used as long as sweet and sharp varieties are blended. The apples should be ripe and juicy and windfalls are ideal, as long as any really rotten parts are removed first. They should be washed and then crushed. Extracting the juice from apples is a problem on a small scale and there is not much alternative to an expensive fruit press. Farmers often pulped small quantities of apples by hitting them with a wooden mallet in a stone trough. Even an old kitchen sink, with its convenient plug hole for draining the juice, would do. Nowadays apples can be pulped easily by freezing and thawing them first.

Harvesting the apples was achieved by shaking the branches with ash poles. Today the shaking is done by machines. This is undertaken about three weeks before the apples are to be milled. This allows the fruit to ripen and the sugars to become concentrated. The apples were merely left to lie in the orchard or, in larger scale operations, taken to be stored in a tallet: a room above the mill.

Not every farm had its own mill and press and usually on Exmoor there was only one for each cider producing parish, which could be hired. William Holland kept a diary during the late eighteenth century when he was parson at Over Stowey on the Quantocks. He well described an occasion in 1799 when the parish clerk gathered his apples to cart them to the press:

They were taken down to Hewletts to be made through his hair cloths, which is not the fashion in this county. Mr Amen thinks it impossible for the cider to be as good as it is not made after the fashion of the county. On the Tuesday Mr Amen was gone again to press out the water cyder. He was very desirous of having Robert to assist him but I would nor permit it. Great wages and little work seem to be the general system of this place. The Somersetshire people are of a large size and strong but in my opinion very slow and lazy and discontented and humoursome and very much given to eating and drinking.

A traditional crusher was a large trugg stone like a millstone, which stood on its edge and was pulled around a circular stone trough by a horse. The juice poured over a lip in the trough into a container. More recently, apples were crushed by the rotating teeth of a geared metal drum, also horse powered. Both types of crusher were used in round buildings referred to as 'engine houses'. Often they were like five sides of an octagon built against the side of a barn. The horse walked around a central post which was like the axle of a horizontal toothed wheel geared to a drive. Several of these survive on Exmoor but may have been used for threshing corn or driving other machinery. The pulp was wrapped in layers of straw or a muslin cheese and placed in a large screw press to extract the remaining juice. The press was usually very simple but massive, as levering to great pressures was involved. The cheese could be built up to four or five feet thick and, once pressed, the protruding edges of a straw cheese would be cut off with a hay knife, placed on top and squeezed again. In other parts of the country the pulp was ground to extract flavour from skin and pips but not locally. The use of muslin or horse hair cloth was not common locally, as it was expensive and difficult to clean. Later, nylon muslins became common.

Improvements in cider mills in Victorian times led to the development of itinerant cidermakers. An all metal mill known as the rotary scratter mill replaced the millstones and both mill and a lightweight press could be carted to the farms where the apples were. Usually the mill and press had their own wheels and were pulled by horse in a little train with a cart for the barrels behind. The practice continued until the Second World War and the horses were replaced by traction engines, then tractors. If horses were used, they would drive the mill, walking around it in a steady circle. Traction engines and tractors were connected with a belt drive. The farm labourers would have to do most of the work, loading the mill with apples, the cheese with pomace (pulp) and filling the barrels with juice. The process suited Exmoor, where orchards tended to be small and the farmers could not justify the expense of milling and pressing equipment.

Cider press in the Minehead area, 1930s

The juice was simply left to ferment for a few weeks. There are many stories about throwing in dead rats to aid fermentation, and it was traditional to add a small piece of meat or even hens, or sheeps, blood, as was common further west. Not surprisingly, milk and cream were commonly added. The fermentation took place in wooden barrels. These had to be cleaned with boiling water to remove the dregs of the previous season and carefully looked after, keeping them damp but not wet to prevent leaks. The bung was left off and, as the juice fermented, most of the impurities, such as pips, stalks, skin, straw and other foreign bodies, came to the surface and frothed out of the hole. The remainder sank to the bottom and the barrel was kept constantly topped up with water or more juice. When fermentation had ceased the barrel was topped right up and bunged tightly as any air would rapidly turn the cider to vinegar.

It was then left in a cool place for another two weeks and racked from the sediment and bottled or barrelled in smaller barrels. Home cider was never strained – it could not be moved and was allowed to clear by settlement. It was ready to drink straight away and preferably not left more than a few weeks as it easily went vinegary, although it could keep for a year if properly stored. For commercial use the cider was tested with a saccharometer so that it was not allowed to ferment right out and kept some of its sweetness. It was racked several times to remove it from the sediment and stop fermentation, fined with isinglass and charcoal and filtered. Latterly, fermentation was stopped with sulphur and other chemicals which also acted as a preservative. Rough cider was the cloudy,

unfined variety which had fermented right out, so was dry and highly alcoholic and inclined to be vinegary. Towards the end of the nineteenth century the rough cider was fetching 2-3 guineas per hogshead, whereas the best sweet cider was fetching up to 10 guineas and was reputed to keep for up to 20 years.

COTTAGE CIDER

Old recipe:

12 lbs apples
1½ - 2 lbs sugar
8 pts warm water
1 lb chopped raisins
Wine yeast, all purpose

Wash and mince or blend apples. Place in a large non-metallic container. Add raisins and sugar and warm water and stir in yeast. Leave in a warm place, cover and stir daily for two weeks. Strain liquid into a fermentation jar with an airlock and ferment to a standstill. Remove to a cool place for 1 month. Rack from sediment and bottle. Drink straight away.

Travelling cider press c1910

APPLE ALE

Old recipe:

3 lbs apples
1 oz root ginger
½ teaspoon cloves
½ teaspoon cinnamon
1½ lbs white sugar
1 gallon water
Yeast and yeast nutrient

Wash the apples, remove the bruised parts and mince. Add the cold water, yeast and nutrient. Cover and leave in a warm place for a week, stirring daily. Strain through muslin onto the sugar and spices. Stir, cover and leave for a further five days. Strain through muslin, store in a cool place for a fortnight. Rack from the sediment and bottle. The ale is now drinkable.

WINES

The West Country seems to have produced large quantities of wine in the Middle Ages. Grapes were probably brought over by the Normans and much wine production seems to have been centred on monastic estates from thirteenth to fifteenth centuries. Dunster had well known terraced vineyards on the south facing slopes of Grabbist Hill and even exported wine to France. Production seems to have declined as the climate changed and seems to have been finished off with the dissolution of the monasteries in the sixteenth century.

Vineyards have started again in the twentieth century with the development of grape varieties more suited to the local climate and wine is once again produced on Exmoor. One vineyard was even started at Parracombe, 900ft above sea level, but never reached commercial production. A vineyard at Dulverton may have been started in the nineteenth century but little is remembered of it. Now converted to gardens, the land is still known as the Vineyard. Vineyards grew up in the Exe valley south of Exmoor in the 1970s and one started at Wootton Courtenay in the 1980s, now producing Dunkery wines. Most West Country wines are white wines resembling German wines. They tend to be drunk young and as a result can be spongy or slightly sparkling. They are generally of high quality but their price compared with the cheaper German wines has not led to a great popularity.

BEECH LEAF WINE

Old recipe:

1 gal beech leaves
3 lbs sugar
1 gal water

Juice of 2 lemons
Wine yeast and nutrient

Boil half of the water, dissolving the sugar in it and pour the hot syrup over the beech leaves. Stir and leave for a day or so. Strain into a gallon fermenting jar. Add the lemon juice, yeast and nutrient and top up with cold water to the bottom of the neck. Fit an airlock and leave in a warm place to ferment to a standstill. Rack into another jar and leave in a cool place for a week before racking into bottles.

SPIRITS

In the eighteenth and nineteenth centuries spirits were relatively cheap but taxed and mostly out of the price range of ordinary people. Smuggling was rife and even wealthier people were involved. The clergy were often included in the concealment of smuggled spirits and Trentishoe church was a regular hiding place. The Rev. William Thornton implied that his friend the Rev. William Fortescue, who lived at Allerford, frequently drank smuggled cognac. Another friend, the Rev. Bailey of Exford, always recommended a sugar lump dipped in brandy to keep off the cold. Brandy Path, at Countisbury Cove, was a well-known smuggling route. The Rev. Thornton stated:

> In all my intercourse with smugglers, illicit distillers, and such like people, I have remarked the peculiarity of their wares either were, or were honestly deemed to be, of extra quality. Was it that the sense of irregularity added extra flavour to the dram, or were the smuggled spirits particularly choice? I do not know; but years later on in my life I sat by the deathbed of a very old smuggler, who told me how he used to have a donkey with a triangle on its back, so rigged up as to show three lanthorns, and how chilled he would become as he lay out winters night after winter's night, watching on the Foreland, or along Brandy Path, as we called it, for three triangled lights of the schooner which he knew was coming to land her cargo where Glenthorne now stands, and where was the smugglers cave. Lord bless you, sir, and the dying man of nearly ninety chuckled, we never used no water, we just put the brandy into a kettle and heated it and drank it out of half-pint stoups, us did, and it never did us no harm whatsomdever, it was of quality it were.

Only recently has anyone been licensed to distil cider and it is strange that the West Country did not market a spirit like Calvados, although it is said to have been produced here in Norman times. Now a Somerset cider brandy is produced in small quantities and is delicious but expensive. Royal Somerset brandy of Brympton d'Evercy produce 5, 10 and 15 year old brandies. There is also a Devonshire apple liqueur. This is not to say that cider was not distilled. There are many accounts of stills from inventories of West Country gentry up until the seventeenth century. Since then it was done so illegally and little is known of its extent. Exmoor seems a likely place to have had illicit stills but there is no evidence for such as there is from surrounding parts of Devon and Somerset. The spirit was known as 'still liquor' and it is unlikely that Exmoor farmers did not occasionally drink some form of moonshine.

Spirit was distilled from the 'snarleygogs' or dregs of the cider – a sticky sort of pulp found at the bottom of cider barrels. Vancouver mentions that these were filtered through canvas bags and the cleared liquid returned to the cider or distilled. Sometimes ox blood was added to the snarleygogs to act like finings to help clear the cider. More often than not, however, the snarleygogs were distilled without treatment. The still was a metal porridge pot, usually with a tin head connected to a pipe which passed through a barrel of water to condense the spirit. The resulting liquid was then passed through the still again. Great care had to be taken to keep the temperature of distillation correct or the result could be, and often was, akin to meths. In more recent times the equipment was more sophisticated, with coiled condensation tubes, although the still itself was often a milk churn so that is was easy to disguise, unlike the disgusting smell which was produced.

The spirit, like most spirits until recent times, was regarded as medicinal and Marshall notes that it was referred to as 'necessity' in that it was used as a cure-all for man and beast. Used as a treatment for colic it was often a kill or cure remedy and could result in severe pain, loss of use of limbs and even death. Marshall hints that it could have even been regarded as a form of euthanasia for untreatable cases. Colic was a severe digestive disorder caused by drinking cider. It was incurable as it was, in fact, lead poisoning caused by the action of the acid juice on the lead linings of cider presses and troughs. The connection was not discovered until the end of the eighteenth century and the use of lead was gradually phased out.

LIQUEURS

NOYAU

Traditional method:

Recipes for this seem to date from the eighteenth century and, with French connections and almond base, did not originate on Exmoor but were locally adapted. The basic one is to pack a jar with young

beech leaves and fill to the brim with gin. The jar is corked or covered and stirred daily for two weeks, after which the gin, now a beautiful green, is strained off. To every pint of gin is added ½ pt (300 mls) of water in which has been dissolved 9 ozs (250 gms) sugar. This is stirred in and the mixture is bottled, adding about a tablespoonful of brandy or sherry to each bottle.

SHRUB

This is a West Country cordial, subject to many secret recipes and local variations. It dates from the smuggling days of the eighteenth century. Contraband brandy or rum was often stored in sea caves or by sinking it offshore and marking it until it was safe to retrieve it. Not surprisingly, the spirits were often rendered unpalatable by being mixed with seawater. Shrubs were invented to disguise the salt taste. They were usually syrupy, herby, fruit cordials, mixed with a little spirit for keeping. The syrup base was usually of treacle or molasses, once thought to be of medicinal value, and shrub was used for chest complaints. The word shrub is actually a derivative of syrup. It is best known today as a liqueur produced by J. R. Phillips of Bristol, who recommend mixing it with double the quantity of rum. The same company makes Lovage, another West Country liqueur, based on celery and herbs.

MAZZARD SHRUB

Traditional method:

Pack an earthenware jar with ripe mazzards and set it in a cool oven or hot water until the juice runs. Pour into a fine muslin bag and squeeze out the juice. Add one part of brandy to four parts of juice and sweeten to taste, stirring well to dissolve sugar. Bottle, cork and store in a cool place. Consume within about 6 months.

SLOE GIN

Sloe gin was the original 'mother's ruin' as it was blended with Penny Royal and Valerian to induce miscarriages. It is found throughout England and France, where sloes are called 'prunelles'. However, it is often associated with the West Country and is still a strong tradition on Exmoor. Here everyone has their own method and there is plenty of advice. Some say that you have to wait until after the first frost to pick the sloes and some that you have to prick them with a silver fork. I freeze then thaw mine. This softens them and I gently squeeze them to break the skin as I pop them into the bottle. This saves the tedium of pricking them. Some say just put them frozen into the gin and there is no need to break the skin as they split with the rapid thaw. A commercial manufacturer on Dartmoor uses this method. I have tried this and it works but I still prefer my own method, as it does not work for all and you need to leave the fruit in the gin for a full year to infuse. If you squeeze too hard, though, you end up with a sediment in the bottle which you have to filter out. It is worth experimenting with differing proportions of sugar and fruit and other fruits such as haws, rowan berries, raspberries, damsons or whortleberries. Sloes are also good in other sprits such white rum or vodka or steeped in a strong sweet wine.

Traditional method:

J. L. W. Page, in his book *The Coasts of Devon* (1895) reckoned that the best place for picking sloes was a lane between Berrynarbor and Hele, near Ilfracombe:
– just the sort for that delectable liqueur known as sloe gin. By the way, the reader may like to know how we Devon folk make sloe gin. I present him (or her) with the recipe. Into an ordinary wine bottle put half a pound of sugar candy, and upon this pour about half a bottle of gin. Then drop in the sloes (puncturing each berry as you do so) until the gin rises within an inch of the cork. The bottle should be shaken daily for about a month, when the liquor may be strained off, and rebottled, or left according to taste. In my opinion the flavour is improved by leaving sloes and gin together.

Old recipe from Mrs J. Furse Sanders of South Molton:

Take a two gallon jar and place therein
A measured gallon of unsweetened gin,
Three quarts of sloes, well pricked with care and pain,
With five half pounds of sugar from the cane.
On almonds bitter essence deftly pounce
And o'er the perfumed whole add half an ounce.
Cork tight and shake, then shake and turn again,
'Till twice three moons have passed to mortal men.
So shall a fragrant liquor, rosy red, reward your toil, and
clear your weary head.

Modern recipe from Winifred Everitt of Wootton Courtenay:

Sloes, about 1 lb
Gin, about ½ bottle
3 oz crushed barley sugar
Noyau, about 1 liqueur glass, or 2-3 drops
almond essence

Half fill a clean, dry wine bottle with sloes previously pricked with a darning needle. Add barley sugar and noyau or almond essence. Fill bottle with good gin, cork securely and allow to remain in a moderately warm place for 3 months. Gently shake the bottle every day. At the end of this time, strain the liqueur through

fine muslin and then through filter paper until quite clear, then bottle it and cork securely. Store in a cool dry place until required for use. It can be drunk straight away but it is far more mature if you can resist drinking it for 6-12 months.

MAZZARD BRANDY

Traditional method:

Steve Guscott

This is made in a similar way to sloe gin, but substituting mazzards for sloes and brandy for gin. The mazzards are bruised rather than pricked and a much smaller quantity of sugar is added, with a cinnamon stick and some cloves. For a more almond flavour, the mazzards are stoned and the stones are cracked and added to the liquor, along with almond slivers.

SINGING JOHNNY

Recipe from Jenny Prior-Wandesforde of Timberscombe:

1 cider flagon – empty
1 bottle of whisky – full
1 cupful Exmoor heather honey
Blackcurrants

Put the honey and whisky into the flagon and top up with blackcurrants. Leave for approximately 6 months, occasionally shaking the flagon to stir the contents. Filter through fine muslin and bottle. A delicious filler for your flask – it can be made into a longer drink by the addition of water.

PUNCHES

Punches were traditional throughout the twelve days of Christmas and on Christmas Eve, when it was traditional to toast the ashen faggot. The faggot was tied with willow bands and, as it burnt, the bands snapped open and each was toasted for good health. The toast was usually of mulled ale into which were dipped wigs. These were small, spiced dough cakes, eaten before mince pies became traditional. This was similar to the wassailing ceremonies, where the word wassail comes from the old English drinking toast 'wes hal', meaning good health. In the case of wassailing, however, the good health was wished to the apple trees for a bountiful crop the next season. The wassailing ceremonies were traditionally on Twelfth Night, which was seventeenth January on the old calendar and 6th January on the new. The oldest surviving wassail in the Exmoor area is at Carhampton on old Twelfth Night. The ceremony includes offering sops in cider to the good spirits of the trees, scaring off the evil spirits with gunfire and toasting with mulled cider and bread sops.

FRUIT CUP

Old recipe:

1 pt cider
1 pt water
2 lemons
2 tablespoons honey
1 cupful strawberries

Thinly slice one lemon and place in a jug. Squeeze over the juice of the other lemon. Cover with the water, add the honey and cider and stir well. Keep cool and add the strawberries just before serving.

MULLED CIDER

Old recipe:

2 pts cider
4 ozs granulated sugar
12 cloves
4 sticks cinnamon
10 whole allspice

Heat all the ingredients in a pan, stirring until the sugar has dissolved. Strain and serve hot.

LAMBSWOOL

This drink is not peculiar to Exmoor or the West Country. It was a common drink for Christmas Eve, eaten with wigs or spiced yule bread and Christmas morning, when landlords would entertain their tenants and farmers their labourers and families. Apples were commonly associated with Christmas and it was a sign of a good crop to come if the sun shone through the trees or snow lay on the branches on Christmas Day. Originally the lambswool would be made with crab apples.

Old recipe:

4 dessert apples
2 pts brown ale
1 pt sweet wine
1 teaspoon mixed spice
Cinnamon stick
Lemon rind
Brown sugar

Core the apples and bake in a moderate oven until soft. Skin and pulp them. Heat the ale, wine, spices and lemon rind in a pan and stir in the apple pulp. Strain and reheat the liquid, adding sugar to taste.

TAUNTON WASSAIL CUP

This is a modern recipe invented for the revived wassail at the Taunton Cider Company at Norton Fitzwarren. Here bananas replace the traditional roast apples.

Ingredients for 10 persons:
3 flagons dry cider
4 tablespoons brown sugar
2 oranges
4 cloves
¼ teaspoon grated nutmeg
¼ teaspoon grated cinnamon
2 bananas

Slice the oranges thinly and heat together slowly all the ingredients except the bananas until nearly boiling. Slice the bananas thinly, add to the liquid and serve at once.

WASSAIL BOWL

Old recipe:

Dissolve 1 lb of brown sugar in a pint of hot beer with a little grated nutmeg and ginger. Add 4 glasses of sherry and, when cool 5 pints of cold beer. Float slices of toast spread with yeast on the liquid and leave in a warm place for a few hours. Strain and bottle with corked bottles. In a few days it should be bursting the corks and ready to drink from the wassail bowl with hot roasted apples floating in it.

STIRRUP CUP

Stirrup cup has no particular recipe as it is any drink which is served to riders before a hunt. Nowadays whisky, whisky and ginger wine, gin and ginger wine, and sherry are popular but punches hot or cold were often offered in the past. This is a recipe for a Christmas stirrup cup from Heather Burnett-Wells:

2 bottles cider
1 bottle brandy
2 bottles red wine
1 lb sugar
1 orange
1 lemon
Spices: ginger, cloves, nutmeg and cinnamon

Heat all except fruit together gently without boiling. Strain and serve hot with slices of orange and lemon.

WHORTLEBERRY PUNCH

Traditional method:

Cook some whortleberries in a little warm water with sugar and cinnamon to taste. Strain, add some sliced lemon and drink hot.

Ashen faggot ceremony at Dunster

Alfred Vowles Collection

❧ Glossary ❧

The following words and phrases are or have been used in Devon and Somerset. Many are or have been in common useage on Exmoor but few can be distinguished as being peculiar to Exmoor.

addle-gutter	stale beer or cider
agger	egger: a collector of eggs, game and poultry
Ale Tuesday	Shrove Tuesday, when church ales were sold
aitch-bone	the beef joint around the rump bone
alabash	boiling
ammit	lunch
andogs	fire dogs: moveable iron plates used to contract the fire to save fuel
apple-chimmer\ chamber	an upstairs spare room where best apples were stored
apple garden	a vegetable garden with fruit trees
apple in and out	a flour pudding in which apples are indiscriminately mixed
apple meat	apple purée
apple muck\ apple pummy\ arisings\ cider muck	the pulp of apples left from cider making
apple trade	apple dumplings, pudding or tart
Argans	marjoram (from Oregano)
arrish goose	a goose fattened for Michaelmas by gleaning amongst the stubble
ash cake	a cake baked on a hearth stone under a lid covered with ashes
ashen faggot	faggot of ash twigs tied with withies, equivalent of Yule log, used for cider toasts on Christmas Eve
back bar\ bar rod	an iron bar fixed from side to side in a chimney for supporting the bar crooks
back house	scullery
back stick	a large log set at the back of an open hearth fire
back stone	a flat piece of stone or iron on which flat cakes are baked
bacon pig	a pig big enough to make bacon
bait	any food but especially a packed lunch
baking ire	a griddle for baking cakes
baking kettle	a saucepan shaped lid put over food on an open hearth
bald-headed sailor	a plain, boiled suet pudding
ballard	a wether

bannock	an oatmeal or barley cake baked on a griddle
bap	plain bread bun
bar ire	horizontal bar of a crane for hanging kettles over an open fire
barm	yeast; froth on fermenting beer
barm cake	cakes made with fresh brewers yeast
Barnstaple oven	a cloam oven made in Barnstaple
barrow pig	a gelt boar
batch loaf	a small, freshly-baked loaf
batting	snaring birds at night using a lantern behind a net and beating bushes and other roosting places
beastings	colostrum: the first, rich, yellow milk from a cow after calving
beasts	cattle
beaufet	buffet, or sideboard
Beauty of Abraham\ Hebron	an old variety of potato
beaver	lunchtime
bed	a forequarter of mutton without the shoulder
bed ale	ale given at a housewarming or birth celebration
bee bole	cavity in wall used to hold bee skip
bee butt\skep	straw beehive
bee spittal	honey
bellises	bellows
beverage	weak cider made by watering the pressed cheese and pressing again; watered cider; hot cider punch with sugar and gin
Bible tripe	tripe from the third stomach which, when folded over, resembles a book
biggin	a metal coffee pot
biskey pie	junket made from colostrum
black butter	potted laver
blow coal	a metal sheet in the chimney throat to control the draught through the fire
blessing	a drop over full measure when buying cider or beer
blue-vinnied	blue veined or mouldy cheese
bobbing	catching eels
bobby-dazzler	a plain bun eaten with cream and jam; jam centred biscuit
Bodley	a type of range patented by George Bodley of Exeter in 1802, often applied to any cooking range
bolt	to seive flour through cloth

bone-orchard	a pasty
bosky	tipsy, of an alcoholic pudding
Boveys\ Chudleighs	names given to the yeast buns eaten with cream and jam
Bowhill	a variety of apple
brack	lard, the fat covering intestines
brandis	an iron trivet with three legs, sometimes four, for standing saucepans over an open fire
brandy mazzard	the wild cherry or gean, used for making cherry brandy
braund	log for the fire
brawn	a large log for the Christmas fire, able to last the twelve days
bread corn	an allowance of corn for making flour, once part of the wages of farm workers
bread and point	thinly buttered bread: with no more butter than can be held on the point of a knife
bread and pull it	poor man's food
break bread	to break fast, commence eating
brick	a small loaf of bread
brimmle	blackberry
britt	whitebait
broad figs	dried, flattened figs
Brown Bett	apple charlotte
bucket	a small pint or quart milk can, with lid, used to carry tea out to farm labourers
buckhorn	dried, salted whiting
Budget	a variety of pear tree
Buffcoat	a coarse kind of eating apple
bull's beef	high quality meat
bullum	bullace or sloe
Burton	ale or beer
bury	rabbit burrow
butcher's figs	large lumps of suet
butter biscuit	plain bun eaten with cream and jam
butter stein	cloam container for keeping butter cool
cast	a handful of three herrings used when counting out a long hundred
casting\cristling cristal\kesting	a small wild plum or bullace
cauch	a meal of stewed or fried leftovers
chats	small, poor quality potatoes
chawl	a pig's cheek
cheese	pile of straw, sometimes covered in hessian, mixed with apples for pressing in cider making
chibbles\ chipples	spring onions
chicksy-pixy	of inferior quality, cream made by separating rather than scalding
chimney crook	a hook hanging from a bar iron for hanging pots and kettles over the fire
chitterlings	small intestines of a pig
chopper	a large cranked knife used to chop potatoes in a frying pan whilst they are being cooked
chowder	a female street/market fish seller
chuck pear	a hard winter pear
cladgy	waxy, of potatoes
clatter	an eel fisher
clatting	catching eels with a bundle of earthworms
clavel	the beam across a fireplace
clavel board	mantlepiece
clear	scalded milk with traces of cream on it
clibby	stodgy, of a cake
clifty	not risen, of a loaf
clit\close	dry, of a cake
clitchy	sticky; a clitch fair had a game like apple bobbing but with buns in treacle
cloam\ cloam ware	coarse earthenware made of clay
cloamen	made of clay
cloam pan	clay pan glazed inside
cloam oven	clay oven
close	not breaking up when cooked, of potatoes
clouted	clothed, of clotted cream
Cobble Dick	an apple variety
codds	shells, of peas
coffin	a raised or dish pie crust
cole pixing	beating apple trees to recover the last few apples after picking the crop
collop	a thick slice of meat
Collop Monday	the day before Shrove Tuesday when collops were eaten to use up meat before Lent
Come-back	a Guinea Fowl
conygar\ coneyary	a rabbit warren
copings	fine\seived flour
copper\ copper kettle	copper boiler holding 10-15 gallons
corbutt	a large, deep, oval wooden tub for salting a pig
corn	once used only for oats
cotterel-cremaster	a chimney crook
coup	a log basket
courge	a basket hung over the side of a boat to keep fish alive, especially sand eels
Cousin Jack	smuggled brandy
cowal	a fish basket carried on the back
cow and calf\ diesel	cider mixed with stout
crabalorgin	spiny or spider crab
crabs eye	not quite on the boil
crack nuts	hazel nuts
cramp	a poor cake made with inferior flour

cream	to spread cream on; to mash, of potatoes
crib	a snack; to eat sparingly
cricket	a three or four legged milking stool
cricks	dry hedge wood
crisling	pork crackling
crock	large earthenware pot for salting meat or butter; large iron cooking pot with three legs; a kind of fruit cake
crock stew	potato stew
crook	an iron hanger with ratchet for holding pots over the fire
crowdy	a pie with mutton chops, apples and onions
crowdy pies	apple dumplings
crowst\crummit	a snack
crumplings	the stunted apples which shrivel on the tree
cuits	cookable, of apples
cullack	an onion
culver	a pigeon
culver house	dovecot
cut round	a scone type bun eaten with cream and jam
daffer	small crockery: cups and saucers
damzil	damson, sloe or bullace
dash and darras	a parting drink, stirrup cup
dibben	a fillet of veal
deave\dreave	empty nut or corn
dolwin	yeast
double bakes	stale bread buttered and baked in the oven to make it more edible
doucet pie	a sweet herb pie
doughboys\ dawbwoy	dumplings, used in stews or puddings
dowdies	large, spiced yeast buns carried out to labourers in the fields
dredge	a shaker for salt or pepper
Ducks Bills	a variety of apple
emptin cloam	drinking
enterlain\ interlean	streaky bacon, cut thickly and usually green
Espaniard	a variety of russet apple
faggot\facket	a bundle of sticks for lighting the fire, usually made of hedge trimmings and about 3ft long and 2ft diameter
faggot wood	brushwood
fairings	presents bought at a fair, commonly including gingerbread
farthing bun\ halfpenny bun	a yeast bun, plain or spiced, eaten with cream and jam
fat shag	fat bacon
fect	a potato disease
figgin	a plain bun eaten with jam and cream
figgy	of dishes made with dried fruit, usually raisins
figgy duff	a pudding with dried fruit

figgy whitpot	a pudding of milk, flour, treacle and raisins boiled or baked
fig pasties	pasties with dried fruit filling
fire dogs	the supports for burning logs on an open fire: andirons
firing	fire wood
firkin	a small wooden barrel carried on a leather thong, for drinking cider in the fields, smaller than the correct firkin measure
Fishers	apples baked in batter, after Dr Fisher, Bishop of Exeter, who is reputed to have invented them
fish jolter	street fish seller or pedlar
flacket	a wooden bottle or keg
flair	a layer of fat in bacon
flat	a large, flat, rectangular basket with lid, used to carry dairy produce to market
flat-poll	a large, dense white cabbage used in soups
flawn	a pancake
Flesh and Blood	an apple variety
flicker meat	a baked pudding made of ½ lb flour, 2 oz treacle and a quart of milk
flinket	a small bundle of wood
flour milk	gruel made with flour and milk
fore-right	made of coarse flour
French hales	brown berries of the rare Devon Whitebeam tree, found on Exmoor and once sold at Barnstaple pannier market
French nuts	chestnuts or walnuts
fries	fried lambs' testicles
frith	small brushwood
frizzle	fried sweetbreads
froize	a thick pancake eaten with bacon
frumity\ frumenty	a porridge of cracked wheat, sugar, spice and currants, boiled in milk and eaten with wedges of bread
frying knife	a long knife or spatula with cranked handle for cutting food in the frying pan
ganny\gander	a turkey\guinea fowl\peacock
girts\grits	groats, grain
glatting	catching conger eels on the shore with dogs
Gracy	an apple variety
granny's pudding	apples baked in batter
grass beef	beef from grass fed cattle
grass fruit	windfall apples
gravelling	young salmon peal, up to 4oz in weight
greast	grist: corn for milling
green	fresh meat as opposed to salted or smoked, especially of bacon
green meat	green vegetables

gribble cakes	cakes made with the sediment from brack after rendering into lard
griddle	a grid iron used on an open fire
groinge	sour fruit
gubbings	fish offal
guzegob\ guzeygog	gooseberry
halse nit	hazel nut
handymaid	a long handle which can swivel on a chimney crook to pour the kettle
hange	the pluck of a sheep: the heart, lungs and liver
hanger	part of a crane for hanging pots over an open fire
hard-a-pan	the rim of cream sticking to the pan after the rest has been skimmed
hard wood	firewood cut into logs as opposed to brush wood bound in faggots
head	the top of the milk, cream
heft	to rise, of bread
herby pie	a pie well seasoned with herbs or made with green vegetables eg spinach, parsley, cress, spring onions and baked in milk with bacon
hoarding apples	apples which keep well
hollering	wassailing apple trees
hollums	wild plums, bullaces
hoppers	maggots of small flies which infest ham or cheese
hull	to shell peas or nuts
humming	frothing, of beer
innards	intestines: skins for hogs puddings
jacky bread	currant cake
Jennet	an early-ripening apple variety, often used as stock for grafting onto
jennie quick	a kettle with a large base to boil quickly
jerking	a form of poaching of salmon whereby the fish is noosed by a pole with slip-knotted cord jerked over the fish's head
josses	small mackerel
junket	sweetened milk curdled with rennet
keemy	cider covered with a thin white mould
keiger	a cider cask
keive	a large wooden tub for fermenting cider of beer, holding two hogshead (120 gallons)
kerle\kiddon	a loin of veal or mutton
kettle bread	bread baked on a hearth under a baking kettle
kettle broth	broth made of cubed bread, a lump of dripping, pepper, salt, and boiling water; can be a sweet broth made with hot milk, sugar and bread
lamb's wool	mulled ale with roasted apples
Lammeys	small July salmon in the River Exe, after Lammas (1st August)
lammint	garden mint or peppermint
laver	usually seaweed of the genus porphyra, of which there are three British pecies, known also as slake kale. Green seaweeds of the genus ulva, including sea lettuce and sea moss, are sometimes included.
laver bread	a mixture of cooked seaweeds, as opposed to Welsh laverbread, which is laver rolled in oats and fried; also a wholemeal bread flavoured with laver
leaf	the inner layer of fat of pork or poultry
leavings	food left on a plate after a meal
leery	hungry
lees	brewer's yeast, sediment in beer
let back	to swallow, either in eating or drinking
lie the livings	to put bread dough in a warm place to rise
lift	to rise, as in dough or cakes
likky broth	leek and potato soup, sometimes with mutton
loady nut	a double nut
lob	molasses
lobby	sweet, sticky
loblolly	a porridge of flour and milk, also known as whitpot
lolly	anything boiled in a pot, usually soup or stew
lolly cock\ lubber cock	a cock turkey
long biders	good keepers, usually of apples
long-tailed rabbit	pheasant 'accidentally' shot whilst out shooting rabbits
make in	to kindle a fire
mang	to mix up or mess up food
market merry	merry and talkative after a few drinks
market basket	a large rectangular basket for taking produce to market
maslin	mixed corn sown in odd corners to feed poultry or game
matrimony	a mixture of gin with whisky or rum
maund\mawn	a large oval wicker basket for taking food to market; a wooden close stave basket with handles each end and holding 40lbs of potatoes; a measure of fish equal to 200lbs or 350 herrings
maw guts	sheeps intestines
mazzard	small, sweet black cherry, also the wild cherry or bird cherry
meat\mate	general word for food
meaching\ mitching	playing truant, hence blackberry, strawberry or wort mitching: staying off school to pick fruit
mease\maise maze	a measure of herrings, thus: 1 handfull of three herrings = 1 cast

	50 casts plus 1 cast for luck = 153 fish, 4X153 = 612 = 1 mease
meat nuts	sweet chestnuts
meatward	tender when boiled, of vegetables
melted	heavy, of bread; of sprouted corn which has become unfit for bread making
metheglin	a brewed drink made with honey
mimp	to toy with food in the mouth
mimser	a poor eater
mock	crushed fruit such as apples in cider making
mood	the pancreas or sweetbread of an animal
morded	fatty, of a pig
mores	roots\root crops such as turnips
mort	lard
mozil	stirrup cup
muggit pie	pie made with the intestines of a sheep, elsewhere a calf's umbilical cord
mug house	ale house
naips\neeps	turnips
naked Jacks	small suet dumplings
nammet	elevenses, a snack
nan	a small cloam jar
natlings\ knotlings	intestines cleaned and knotted (plaited) ready for cooking, especially of a pig
naty	meat with closely intermingled fat and lean: good for cooking
necessity	moonshine spirits made from the dregs from cider or beer fermentation
neck	necklace shaped corn dolly made from the last sheath of corn to be reaped
nib	to top and tail gooseberries, currants etc.
nickie	small bundle of sticks used to light a fire or heat a bread oven
nine and one	pasty having nine parts of vegetables to one of meat
nobs	Brussels sprouts
nog\noggin	a small cask\firkin
No-pips	an apple variety
nott\nat	a sheep or cow without horns
nubbies	small yeast buns flavoured with saffron; plain nobbies yeast buns eaten with jam and cream; small currant buns or cakes
orts	bits of left-over food
pad	an open pannier basket for fish
paikse	to toy with food
pannier market	market for farm produce brought in panniers, often co-inciding with market for farm stock
patch	the stone of a fruit
paunch	guts, especially of a rabbit

peal	the sea trout: brown trout which have taken to feeding in the sea and return to Exmoor rivers in summer to spawn
peal chad	younger version of the sea trout or salmon peal, but larger than a gravelling, equivalent to salmon smolt
peas	the hard roe of a fish
peds	wicker panniers carried on each side of a pack horse
peel	a batch of bread
penny brick	a brick-shaped loaf
pestle pie	a huge pie made for revels, often containing a whole gammon, tongue, turkey and a couple of chickens
pick	to pluck feathers
picky\picksome	fussy in eating
Pigs' Noses	apple variety
pile	a heap of ten faggots of wood
pill\peel	the long wooden spade used by bakers to take bread in and out of an oven
pinded	stale, musty
pitcher	cloam jug holding about a gallon, used to top up kettles
pith	the soft centre of a loaf, other than the crust
pixy whorting	gleaning a few apples after the crop has been picked
pluff\plum	to rise or swell, fluff up
pluffy	of bacon, fresh, not too dry
plumming	yeast
pomace	the pulp from pressed apples
ponted	bruised, of fruit
poor ground	allotment gardens given to the poor
posset	a warm drink of milk and bread, sweetened often with treacle and flavoured with ale or cider
pot	pudding
pot an'\ potten pudding	a baked pork sausagemeat pudding
pot crook	a chimney hook for hanging pots over an open fire
pot herbs	herbs used for cooking
pots	intestines
pot water	potable water
poult\heath poult	the male and young of the black grouse
pound	an apple press; 18ozs, as applied to butter
prilled	sour, of beer or cider
proddling	milk with small bubbles – just rising to the boil
puddings	pork sausages
pug	a young salmon or sea trout
pullers	small crabs when their shells can be pulled and the bodies used as fishing bait

pully-alley	raw sinews of beef given to babies to suck
pummy	the froth on fermenting cider
Quarrender	an apple variety
queens	scallops
Quinch	an apple variety
rabbit-part	the undercut of sirloin beef
ragged jack	small suet dumplings
rail	a revel or fair
rammil	a cheese made from whole milk
rand	a cut of beef
ranging	collecting windfall apples
raunch	raw, uncooked
rasher wagon	frying pan
raw cream	separated, as opposed to scalded, cream
raw-reamed butter	butter churned from raw, not scalded cream
raw head	the top of the milk
raw tetty fry	raw potato slices, bacon pieces, onion, milk, water and seasoning simmered in a frying pan with a lid
raygrater	a door to door salesman for farm produce
raymy	of cider: sour, cloudy
reasty	rancid, particularly of bacon
ream	cut and dried turf for burning
reamy	creamy consistency
rear bit	elevenses snack
red noses	cockles used as bait
rennet\runnet	enzyme from calves' stomachs for setting milk to make junket
ride	to digest food or drink
right-vore	grinding wheat with meal and flour mixed, but bran extracted; hence, right-vore brown bread as opposed to wholemeal, which includes the bran
rizzled	shrivelled apples
roading time	season when woodcocks use regular routes for feeding and so can be easily netted or snared
rodden bine	sticks used to bind faggots
rookler	young pig
roots	root crops for culinary purposes
roove	to dry meat in a chimney
ropey	glutinous, stringy, of bread, stale cider or beer
rouched	bitter, of beer
rough meat	green vegetables
round robin	a small pancake
ruck	a covey of game birds
running about	free range
salet	salad
salmon peal	the grilse: a young salmon that has been feeding in the sea locally for a short period and returns to Exmoor rivers in the summer, weighing between 3 and 7lbs

salter	a wooden or cloam cask for holding pork in brine
samsawed	food half cooked and warm; stewed tea
samsoakey	lukewarm, tepid
samsoe	a dough cake
scad	a slab of peat or turf used as fuel
scald cream	clotted cream
scald milk	skimmed milk remaining from making clotted cream
scallups\ scriddlings\ scrippings\ scratchings	scraps after rendering lard or deep frying
school peal	young peal, equivalent to the salmon peal
scoop	the neck and breast of lamb cut as one joint
Scotched collops	slices of meat stewed with onions
Scotch hands	ribbed wooden boards with handles used to work and roll butter
scrap pudding	pudding made with flour and the remains of fat after rendering for lard
scraps\scrips	scraps of fried batter
scrivvens	the solid remains after rendering fat for lard
scrowle	to dry fish in the sun\grill fish
scrumpling	a small shrivelled apple
scrumpy	farm cider, made from scrumplings
seam	a measure of wood, ten faggots
settle	high backed wooden bench to keep the draught away from the fireplace
shagapenter	shoulder of pork roasted whole
shaky trade	jelly
shammel mate	meat bought fresh from a butchers as opposed to home killed and salted – from a shambles or row of butchers shops
sherbit	euphemism for strong drink
shoe nut	Brazil nut
shuck	shell
skill	to shell peas, beans, nuts etc
skillet	a small saucepan with three legs and a long handle, for use over an open fire
skits\splits	the plain yeast buns eaten with jam and cream
skivver	skewer
slattery	derisory term for thin, runny food, slops
slingers	invalid food, slops
slob trout	a variety of peal, looking like a cross between a brown trout and sea trout
snarligrog\ snarleygogs	an organic growth in vinegar; the slimy sediment of cider fermentation
snatching	a form of poaching of salmon whereby a weighted multiple hook on a line is thrown over the fish and used to snatch it by any part of the body

soak	to cook thoroughly; to return a cake to the oven for further baking
sodger	a smoked and salted herring
sour grabs	crab apples
soursap pie	sorrel pie, sweetened with sugar and eaten with cream
spence	a large store cupboard or pantry
spill	the front part of a tongue
spine beef\ spine pork	meat with the outside fat and skin attached
squab	young pigeon
stalk	to steal potatoes by digging out the tubers and leaving the stalks
standard	an oval oak salting tub
standing pie	a large game pie with a thick crust
stane\stein	an earthenware pot, about 10" high, used to store cream, lard, butter etc
sticker	a butcher's killing knife
stickjaw	chewy food
still liquors\ waters	moonshine distilled from cider dregs
stoddy	clotted, of cream
stodgy	badly mixed or half cooked, of cakes and puddings
stodgers	large, filling cakes or buns
stoodle	to simmer
stoog	a small jar or pitcher
stotty	lumpy
Stretch my Girdle	an apple variety
stinkibus	the sour and vile smelling spirits which smugglers had let lie in salt water for too long
strubbing	robbing birds nests for eggs
Stubbard	a variety of apple favoured for making squab pies and lamb's wool
squab pie	originally a pie of young pigeons, applied to a pie with layers of meat, apples and onions
squench coal	charcoal
sugar toast	cake toasted and covered with sugar and cider, for christenings
sunburnt	potatoes turned green by exposure to light
swale	to singe the bristles off a killed pig
swap-at	Guinea fowl
tab	a piece of turf dried for fuel
table board	the top part of a table made to rest on trestles as opposed to having fixed legs
taffety	dainty with eating
tag\tagend	a joint of beef from the rump
tame	to start a loaf or cake by cutting the first slice
target	a fore-quarter of lamb or mutton without the shoulder joint
tatties\teddies\ tetties	potatoes

tatie bashing	digging or peeling potatoes
tatie oggie\ tatie huddy	pasty including potatoes, in Cornish style
Tay fish	dried Newfoundland cod
teddy basket	slatted wooden basket for carrying potatoes
Tiverton	boiled sweets made of barley sugar and almonds, humbugs once sold four for a penny
tea kettle	weak broth: boiling water with a diced slice of broth bread, dash of milk and seasoning
teagle	tea kettle or teapot
thunder and lightning	treacle and cream, eaten on splits
tich	to set peat turves on end to dry for fuel
tich crook	a tool for turning peat turves
tiddly-wink	an unlicensed pub, drinking place
timber dish	trencher
tinner\tunner	metal funnel for filling cider flasks
titch crook	a hook for pulling faggots from a wood rick
toad in the hole	not just sausages in batter, but any meat baked or fried in batter
toe rag	salt cod
Tom Putt	an apple variety named after Thomas Potter, often used in apple dumplings
tough cake\ tuffs\chuffs\ touchers	plain yeast bun used for cream teas
traunchard	trencher
treacle posset	a hot drink of milk and treacle, or cider and treacle
trennel\trendle\ trundle	a large oval oak tub about eight inches deep, four feet wide and six feet long, used for salting a pig, sometimes an earthenware pot
tribute fish	John Dory, named after two black marks looking like finger marks on its sides
trin	a flat tub for fermenting apple juice, a kieve
trip stick	a prop to hold a barrel inclined
trivet	three legged stand for holding pots over an open fire, with a circular top unlike a brandis, which had a triangular top
trout	the native brown trout
truckle	a small, barrel-shaped farmhouse cheese
tub	a four gallon spirit keg, used by smugglers
tun	to pour liquid into a cask
Turkey fig	a dried fig, as opposed to anything figgy, which contained other dried fruit, usually raisins
turnover	a fruit pasty, usually contains apple

turf spade	a curved or angled spade used to cut peat
turvey\turbary	the right to cut peat
Twelfth Day\ Night	the Twelfth Night of the old calendar, now 18th January, traditional time for wassailing
Twelthy Eve	the evening before old Christmas Day, now 6th January, also time for wassailing
tye-pit	a drinking well
underlane	a female crab used as bait, found under the males in summer
undo	to peel
vags	turves for burning, as opposed to peat from a bog
vigging	digging about in the garden
wadge	a large hunk of bread or cheese
wairsh	insipid, insufficiently seasoned
wallage	a large helping
walsh	insipid, lacking salt
wangary	tough, of meat
wash brew	an invalid food consisting of oatmeal porridge often eaten with ale, wine or sugar
wassail cup	a spiced and sugared punch of ale or cider

wats	oats
waysgoose	a stubble fed goose originally eaten at an annual printers' holiday, now an outing
werts\whorts\ worts\orts\urts	whortleberries
whelpy	stale, sour – of milk
whift	to fish from a boat with hand lines
whig	wood pigeon
whit	crab apple
whitsole	dairy produce, especially curds and cheese
whitpot	drink made from flour mixed to a paste with water and adding boiling water and treacle
wig	a small bun, plain, spiced or with currants
wood hook\ 'ood 'ook	a small bill hook for hedging
wood rick\ 'ood rick\ yude rick	pile of faggots, usually kept outside the kitchen door
word apples	keeping apples
wring	a press for cheese or cider apples

❧ Index to Recipes ❧